# BY THE EDITORS OF CONSUMER GUIDE®

## THE COMPLETE BOOK OF
# PREFABS, KITS, AND MANUFACTURED HOUSES

FAWCETT COLUMBINE ● NEW YORK

# Table of Contents

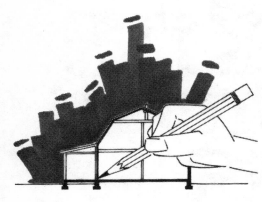

If your idea of a prefabricated house is a tiny box or a trailer, you're in for a surprise. Manufactured houses come in almost any size or style you can imagine—they're frequently constructed with the same high-quality materials found in the finest custom-built homes.

There are seven basic types of manufactured houses, and most offer a wide choice of design possibilities. Besides type, you'll have to decide on the house package. Some house packages are more complete than others; they include more of the materials you'll need for house construction.

Deciding on a manufacturer requires a calculated plan of attack. You'll need to know what to look for in house design and construction, how to read the catalogs, and the best ways to compare one manufacturer against another. Most of all, you'll need to know how to estimate the total cost of any house.

No matter how inexperienced you might be, you can still take advantage of at least some of the do-it-yourself possibilities of manufactured houses. Do-it-yourself construction offers the greatest opportunity for cash savings—but before getting in over your head, be sure of what is involved.

THE COMPLETE BOOK OF PREFABS, KITS, AND
MANUFACTURED HOUSES

Published by Fawcett Columbine Books, a unit of CBS Publications, The Consumer Publishing Division of CBS Inc.

Library of Congress Catalog Card Number: 80-84047
ISBN: 0-449-90051-7

Printed in the United States of America
First Fawcett Columbine Printing: May 1981
10  9  8  7  6  5  4  3  2  1

Cover Design: Frank E. Peiler
Illustrations: Benson & Benson Design
Technical Consultants: Burch, Burch & Burch, A.I.A.

Cover Photo Credits: Acorn Structures, Inc., American Timber Homes, Inc., Beaver Log Homes, Inc., Boise Cascade Corp., Deck House, Lindal Cedar Homes, Monterey Domes, Inc., Northern Homes, Pan Abode, Inc., Scholz Homes, Wickes Lumber.

We would also like to thank the following manufacturers for supplying us with photographs and artwork for sections I and II: Acorn Structures, Inc., 15; Alta Industries, 14; Deck House, 15; Evans Products Co., 25, 26, 49, 50, 51; Helikon Design Corp., 55; Monterey Domes, Inc., 15; New England Log Homes, Inc., 14; Wickes Lumber, 17.

# Planning

Consider the benefits
manufactured houses have to offer—
time and money savings,
do-it-yourself opportunities,
energy saving features,
and even solar technology

# Why Buy a

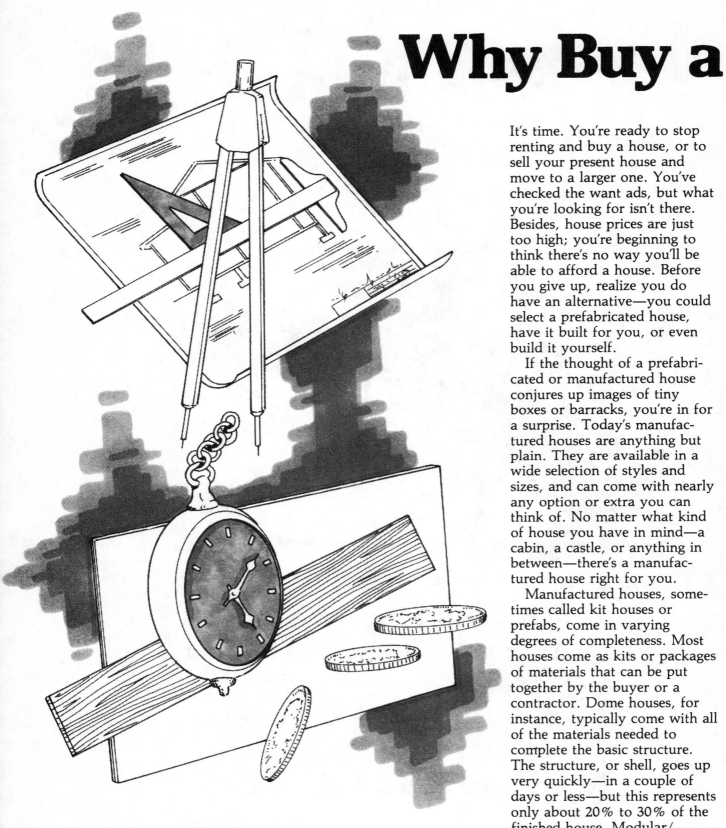

It's time. You're ready to stop renting and buy a house, or to sell your present house and move to a larger one. You've checked the want ads, but what you're looking for isn't there. Besides, house prices are just too high; you're beginning to think there's no way you'll be able to afford a house. Before you give up, realize you do have an alternative—you could select a prefabricated house, have it built for you, or even build it yourself.

If the thought of a prefabricated or manufactured house conjures up images of tiny boxes or barracks, you're in for a surprise. Today's manufactured houses are anything but plain. They are available in a wide selection of styles and sizes, and can come with nearly any option or extra you can think of. No matter what kind of house you have in mind—a cabin, a castle, or anything in between—there's a manufactured house right for you.

Manufactured houses, sometimes called kit houses or prefabs, come in varying degrees of completeness. Most houses come as kits or packages of materials that can be put together by the buyer or a contractor. Dome houses, for instance, typically come with all of the materials needed to complete the basic structure. The structure, or shell, goes up very quickly—in a couple of days or less—but this represents only about 20% to 30% of the finished house. Modular/sectional houses are almost completely finished at the

# Manufactured House?

factory. These houses are delivered to a site, placed on the foundation, and the sections are attached. They can be made ready to occupy in a couple of days, and are up to 95% complete when you move in—they can contain furnaces, plumbing, appliances, and even drapes and carpeting.

Of importance to house buyers are the many advantages that manufactured houses have to offer. They can be built much faster than conventional houses. They offer money-saving opportunities for anyone interested in building the house on their own. They often come with a variety of energy-saving features that aren't always available with other houses. And they offer tremendous flexibility in house plans. When this flexibility is combined with the wide selection of styles and sizes that are available, manufactured houses end up having what is probably the greatest number of choices for you, the new house buyer.

## Time Savings Add Up

Because of the way they are constructed manufactured houses usually can go up much faster than a conventional house. On-site construction time is the most important time savings, because it is expensive and subject to weather delays, materials damage, and vandalism. If the house will be built by a contractor, the more preassembled it is when it

reaches the site, the less time it will take for a contractor to finish. Any reduction in construction time results in savings because labor costs are reduced.

Purchasing a precut manufactured house produces considerable time savings. Materials don't have to be cut at the building site, and the time needed to fit parts together is reduced. More time can be saved if a house is partly panelized. Sections of such houses are preassembled in the factory and have only to be stood in place and secured at the building site. Houses made up of large panelized wall sections can usually be erected and made weathertight in a day or less, leaving only the interior to be finished.

A manufactured house can be chosen from your living room, and made ready for delivery in anywhere from 30 to 90 days. Two or three weeks before the delivery date the house site is prepared and a foundation is built. When the house arrives it can often be completed in from three or four days to one or two months. This short interval, from the time you order until the house is completed, virtually rules out the possibility of price increases that are so common when house construction drags on over a period of many months.

If you must sell your current house before moving in there is another possible advantage. Because construction time is shorter you can sell your old house and close without worrying about whether the new

house will be completed in time. The possibility of having to find alternative housing because your new house isn't ready when scheduled is practically eliminated.

## Money Saving Possibilities

A cash savings is possible when you buy a manufactured house. It depends on what type of house you buy, who builds it, and where. The most money can be saved if you, with the help of family and friends, do some or most of the construction and finishing yourself. Depending on the type of manufactured house, the possibility for involvement in construction ranges from the entire job to only a few bits of trim.

Dome houses, for instance, typically come as kits with all the materials you need to complete the basic structure or shell. These dome house shells can usually go up quickly with a crew of four or five do-it-yourself builders. The kits are low priced because they represent only about 20% to 30% of the materials needed to complete the dome. You'll have to purchase the materials needed to build, insulate, and cover the interior walls and roof; install heating, plumbing, and electrical systems, kitchen cabinets, floors, and appliances. If you complete the interior yourself you can save 30% to 40% of the remaining cost.

Panelized houses can be as

much as 50% to 60% complete, but offer fewer opportunities for savings. They often must be assembled by a manufacturer's crew or builder, and may include complete walls and floors, plumbing and electrical systems, and sometimes appliances and cabinets. When the house is ready for you to take possession, sometimes it's possible to move right in. What remains for you to do is to put a final covering on the walls, floors, and ceiling, put up moldings and trim inside and out, and decorate the interior. Obviously, the more work you choose to do yourself, the less a contractor or tradesperson will have to do, and the greater the savings will be. Panelized houses can easily cost three or four times as much as dome houses. But the possibility to save by doing the rest of the work yourself will be no more than roughly 20% of the complete cost for the house.

Do-it-yourself construction is not a necessity, however, when you purchase a manufactured house. You can always decide to hire a contractor or builder to assemble the house. Some manufacturers will only sell you the house if they or a contractor builds it for you. The do-it-yourself opportunities with these houses are limited. But even when a house is completely built by a contractor there is a possibility of slight savings compared to the cost of a conventionally built house, because construction time is shorter.

Contracting the house with a builder offers the additional advantage of keeping responsibility for construction with just one company. Most house manufacturers will either provide a factory crew or will recommend a builder to complete the house. In either

case the manufacturer can clearly be held responsible for any problems or difficulties that arise. With a conventionally built house usually a number of subcontractors are used to complete the various parts of construction such as plumbing, heating and cooling, floor covering, or roofing. If a subcontractor makes a mistake, responsibility can be hard to establish. The general contractor often won't bother to track down mistakes—once he turns over the house to you his responsibility ends. But if the contractor was recommended by a house manufacturer, future business with that manufacturer is at stake. Under such circumstances, the contractor is likely to be more responsive.

If the house is completed on a do-it-yourself basis there's the added possibility of it producing a profit for the buyer when the time comes to sell. The house will appreciate in value in direct proportion to local real estate prices. How much money you can make on the sale of the house will depend on how much of your labor you substitute for paying someone else. For example, a buyer who completes a house on his own can easily save as much as $20,000 in labor charges. When the house is sold, some or all of that $20,000 is added to its

value and increases the price of the house. While this sort of profit is possible, there is no guarantee that you will make any money on the sale of a manufactured house.

## Design Advantages: Choose Exactly What You Want

There are several advantages, other than savings, that should also be given consideration in the selection of a manufactured house. The most important are the large choice of designs from which to make your selection, the availability of custom design and engineering services, and the choice of energy-saving designs and technology.

When you set out to purchase an existing house, your choices are limited to whatever happens to be on the local real estate market at that time. You can have a house custom-designed for you by an architect, but a proper job requires a substantial amount of time, effort, and expense. But with manufactured houses, the situation is different. There are literally hundreds of manufacturers in the field today, with a large assortment of stock house plans. You can choose from practically every architectural

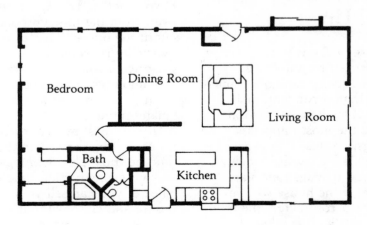

style that exists—from traditional to contemporary to futuristic.

The best part is that all of the details can be absorbed at your leisure, through the manufacturers' literature and discussions with factory personnel and dealers or representatives. There's no need for lengthy sessions with architects, or for hours of searching for just the right existing house. There's no better way to determine exactly what you want and need in the way of a house than to thoroughly investigate, compare, and contrast a broad spectrum of information about manufactured housing.

## Customize Your Own Design

Most manufacturers offer some degree of custom design possibilities; the service can be loosely separated into two different types. One consists of changes that can be made to standard houses. Floor plans can be flip-flopped or rearranged, partition walls can be moved or deleted, a garage can be added, or a wing from one model can be grafted onto another. Much is done through the selection of options and extras such as different exterior siding or windows. There may be no charge for the custom change, a small flat fee, or an hourly charge where actual design and drafting work must be done. There might be additional charges for extra or more expensive materials, over and above the standard items.

The other possibility is a complete design and engineering service. The starting point might be just a few expressed ideas, a picture or a floor plan you have sketched, or a stock model from that or some other manufacturer. The designs and plans are then developed by you and the manufacturer's staff working together, just as it would happen with an independent architectural firm. But there is a difference; the cost

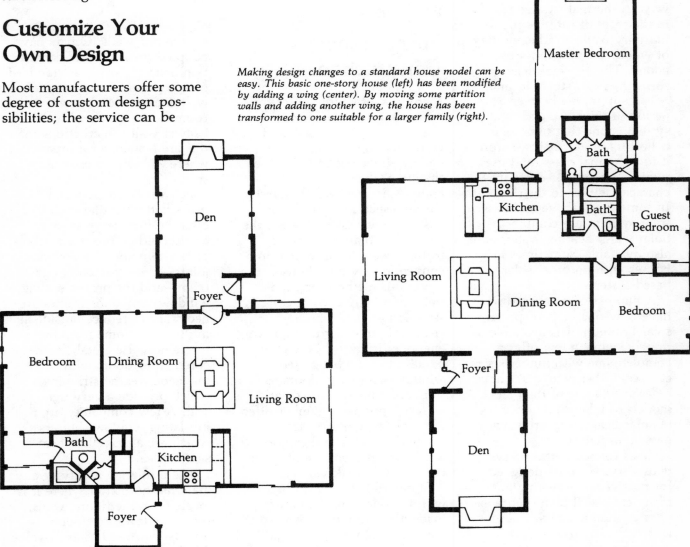

*Making design changes to a standard house model can be easy. This basic one-story house (left) has been modified by adding a wing (center). By moving some partition walls and adding another wing, the house has been transformed to one suitable for a larger family (right).*

of the service is likely to be less than independent architectural fees.

# Solar Features

Viable active and passive solar heating systems are among the most important developments to come along for house buyers in years. A number of house manufacturers offer both types of systems.

Passive solar systems make direct use of sunlight coming through windows. Windows are liberally placed on the south side of the house, and on a sunny day much of the needed heat can be provided in this way. A thermal storage mass, in the form of ceramic tile, a masonry wall, or a heavy mass of wood can sometimes be added. This thermal mass absorbs the heat, stores it, and releases it gradually over a period of time. An active solar system is one that uses solar collectors to gather heat; stores it in a thermal mass; and uses pumps, motors, or other mechanical devices to distribute it. In some cases active and passive solar systems are combined. Solar water heating systems are also available, sometimes in houses with no other solar-based systems.

A number of manufacturers have only one or two special solar house models available at present, while a few offer a complete line with numerous choices. Other companies have redesigned some of their stock models to take some advantage of solar heat; these are usually passive in nature.

Costs for solar heating systems vary. A house designed for passive solar heating in many cases will be no more expensive than a similar house without solar. If a storage medium needs to be added, this

will increase the total house cost usually by about $1,000. Active solar systems, however, can add several thousand dollars, or more, to the cost of a house. Generally, active solar systems must be installed by professionals, and this increases costs even further.

Obviously, some areas of the country are more advantageous for solar designs, but solar heating systems can provide at least a part of the total heating needs of a house, no matter where it is located. With the possibility of saving money on energy costs, there's no question that you should give serious consideration to solar heating possibilities.

# Energy Saving Construction

Many manufacturers offer the opportunity to choose options that incorporate designs and construction that improve energy efficiency and increase the life of the structure. These features are well worth investigating, especially since their cost is not excessive. Often, the cost is less than if the same features were incorporated in a conventionally built house.

Various methods and materials commonly used in construction are used more effectively in order to improve energy efficiency. Many companies offer double-glazed windows and patio doors as standard components, or at least as options; a number offer triple-glazed units. Metal-framed windows and exterior doors, when used, are often of the thermal-break variety.

Standard 2×4 walls filled with fiberglass insulation are inadequate in many areas, so many companies offer an additional layer of sheathing board

on exterior walls. Others have adopted the 2×6 wall construction method, either as standard or an option. This system of wall construction allows more room for insulation. Much heavier wall constructions than this are available for areas where winters are especially severe.

Full vapor barriers and proper attic ventilation are essential for energy saving and should be provided. Complete sealing of all seams and joints—a few companies gasket them—and the proper sealing of windows and door frames are necessary to reduce outside-air infiltration. Some manufacturers now use metal, foam-cored entry doors with magnetic weatherstripping, which provide a very tight seal. A few companies offer insulating window shutters, which are an excellent heat-saving idea.

The insulating ability of any material, no matter where it is located—in the floors, walls, roof, windows, or doors—is usually expressed as an R-value. An R-value is a material's abil-

*Passive solar houses, like the one above, make direct use of sunlight coming through groups of windows. Sometimes a thermal mass is added to keep the house warm through the night. The active solar house, below, uses solar collectors to gather heat, stores it in a thermal mass, and uses pumps, motors, or other mechanical means to distribute it.*

ity to resist the passage of heat. The higher the R-value the more effective the insulator will be at keeping heat from escaping, and cold air from infiltrating. Even more important than an insulator's R-value is how thoroughly it is installed. Insulation materials should be packed into even the smallest places, especially around windows and doors and behind electrical switches, and should always be used with adequate vapor barriers. The vapor barrier keeps moisture off the insulation, which can reduce its effectiveness, and serves as an additional barrier against outside air infiltration.

Design factors that affect energy efficiency should also be considered. For example, a house can be designed with wide eaves overhangs to admit winter sunlight through windows, but shade them and the house walls during the summer months. Double entryways can be included so that the outside door can be closed before the entry door to the interior proper is opened. And, the number, size, and locations of windows and doors on the north and south sides of a structure can be planned so heat loss will be minimal in winter, and still take full advantage of solar warmth.

# What Are the Choices?

Buying a manufactured house involves a number of choices. How big a house do you need, where do you want to build it, or how much do you want to spend; these are some of the decisions you will have to make. The basic choice, however, is one of style; what type of house fits your needs and desires.

Deciding what type of manufactured house to buy can be a challenge because of the many different houses available. But choosing the house type you want isn't the only decision you'll have to make. Manufactured houses come as packages, or kits, that include some or most of the materials necessary for construction. The amount of materials included varies from just the basic parts to nearly everything you will need to finish house construction. The completeness of the packages you choose will deter-mine how much more material you will have to buy from other sources, and what the total cost of the house will be.

## Types of Manufactured Houses

To make your selection of a manufactured house easier, houses have been arranged into seven basic types: log, timber, dome, post-and-beam, panelized, precut, and modular/sectional. All types of manufactured houses are available as kits or packages. And most basic packages are similar in the amount and kinds of materials included—there are some differences, however. Most log, timber, dome, post-and-beam, and precut houses are made up of precut pieces. A basic package for any of these houses would include materials for exterior walls, a first floor, and the roof. Panelized houses come with some precut pieces, but also include partially or completely assembled components, normally walls, floors, and roofs. Modular/sectional houses are different from all other manufactured houses in that they are almost completely finished when they are delivered.

## Log Houses

Houses made of logs can be divided according to their exterior appearance into two groups: hand-peeled logs and machine-peeled logs. Hand-peeled logs have a characteristic mottled and rustic look because some of the inner bark is left in place. Such logs also retain much of their natural contours. Machine-peeled logs are milled to a uniform shape; occasionally some of their natural contours remain, but they usually have little, if any, bark left on.

Most log house packages consist primarily of the basic shell—the walls and the roof—although some packages are more complete. Assembly is not technically difficult because most components are precut, and complete plans and instructions are included. Construction, however, can be physically demanding due to the weight of the logs. Despite this, log house kits are very popular because construction is relatively simple, and they offer the do-it-yourselfer a good opportunity to do more.

Many different sizes and styles of log houses—from rustic to modern—are available. Many of the stock houses offered can be modified substantially, and most can be changed to some degree. Interiors also can be altered. Custom design services are available; some options and extras are also offered. Log structures are heavy and are soundproof to a high degree. They also have a considerable amount of inherent energy efficiency that can be easily improved. Another advantage is low maintenance.

## Timber Houses

Timber houses are also called solid-wall houses, solid-wood houses, and flat-milled log houses. Whatever they're called, they offer all the advantages of log houses, including low

*Log houses, like this one from New England Log Homes, Inc. (top), have a natural warmth and charm not often found in conventional houses. A timber house, such as this one by Alta Industries, offers the benefits of logs with a different look.*

maintenance and high energy efficiency, but look distinctly different. The walls are made of flat-faced timbers that may be solid or laminated wood. When assembled, exterior walls look like wood siding; the interior resembles tongue-and-groove wood paneling.

Timbers may be placed horizontally or vertically, or in combination. Conventional methods are usually used to build floor and roof systems.

Timber house packages are available in basic or complete shells. Assembly is similar to that of a log house, but timbers are lighter and easier to handle than logs. Typically, timbers are about three or four inches thick. Most package components are precut and simply have to be fitted in place and secured. Plans and instructions are generally good, and no special equipment or tools are required. In most cases, interior finishing is minimal. Timber houses offer plenty of opportunity for the do-it-yourselfer to assemble and finish the structure.

Traditional and contemporary designs are available in timber houses; interiors range from rustic to modern. Minor modifications can be made to stock models. Custom design and engineering services are usually available.

## Dome Houses

Dome houses are built in the form of a hemisphere, with a special framework based on a geodesic system developed by R. Buckminster Fuller. The pure geodesic dome shape has been architecturally modified by extensions, dormers, and other features to provide an extremely livable structure. Riser walls that lift the entire dome off the ground and increase interior head room are a common addition.

A dome house's framework must be precision-engineered, and the components accurately cut and fitted. On-site alterations, generally, are not possible. The outside covering must be carefully installed for a weathertight seal. Explicit instructions are included with each precut and sometimes partly panelized dome house package.

Assembly of a dome house frame is simple; it can be done quickly with a few hand tools, although scaffolding and ladders are usually required. Applying the exterior skin isn't difficult, but it is somewhat awkward and physically demanding because of the shape of the structure; much the same is true for the interior finishing, which can be a lengthy chore. Dome house packages are very popular with do-it-yourselfers because they offer considerable opportunity for buyer involvement in assembly and finishing.

Dome structures have some excellent advantages over conventional structures. They are highly resistant to storm, wind, or earthquake damage. Dome houses are freestanding and require no interior load-bearing walls; this allows the buyer complete freedom in designing the interior. Dome structures use considerably less material to enclose a living area than do conventional structures, and expose less exterior surface to the weather. Energy efficiency ranges from high to extremely high. Heating and cooling costs are substantially lower than for a conventional house with comparable living space and insulation. Low maintenance is another plus.

There is a good variety of dome house packages. Because domes are modular units, the number of house design variations is considerable. Styles, however, are quite similar, but modifying is a simple matter. Numerous modifications can be made; a variety of options and extras is available; and custom design and engineering is readily obtainable. Packages can be bought in framework-only form, or even in hardware-only form, but most consist of basic shells; a few packages are fairly complete and include many interior components. Costs range from low to moderate, and completed-house costs are quite likely to be less than for a conventional house with comparable living-space.

## Post-and-Beam Houses

Conventional framing techniques are not used to build post-and-beam houses. Instead, a skeleton of heavy posts and beams is used to support the walls and roof. Two different frame styles are employed: traditional, patterned after the centuries-old, braced-frame method of house, barn, and mill construction; and contemporary, a lighter, more open, and modern framework. In both cases, much of the post-and-beam framework remains exposed and is finished to complement the decor.

Post-and-beam houses are inherently strong, and the structural design allows considerable flexibility in size, shape, and styling. Interior walls are non-load-bearing, so the floor plan is very flexible; open interior plans are common, as are vaulted ceilings and an extensive use of glass. Construction is not technically difficult, but can be physically demanding; frame erection with a crane or boom truck is often advisable, especially with larger houses.

Construction of the house sections that overlay the framework is mostly conventional; sometimes these sections are panelized to reduce on-site assembly time and difficulties. There is some opportunity for buyers to do their own assembly and finishing. Energy efficiency can be increased, and maintenance is low to average depending on how the house is made.

Post-and-beam house packages are available as a frame assembly only, which is a basic shell with or without first floor; as a complete shell with some interior components; or as a reasonably complete house lacking only utility systems and finishing. A sizable array of stock models is available ranging from small to large. Modifications can be made. Many post-and-beam house manufacturers offer custom design and engineering services.

### Panelized Houses

Panelized-house packages are considerably different than house packages made up of precut and uncut components and materials because some—and sometimes a considerable amount—of the assembly work is done at the factory. Typically, panelized houses come with preassembled exterior wall sections that have been framed and covered at the factory. Consequently, such houses require less time and labor to assemble at the job site. There are two kinds of panelized houses—open-wall or closed-wall. On open-wall panelized houses, wall sections are left uncovered on one side for on-site installation of plumbing and wiring, and subsequent inspection by local building inspectors. Sections of closed-wall panelized houses contain electrical wiring, plumbing, and insulation, and are covered on both sides at the factory. Panelized houses may or may not include panelized roof or floor sections.

Most closed-wall models are made with large wall sections—

*The rounded structure of a dome has no right angles (above); even when partition walls are added, rooms in this house from Monterey Domes don't have a rectangular shape. The heavy wood timbers used to build the framework of post-and-beam houses are often left exposed. Because the post-and-beam frame is self-supporting, load-bearing partition walls aren't needed, and interiors such as in this house by Deck House are frequently left open (top right). While the construction of panelized houses is unlike that of most other houses, interiors, like this one in a house by Acorn Structures, Inc. appear conventional (right).*

40 feet or more if needed. And many include completely pre-assembled and prefinished utility core modules that incorporate a kitchen, bathrooms, most of the plumbing system, the main electrical panel, basic appliances, and perhaps the laundry room. Open-wall models may feature large wall panels, but usually they are 8×8 feet or less; most interior components are options. Either kind of panelized house may have factory-installed windows.

The closed-wall panelized house must be erected by a professional crew with a crane or boom truck; typically, the entire job takes less than a day. Interior work is carried out conventionally. The same applies for a few open-wall models, but most are delivered as kits ready to be assembled by the buyer. While much of the interior work is already done in the closed-wall panelized house—the amount varies with the manufacturer's line—most open-wall models are basic shells that require about the same amount of interior and finishing work as any other kind of house. The advantage is that shell assembly is faster and easier.

Panelized houses is the most varied category. It has the greatest number of stock models. All styles, sizes, and types are represented; many options and extras are offered; modification possibilities are vast; and custom design and engineering services are common. The opportunity for the do-it-yourselfer to assemble and finish a model ranges from doing the entire job to doing very little except for some interior decorating.

Panelized house packages range from bare shells to models that are nearly complete; even foundations are available. Energy efficiencies of panelized houses range from average to exceptional, and maintenance factors range from low to a bit above average. And as you might expect, package costs and completed house costs cover a wide range.

### Precut Houses

A precut house isn't any particular style of manufactured house; it is a type of house package. By strict definition, log and timber houses are precut houses. But in this category are houses with a conventional appearance that are built by the conventional platform-framing method—joist floors, stud walls, rafter or truss roofs.

Precut house packages are true kits; they contain most of the necessary components to make a complete house. There are some variations; some uncut materials may be included and a few items may be partially assembled for you beforehand. Although a basic house shell—floors, walls, roof—can be bought, most packages are quite complete. Some manufacturers offer virtually everything necessary to finish the house including plumbing and electrical supplies.

Most precut house packages are designed so that the buyer can do a substantial amount of construction and finishing. Most do at least the major portion of the finishing work, and many do the entire project.

A good selection of stock models in traditional and contemporary styles is available, and most can be modified to some degree. Custom designing, however, is less common in the precut house category than in others, but it is available from a few manufacturers.

Assembling and finishing a precut house isn't physically demanding or technically difficult—excellent plans and instructions are included; special tools and equipment are not required. Energy efficiencies range from average to good. Maintenance for such houses is average; it is about the same as for any conventional frame house. Some manufacturers offer financing.

### Modular/Sectional Houses

The modular/sectional manufactured house is the only type that is almost entirely factory-built. Each house consists of two or more modules that are connected together at the building site with only a minor amount of trimming and finishing left to do. Wiring, plumbing, final flooring, painting, papering—virtually everything is done at the factory. Whatever needs to be done when the sections reach the site is taken care of by the dealer or builder, and the buyer is presented with a virtually finished house. The only exception might be some interior decorating. Most of these houses, however, are sold to dealers or builders, not to individuals. Except for some minor finishing, there is little opportunity for owner involvement, although there are some do-it-yourself possibilities such as foundation construction, a garage, and add-ons like decks.

There are plenty of different models from which to choose, though many designs look alike. Minor modifications, however, can be made in most models. Although there is a wide range of options, extras, and some choices in detailing and materials, custom design possibilities are limited and not offered by most manufacturers. Most modular/sectional houses are no larger than 2,000 square

*Precut houses, like this one by Wickes Lumber, have interiors not unlike a conventionally built house.*

*Modular/sectional houses, such as this one from Fleetwood Enterprises, typically have low ceilings and small rooms.*

feet; very few two-story models are offered.

In most cases, conventional building materials are used, but with advanced construction procedures such as glue-bonding of components. As a result, most modular/sectional houses are well-built. Energy efficiency runs from average to good, and in some instances excellent. Maintenance for such structures is about average. Costs are low to moderate.

## The Package

When you buy a manufactured house package, you never buy a completely finished house. At the very least, you must supply some items. Often, the package will include only plans and the components for the basic shell of the house; you will have to buy much of the other components locally to complete the structure. There really is no typical house package; the only accurate method is to examine a complete bill of materials for each specific house. But there are certain general categories that will give you a basic idea of what's included and what is not.

Note that we will be discussing the standard, as-advertised offerings of manufacturers. But in fact, most companies are flexible as to what can be included in, or left out of a so-called "standard" package. Many packages can be developed to suit a buyer's needs by adding or deleting various materials or products.

### Walls Only

Walls-only house packages are offered by some log house manufacturers; they may also be called "logs-only" packages. They include just the logs—usually precut and with the joints formed as required—necessary to build the walls of the structure. In the case of logs-only packages, other components that are made of logs are included, such as a second floor or loft frame, porch posts and rafters, or perhaps log roof trusses. Usually, the hardware needed to assemble the log-work, as well as sealing or caulking materials, is included too. Windows, doors, roofing, floor assemblies, partition walls, trimwork, or other materials are not included.

### Frame Only

As far as standard packages are concerned, frame-only packages are peculiar to dome and post-and-beam houses. A dome frame-only package includes all of the space-frame members for the dome hemisphere itself, along with all necessary hardware to assemble it. Framing materials for riser walls, extensions, dormers or other dome elements are not included; neither are the exterior sheathing, insulation, or any other parts. A frame-only package for post-and-beam houses consists of all the support posts and beams needed to make the complete house skeleton. The members are precut and the joints formed; necessary hardware may also be included.

Because many manufacturers of house packages also make and sell component parts of houses, you might—if you wish—be able to contract for a frame-only kit for a conventional, platform-framed house. Such a kit might consist of a floor frame assembly, stud wall frames, and a rafter or truss roof frame assembly.

### Basic Shell

A basic shell package usually consists of the walls and the roof frame. A first-floor frame with subflooring might be included, but usually is not; a second floor or loft frame, where applicable, is usually included. Windows and exterior doors are generally part of the package. Similarly, roof sheathing is sometimes included; roofing material seldom is. Exterior siding may or may not be supplied, but sheathing is—except for log or timber houses. Hardware and supplies needed to assemble the basic shell package are almost always included.

### Complete Shell

A complete, or weathertight, shell comprises all exterior walls, usually with exterior siding, windows and exterior doors, exterior trim—and sometimes some interior trim—and a complete roof system. A floor system may be included, but often is not. Interior partition wall framing materials are usually included in such a package, especially for load-bearing walls that form a part of the structure. All necessary hardware and supplies are also included.

### Complete House

A complete-house package is not really complete, but goes several steps beyond a complete shell package. A first-floor frame, subflooring, and sometimes a wood foundation are part of the package. Interior wall coverings, ceiling materials, insulation, interior partition walls, and interior trim and doors are included. Sometimes trim and flooring are provided, and inside stair assemblies usually are, too. In short, just about everything is present except for the utilities systems, applied finishes, and similar detailing. Not much in the way of additional materials or labor is required.

### Finished House

Finished houses are not quite finished, but almost so. These are found in two categories: the panelized closed-wall houses that come complete with integral preassembled utility modules or mechanical cores, and the modular/sectional types. With a panelized closed-wall model, the house is assembled and virtually completed by a contractor leaving only the interior decorating for the buyer. In the case of modular/sectional houses, a builder or dealer usually completes the house and also most of the finish work—only a few minor details of interior decorating, if any, are left to the buyer.

# Make the Changes You Want

One nice thing about buying a manufactured house is that you can have a good deal to say about the final design. True, most manufacturers offer complete lines of stock house models, but they're almost never purchased just the way they are presented in the catalog. Everybody makes changes, especially minor ones. Manufacturers expect that, and many of them welcome it since they would prefer to do custom work anyway.

Stock house designs can be changed in hundreds of different ways. You can add extras, choose various options, shuffle the floor plans around, make changes in colors and materials, and even change the structure of the house itself. You can also opt for a brand-new custom design. Much can be done simply by using the information in the manufacturer's literature. Various choices and possibilities will be listed and you can pick and choose among them.

Many manufacturers offer energy efficient features and designs that should be considered too. Extra insulation, thicker exterior walls, and solid-fuel heaters—stoves and fireplaces—are some of the options that you might want to add to the house you select. Solar heating systems, solar hot-water systems, or house designs that can be fitted with solar equipment are offered by some manufacturers and are also worth looking into. While any energy efficient option will cost extra, it's likely to result in long term savings.

Some manufacturers provide complete planning kits with instructions that explain how to make either minor or major changes in any of the stock plans. In effect, you make up your own set of rough drawings and general specifications. These are then refined and translated into working drawings that come back to you for approval or further changes, and so on until the final design is reached.

Where the literature or planning kit is not sufficient, or you have unanswered questions, in most cases you can get direct help from the manufacturer. Sometimes direct contact with factory personnel, either by mail or by phone, is necessary. In many cases factory representatives or dealers will help with all the planning and design details.

# Choosing the House That's Right for You

To choose a manufactured house, you must know what's available. So, the first step is to request information from at least a dozen manufacturers. Although your requests for information may result in telephone calls from local dealers, most manufacturers will send you literature about their product line. This can be a small brochure, a thick packet of detailed information sheets, or a substantial catalog. Manufacturers charge several dollars for more extensive catalogs.

If some of the literature contains little useful information, you'll have to decide whether to send another request for more complete printed information or to cross those companies off

your list of possibilities. Because you have very little to go on at this point, your decision will have to be made largely by your reaction to their original response.

## How To Read the Catalogs

Eventually you'll collect a stack of catalogs and information packets that you will have to sort, study, and compare. This can be a confusing chore, because each manufacturer presents his products differently. The process can be even more difficult if the material covers different types of manufactured houses. The trick is in knowing how to read the

catalogs—how to get to the hard facts and how to determine what important information is lacking.

**Interpreting Illustrations**

Curiosity being what it is, you'll first look over the pictures of the houses offered. Some companies illustrate each house they make, others only a selected few; a few don't include illustrations or photographs at all. If there are no views of houses, you may want to get further information or drop that company from further consideration.

Sometimes a catalog will show full-color photographs, but more often they use artists' renderings or simple line draw-

19

ings. Although photographs present exact detail, artwork often depicts a generalized and sometimes stylized version of a house. Keep in mind that the actual house, built on your lot, will not look the same. Also, a photograph or drawing may show a house with custom features or design modifications not included on the manufacturer's stock models; this fact may not be mentioned in the catalog.

### Evaluating Floor Plans

The next step is to study the floor plans of houses that interest you. Floor plans show the layout of the walls, room spaces, major architectural features, and main fixtures, appliances, and cabinetry, just as though you had removed the roof off a house and were looking down into its interior.

The heavy solid lines on floor plans represent the walls—interior and exterior. The overall outside dimensions of the house are indicated along the finer lines that end in dots or arrowheads, outside the outline of the house. The dimensions noted below each room name are the length and width of the living space inside the room; you can determine the square footage of each room by multiplying these two figures. Often a total square footage figure is listed. Knowing the gross area of the house will be helpful because many building codes specify maximum lot coverages for structures that may not be exceeded.

Windows are shown on floor plans as fine-lined open rectangles in the wall lines; doors are indicated by a fine line across a wall opening, with another line off at an angle to show the direction of the door swing. If there is just a blank space in the wall line, there is an entranceway without a door, or a cased opening—a larger open space in the partition that may go from the floor almost or all the way to the ceiling. Sliding doors or patio doors are shown by double sets of fine parallel lines across openings in wall lines. Stairs are indicated by sets of parallel or sometimes fan-patterned fine lines, with an arrow through them to show whether the stairs go up or

down, and in which direction they go from the level of the house shown in the plan. Other items, such as cabinets, closets, fireplaces, and plumbing fixtures, are often labeled.

Keep in mind one important point as you examine floor plans. In most cases, but not all, the floor plan of any standard house model can be altered to suit your wishes. For example, it may be possible to change window and door locations, or to move closets. Interior walls can usually be moved a few feet or removed entirely; sometimes even exterior walls can be altered. Remember, too, that a room doesn't have to be put to the use that is indicated; a bedroom can be used as a den, two bedrooms can become a large one, family rooms and living rooms can be transposed, and so on. And in many cases, a floor plan can be set up in a mirror image of the original.

As you mull over a floor plan to determine if it might be right for you, there are several points to consider. Are there enough rooms—bedrooms, bathrooms, closets—to accommodate your

*A floor plan shows walls, architectural features, and fixtures.*

family? Are the rooms large enough? You can determine this by comparing room dimensions on the floor plan with the sizes of the rooms you currently occupy. Is there a workable, smooth traffic pattern? Check to see that noise-producing areas (kitchen, family room, workshop) are well separated from quiet areas (bedrooms, den, study). The final factor is entirely a matter of personal judgment. How would you feel in that house? Project yourself, your family, your furnishings, and your lifestyle into the floor plan. Walk through the house in your mind. Will it be a convenient and comfortable house?

If you anticipate some problems with a house but still like it, it's worthwhile to spend time trying to solve the problems by making minor modifications to the plan. If this doesn't seem to be feasible, however, the plan may not be right for you; evaluate another.

### Checking Specifications

After you've selected several possible house plans, you'll have to check the specifications. Before you decide on a house, you should know whether the manufacturer's standard models conform to local governing building codes and ordinances. Look for a statement that says the manufacturer will make any changes or modifications required by municipal building codes—changes may not be needed, but the manufacturer should be willing to adapt to local requirements or furnish additional information that may be requested by your local building department. Then make a list of all the specifications listed in the catalog. These might include type and thickness of shingles; brand names of windows, doors,

carpeting, or other items used; whether windows are single- or double-glazed, and wood- or aluminum-framed; the thickness and R-value of insulation; fire ratings; flame-spread data; and so on. Compile all of the details of this sort for each manufacturer, and then compare your lists.

At the same time, make notes of whatever you can think of that isn't specified. You'll probably raise more questions than you answer during this process, but you'll have a much better idea of the house you're looking at. It's good to know, for instance, just what kind of exterior siding is used, how thick the floor underlayment is, whether shelves are metal or wood, what brand of equipment or appliances may be installed, whether window sashes are removable, and so on.

Some of the information that you turn up when you list these specifications may not have much meaning for you, and you may not be able to compare houses effectively yet. At this point, further investigation is necessary. For example, suppose one manufacturer offers Brand X windows, and another offers Brand Y. A few questions at two or three local building supply outlets should give you some idea of the differences between, and the quality of, the two brands. If you're not sure whether you'd be better off with a certain roof structure, for instance, you can ask a local builder or architect to advise you. In fact, there's no reason why you shouldn't seek professional help if there is any part of the process you don't understand. The fees you are charged for these services can be well worth the expense.

Remember, you should have the same information for each house you're considering, as far

as possible. Otherwise, you won't be able to make valid comparisons. Of course, you'll have to use a little judgment too. Just because the exterior walls of a log house are thicker than those of a dome house doesn't necessarily mean that one is better than the other.

## Who Supplies What?

Perhaps the most important information you can gather is a list of who provides what. Sometimes this is rather difficult to determine, at least in detail. But to get a reasonably accurate estimate of how much a house will cost and how easy it will be to build, you must have this information. Some catalogs are quite explicit about what is included and what is not, but you'll always have to do a certain amount of careful investigating. Unfortunately, many catalogs provide only minimal information of this sort, which means that if you're really interested, you'll have to ask the manufacturer for more data.

As you did with the specifications, the best method is to list everything that's provided by each manufacturer for each house you're considering. Different house models don't necessarily include the same list of materials, even when the houses are made by the same manufacturer. You'll have to refer back and forth from list to list. Naturally, parts or materials that are applicable to one type of house but not to others shouldn't be considered. Eventually, you'll end up with a fairly complete materials list for each house.

### Permits and Preparation: What You Always Provide

The items or materials provided by a manufacturer can vary

 **Planning**

## What to Look For:

### What the Buyer Always Provides

*Building site*

*Survey—parcel and improvement*

*Soil tests*

*Access road/driveway*

*Turnaround/parking area/ unloading area*

*Any necessary local architectural/ engineering services*

*Site preparation*

*Building permits*

*Septic system and permits (where applicable)*

*Well permit (where applicable)*

*Water well installation (where applicable)*

*Water and/or sewer tap permits and fees (where applicable)*

*Water and sewer main installation (where applicable)*

*Electric lines*

*Temporary electrical service (construction loop)*

*Gas supply line (where applicable)*

*Oil or gas storage tanks (where applicable)*

*Telephone service*

*Construction of complete foundation*

*Rubbish removal*

*Landscaping*

*Miscellaneous incidentals*

*Tree removal*

*Drain tile, pits, and pumps*

*Insurance*

*Masonry (chimneys, patios, retaining walls, veneer, etc.)*

*Shipping charges*

*State and local taxes*

*Decorating*

greatly from house to house, and there is even greater variation among different types of manufactured houses. But there are certain items that house manufacturers never provide; you, the buyer, must always provide these. Whether you personally furnish them or your contractor or architect does, they are your responsibility when it comes to paying the bills. The items listed in the accompanying check list are never included in a house package price, but must be provided by the buyer.

First, of course, you need a building site. If you own a parcel of land, you should have an overall land survey. You'll most likely need a recent improvement, or spot, survey that shows existing site improvements. It's a good idea to ask for topographical features and large trees to be included on the survey. There will be an additional fee, but it can be a big

help. Some building departments require an improvement survey after the foundation is in but before construction of the house is begun.

Then you should have a plot plan prepared. You'll need two plans for a large parcel—a broad-scale plan and a plan for the house and its immediate surroundings. You'll also have to obtain whatever building permits are needed, and in most cases this may require a recent survey and in some cases a zoning variance. These procedures require the payment of fees. You must arrange for suitable insurance coverage such as a "builder's risk" policy; the exact details can be sorted out by your insurance agent.

Other permits may be needed, too. In areas where there are no municipal water and sewer mains, you may have to obtain a water well permit, or a septic system permit; if you'll be using a septic system,

you'll also have to have percolation tests made. If there are water or sewer lines available to serve your building site, you'll have to make arrangements to tap onto them. This nearly always involves tap fees and perhaps permits too.

Besides all the paperwork needed to comply with the legalities, you'll also have to make improvements to the site. There must be a driveway or access road so that you or the builder can get to it. Traffic to the building site will compact the soil so it's best to put your driveway base in and use it for access. The roadway should be at least 12 feet wide—the width of most driveways—and well graded. It is better to base the access road with gravel to withstand the weight of a 30-ton tractor-trailer rig, even in wet weather. Any curves in the road must be gentle enough so that a 60-foot truck can negotiate them easily, and there must be plenty of room at the building site for unloading.

Site preparation is also your responsibility. This includes removal of trees, brush, vegetation, and anything else that might be in the way, and site grading or contouring and excavation for the foundation. You must provide a complete foundation for the house you choose; seldom is a foundation provided, and when they are they are usually of the All Weather Wood variety.

You'll also have to arrange for installation of the electric and telephone lines, for temporary electrical service, for a gas supply line or storage tank or an oil storage tank, and for a water supply line or well if required. The sewer main or septic system can be installed when the backfill for the foundation is put in or at any other time during construction.

Although most contractors will leave a house site in reasonably presentable shape, you are responsible for any cleanup chores. Landscaping is also left entirely up to you. And, you can be sure that there will be additional miscellaneous costs—required materials that were overlooked. It's best to allow a contingency for such things—perhaps an amount equal to about 10 percent of the house's cost.

### Hidden Costs:
### What You May Have To Provide

Buying a manufactured house involves other costs, which may not always be obvious. No manufacturer provides a completely finished house; your extra costs depend on the type and model of house you choose. Modular/sectional houses generally involve the least additional cost, because they may be as much as 95 percent complete when they're delivered to the site. Closed-wall panelized homes are also substantially complete, but open-wall panelized homes require a considerable amount of on-site work. Precut house kits, and kits for log, timber, dome, and post-and-beam houses are the least complete and involve the most additional expense.

To determine exactly who supplies what, start with the "manufacturer provides" lists in the catalogs, and make a list of your own for each house that you're considering. Next, if there are "provided by others" lists, copy them too, separately. Now, compare each set of lists; you may find items on one list that aren't mentioned on others. If you can't tell who's supposed to supply an item, make a note to ask the manufacturer.

When your lists are as complete as you can possibly make them, study them carefully to see what items have not been mentioned at all. Some basic knowledge of house construc-

---

## What to Look For:

### Items the Buyer May Have to Provide

Sills (mud sills, sill plates)
Sill seal
Sill flashing
First-floor girder(s) (if required)
First-floor girder support posts/ columns (if required)
First-floor joists/beams
First-floor header and end joists (band, ribbon joists)
First-floor joist blocking/bridging
First-floor subflooring/decking
First-floor underlayment
First-floor finished floor coverings
Exterior wall system, complete
Gable walls, complete (if required)
Interior wall framing
Interior wall surfaces
Windows (storm sash, screens)
Skylights (if required)
Exterior doors
Exterior storm/screen doors
Window/door flashing
Interior doors
Closet doors
Closet separating partitions

Second-floor/loft girder(s) (if required)
Second-floor/loft joists/beams
Second-floor/loft subflooring/ decking
Second-floor/loft finished floor covering
Ceiling framework
Finished ceilings
Tie beam(s) (if required)
Stairway, or stair components
Railings/banisters
Roof trusses, rafters, beams, purlins (as required)
Collar tie beams (if required)
Roof sheathing/decking
Roof underlayment
Roof flashing
Roof drip edge
Roof finished covering
Roof guttering and downspouts
Dormers (or dormer components)
Interior trimwork
Exterior trimwork
Insulation (floor, walls, roof/ ceiling)
Vapor barrier (floor, walls, roof/ ceiling)
Porch, complete
Stoop, complete
Decks, complete
Garage

Garage door(s)
Garage door opener(s)
Exterior applied finishes
Interior applied finishes
Builders' hardware (door latches, hinges, etc.)
Fasteners (nails, spikes, lag screws, washers, etc.)
Weatherstripping
Caulks and sealers
Gasketing
Splines
Brackets, hangers, straps, etc.
Freestanding fireplace/stove with chimney
Electrical system, with lighting fixtures
Appliances
Heating/cooling system
Plumbing system, with fixtures
Ventilating system (if required)
Vent louvers (soffit, eaves, gable)
Bathroom fixtures
Closet fixtures
Shelving
Kitchen (and other) cabinetry
Smoke detectors
Telephone prewiring
Fire/intrusion security system
Drapery hardware
Foundation plans
Mechanical plans

tion would be helpful, so that you can mentally go through the entire process of building a house to visualize all the parts, supplies, and materials that are needed, step by step, for a complete structure. Refer to the accompanying list—"What to Look For: Items the Buyer May Have to Provide"—as a starting point.

If you still have questions, you can contact the manufacturer or dealer for specific details, or you can consult a local contractor or architect. In most cases, going to the manufacturer can give you more accurate information, even though it would probably be faster and more convenient to go to a contractor or architect. A manufacturer, however, isn't likely to point out any deficiencies in his products. The manufacturer, meanwhile, will answer your questions at no charge, but a contractor or architect would probably charge a fee. However you decide to do it, make sure your lists are complete, and make sure you know exactly who is responsible for all the parts and materials.

# How To Estimate Price

Making an accurate estimate of the cost of a completely finished manufactured house can be difficult. It's impossible to arrive at an accurate total from a manufacturer's literature alone; you'll also have to do some work yourself, and get some help from other people in your area. It's not practical, of course, to go through this involved procedure in detail until you're serious about buying a certain house, or until you want to compare several houses. But you can make some

reasonable preliminary cost comparisons. Your estimated prices won't be valid for very long—probably not more than two months or so—but your estimates will be realistic if you know how to figure them.

### The House Package

The apparent cost of a manufactured house—the price you pay the manufacturer—can be misleading. Most manufactured house prices sound attractive, especially when you compare them with prices in real estate ads. If you're not careful, the package price can really fool you. This is less true of modular/sectional or closed-wall panelized houses, but for other types of houses, the package price may be a far cry from the total cost. For example, some log house kits actually consist of only the logs for the walls—you're not buying a complete house, but only part of one. The difference between the cost of a house package and the total cost of the completely finished house can be a considerable amount.

What is the total cost? Besides the house package, you'll have to pay for shipping, for all of the permits and site preparation discussed earlier, and for other materials that may be needed. Unless you're building the house yourself, you'll have to pay for labor, too—for a general contractor, subcontractors, and unskilled labor. And, if you want to make any changes in the house plan, you'll also have to pay the manufacturer's charge for design modifications or custom design, and sometimes, architects' or engineers' fees. All these costs can add up to much more than the cost of the house package itself. Although a manufactured house package may cost a lot

less than a conventional house of comparable size and quality, the completed house can cost as much as a conventional house.

Most catalogs or information packets include the price of each basic model offered, and a list of any special options offered. If you're interested in getting the most space for the least cost, divide the price of each house, without options, by the square footage. This gives you the basic cost per square foot. You'll find considerable differences, not only among the different manufacturers, but also among the various models listed by each manufacturer. And you'll find that the per-square-foot costs usually increase as the house gets smaller. Variations are due to differences in house design, and the kind—and quantities—of materials supplied with each house.

You can use your initial cost-per-square-foot figures in several ways. First, by comparing models offered by the same manufacturer, you can determine which appear to be the best buys, as far as obtaining basic shelter on a per-square-foot basis.

Second, it becomes obvious that if one house costs $5 a square foot less than another with the same amount of living space, the lower-cost house must include less materials. Ask yourself why. Is this because the different design requires less material, or does it mean that more materials must be supplied by the buyer? Or, is the material supplied of less quality; for example, lauan instead of oak?

Third, you can find out how much extra you're paying for added non-living space and a fancier design, either or both of which you might not want.

And fourth, you can compare the per-square-foot costs for

different manufacturers or for different houses. At this point, however, such a comparison can be tricky unless the comparable materials, or at least the same component systems, are included in all of the houses you're comparing. Otherwise, your conclusions will be invalid. If all the kits, for instance, have full floor systems, interior and exterior walls, comparable doors and windows, a complete roof system, similar porches, and so on, they can be reasonably compared. But if one lacks an entire first-floor system, it can't be compared with the others unless you add the cost of building the floor system.

## Buyer-Supplied Materials

The cost-per-square-foot prices may lead you to discard some of the houses you've been considering. After you've reconsidered your list of manufactured houses, go on to the next step—making rough estimates of the total cost of the houses you like. With two exceptions, the entire list of "owner always provides" items can be set aside for the moment. Those excep-

tions are the shipping costs and the cost for the construction of the foundation.

Shipping should be the last consideration; only occasionally does it tip the balance in favor of one house over another. The foundation cost depends on the building site conditions, the size and shape of the house you choose, and the general style of house. For example, a rambling one-floor house might be suited for a slab foundation, but a smaller one might be best set on a full basement that would provide additional living space.

Nearly all house models can be set on any kind of foundation—piers, perimeter crawl space, full basement, pedestal and post, slab, or wood. A pier is a concrete column—normally

above ground—that is reinforced with steel rods; a number of these are used to support the house. Generally, a pier foundation is used where the terrain is irregular or slopes sharply.

A perimeter crawl space consists of 18-inch or 24-inch masonry walls built on a concrete footing or support. A full basement is similar in construction to a crawl space, but because the walls are usually seven feet high, the full basement provides extra living space.

A pedestal and post foundation is made of large wood beams, no smaller than 8 by 8 inches, that are used to support the house. A slab foundation is composed entirely of concrete

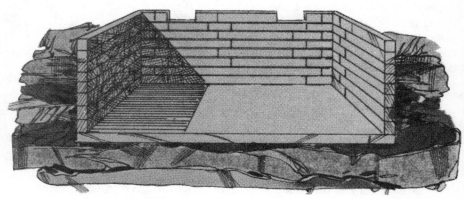

*A full basement (above) usually has 7-foot walls, and is built on concrete footings. The full basement provides extra living space. A daylight basement (left) has at least one wall fully exposed. Windows can be installed in this wall to let in light.*

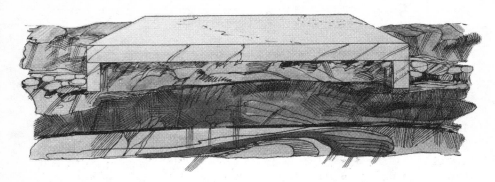

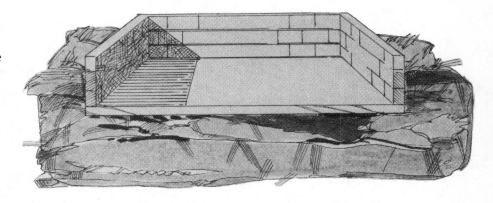

A slab foundation (left) is composed entirely of concrete poured directly onto the soil; it's not excavated, but it is supported by concrete footings. A crawl space (below) consists of 18- or 24-inch masonry walls built on concrete footings for support.

poured directly onto the soil; it's not excavated, but is supported by concrete footings. And, with this type of foundation, a supporting frame for the first floor isn't necessary.

When you've boiled your choices down to three or four houses, you can add the foundation costs for each one to arrive at final cost figures.

Next, assess the cost of the items that must be supplied by you the buyer. Often, it's the cost of these items that really determines what the total cost of a house will be.

First, consider the list of parts and materials that you must supply. You can easily get accurate figures for such items as 24 sheets of ½-inch CDX plywood, 50 pounds of 10d nails, or a case of acrylic latex caulk by calling a local building supply center. Other items, like a complete floor system or a complete partition system, will be more difficult. If you have some knowledge of or experience in residential construction, you can roughly assess what will be needed in the way of floor joists, plywood subflooring, particle board underlayment, or 2×4 studs and drywall. Then work out the quantities, and obtain the prices from a lumberyard. Chances are you don't have such experience so it's best to ask for help from a local builder, an architect, or even a building supply dealer to

determine just what materials will be needed and what their approximate cost will be.

Many of the items that you must supply for the house must also be specified by you. This commonly includes carpeting or other floor coverings, interior finishes like paint and wallpaper, kitchen cabinets, appliances, bathroom fixtures, closet rods, and the like. Since you probably don't know at this stage just what you'll want, all you can do is make estimates, or allowances. For cost estimating purposes, set base figures, and then use the same figures for all of the house estimates you're working on.

For example, if you must specify and supply a finished ceiling covering, there's a wide range of choices—acoustic tile, suspended panel, plaster, drywall, wood plank—and an equally wide range of prices.

Choose the ceiling type that you'd like, and then consult catalogs, inquire at building supply dealers, browse in home centers, and settle on a reasonable per-square-foot cost. Your cost figure can be at the extravagant end, a middle-of-the-road choice, or so low you'll just scrape by. As long as it's the same for all estimates, it doesn't matter if it's exactly accurate. If you have to supply a ceiling for a 1,000-square-foot house, and you've settled on $1.25 per square foot as a reasonable cost, you can set an allowance of $1,250 for ceiling costs in estimating the total price of each house you're considering. Follow this same procedure for the other materials you must supply.

Some items that you must specify and provide are considerably more complex. These include the heating, cooling,

# Cost Estimating Worksheet:

## *What the Buyer Sometimes Provides*

This checklist can be used to estimate how much money you'll have to spend in addition to the package price of a manufactured house. The cost for any materials not included with the house, but still necessary to make your house livable, will have to be estimated and added to the manufacturer's price. Where possible, house components have been broken down into their various pieces; you can estimate the cost for each separate material. For some of the materials or systems you will need—plumbing and electrical for example—it will be difficult to estimate costs on your own. Get an estimate from a contractor that specializes in that work. Then use that estimate to determine the total estimated cost of everything you will have to provide.

**FIRST FLOOR** (includes hallways, foyers, and closets)

**Structural**                                          Cost
___ Sills
___ Main beam *(wood or steel)*
___ Support columns *(wood or steel)*
    Cost/sill        _____ × No. required = _____
    Cost/beam        _____ × No. required = _____
    Cost/column      _____ × No. required = _____

**Frame** *(based on joists placed 16-inch on center)*
___ 2 × 10's
___ 2 × 12's
___ Other
    Cost/joist       _____ × No. required = _____

**Bridging** *(needed every 8 feet in the floor frame)*
___ Solid *(wood)*
___ Cross-bridging *(wood or steel)*
    Cost/unit        _____ × No. required = _____

**Insulation** *(not required with heated basement)*
___ Batt
___ Blanket
___ Rigid
___ Other
    Cost/sq. ft.     _____ × No. sq. ft. = _____

**Vapor Barrier** *(not required with heated basement)*
___ Building paper
___ Vinyl rolls
___ Rosin paper
___ Other
    Cost/sq. ft.     _____ × No. sq. ft. = _____

**Subflooring**
___ Plywood
___ Planks
___ Other
    Cost/sq. ft.     _____ × No. sq. ft. = _____

**Underlayment**
___ Plywood
___ Fiberboard
___ Particle board *(advisable only under carpeting)*
___ Other
    Cost/4 × 8 sheet _____ × No. required = _____

**Floor Covering**
___ Wood
___ Ceramic tile
___ Other tile
___ Linoleum
___ Carpet
___ Other
    Cost/sq. ft.     _____ × No. sq. ft. = _____

**SECOND FLOOR** (includes hallways and closets)

**Frame** *(based on joists 16-inch on center)*
___ 2 × 10's
___ 2 × 12's
___ Other
    Cost/joist       _____ × No. required = _____

**Bridging** *(needed every 8 feet in the floor frame)*
___ Solid *(wood)*
___ Cross-bridging *(wood or steel)*
    Cost/unit        _____ × No. required = _____

**Subflooring**
___ Plywood
___ Planks
___ Other
    Cost/sq. ft.     _____ × No. sq. ft. = _____

**Underlayment**
___ Fiberboard
___ Plywood
___ Particle board *(advisable only under carpeting)*
___ Other
    Cost/4 × 8 sheet _____ × No. required = _____

**Floor Covering**
___ Wood
___ Ceramic tile
___ Other tile
___ Linoleum
___ Carpet
___ Other
    Cost/sq. ft.     _____ × No. sq. ft. = _____

**Ceilings** *(first floor and second floor)*
___ Acoustical tile
___ Drywall
___ Suspended ceiling
    Cost/sq. ft.     _____ × No. sq. ft. = _____

 **Planning**

EXTERIOR WALLS

**Cost**

### Sheathing
____ Plywood
____ Planks
____ Foam sheets
____ Other
Cost/sq. ft.  _____ × No. sq. ft. = _____

### Exterior Covering
____ Siding
____ Brick veneer
____ Shingles
____ Other
Cost/sq. ft.  _____ × No. sq. ft. = _____

### Exterior Finish
____ Paint
____ Stain
____ Other
Cost/sq. ft.  _____ × No. sq. ft. = _____

### Insulation
____ Batt
____ Blanket
____ Blown
____ Rigid
____ Other
Cost/sq. ft.  _____ × No. sq. ft. = _____

### Vapor Barrier
____ Vinyl rolls
____ Other
Cost/sq. ft.  _____ × No. sq. ft. = _____

### Interior Wall Surface
____ Drywall
____ Plaster
____ Other
Cost/sq. ft.  _____ × No. sq. ft. = _____

### Wall Covering
____ Wood panel
____ Laminated panel
____ Paint
____ Wallpaper
____ Other
Cost/sq. ft.  _____ × No. sq. ft. = _____

## PARTITION WALLS

### Frame *(based on studs 16-inch on center)*
____ 2 × 4's
____ 2 × 8's *(for plumbing walls)*
____ Other
Cost/stud  _____ × No. required = _____

### Wall Surface
____ Drywall
____ Plaster
____ Other
Cost/sq. ft.  _____ × No. sq. ft. = _____

### Wall Covering
____ Wood panel
____ Laminated panel
____ Paint
____ Wallpaper
____ Other
Cost/sq. ft.  _____ × No. sq. ft. = _____

## ROOF

### Frame
____ Rafters
____ Truss
____ Beam
____ Other
Cost/unit  _____ × No. required = _____

### Insulation
____ Blown
____ Blanket
____ Rigid
____ Other
Cost/sq. ft.  _____ × No. sq. ft. = _____

### Vapor Barriers
____ Vinyl rolls
____ Other
Cost/sq. ft.  _____ × No. sq. ft. = _____

### Sheathing/Decking
____ Plywood
____ Wood planks
____ Tongue-and-groove decking
____ Other
Cost/sq. ft.  _____ × No. sq. ft. = _____

### Roof Protection
____ Building paper *(rolls)*
____ Other
Cost/sq. ft.  _____ × No. sq. ft. = _____

### Sheet Metal
____ Flashing
____ Gutters
____ Downspouts
Estimated cost = _____

### Roofing Materials *(one square = 100 sq. ft.)*
____ Asphalt
____ Slate
____ Tile
____ Fiberglass
____ Wood *(shingles or shakes)*
____ Other
Cost/square  _____ × No. squares = _____

## GLASS AND GLAZING Cost

**Windows**
____ Double-hung
____ Awning
____ Casement
____ Sliding
____ Jalousie
____ Fixed Windows
____ Other
____ Screens *(sold as options with windows)*
Cost/unit _____ × No. units = ____
Cost/unit _____ × No. units = ____

**Storm Windows** *(sold as options with windows)*
____ Insulating glass
____ Double glazing
____ Triple glazing

**Miscellaneous**
____ Mirrors
____ Other
Cost/unit _____ × No. units = ____

## DOORS

**Exterior Doors**
____ Wood
____ Metal
____ Sliding glass
____ Other
____ Screens *(sold as options with doors)*
____ Storm doors *(sold as options with doors)*
Cost/opening _____ × No. required = ____

**Interior Doors**
____ Wood
____ Metal
____ Other
Cost/opening _____ × No. required = ____

**Miscellaneous Doors**
____ Garage
____ Outbuilding
____ Other
Cost/opening _____ × No. required = ____

## INTERIOR TRIM

**Moldings**
____ Cove
____ Casing
____ Corner
____ Base
____ Chair rail
____ Other
Cost/ft. _____ × No. ft. = ____

## Cost

**Closets**
____ Rods
____ Shelves
____ Shoe rack
____ Other
Cost/item _____ × No. required = ____

**Kitchen**
____ Cabinets
____ Countertops
Estimated cost = ____

## STAIRS
____ Carpenter-built
____ Manufactured
Estimated cost = ____

## CONCRETE MASONRY
____ Porches
____ Stoops
____ Patio
____ Stairs
Estimated cost = ____

## PLUMBING SYSTEM AND FIXTURES

**Bathroom Fixtures**
____ Toilet
____ Lavatory
____ Tub/shower
____ Trim *(faucets, valves, etc.)*
____ Other

**Kitchen/Laundry/Utility Fixtures**
____ Sink
____ Washtub
____ Water heater
____ Appliance connections

**Drain-Waste System**
____ Water Supply System
____ Waste System
____ Trim
Total estimated plumbing cost = ____

## ELECTRICAL SYSTEM AND FIXTURES
____ Wiring
____ Outlets
____ Switches
____ Fixtures
____ Service Panel
Total estimated electrical cost = ____

HEATING COOLING SYSTEM                                    Cost

____ Furnace

____ Coils

____ Condenser

____ Controls

____ Humidifier

____ Air cleaner

____ Filters

____ Flue

Total estimated cost =                                    _____

MASONRY

____ Fireplace

____ Chimney

Total estimated cost =                                    _____

MISCELLANEOUS MATERIALS

**Rough Hardware**

____ Nails

____ Screws and bolts

____ Staples

____ Joist hangers

____ Miscellaneous fasteners

Estimated cost =                                          $300–$500

**Finish Hardware**

____ Door hinges

____ Door knobs

____ Door stops

____ Locks

____ Cabinet hinges                                       Cost

____ Cabinet drawer slides

____ Cabinet handles

____ Metal closet rods

____ Closet shelf supports

____ Bi-fold door hardware

____ Ornamental hardware

____ Miscellaneous hardware

Estimated cost—1% to 2% of the total cost of construction

**Adhesives and Other Materials**

____ Glue

____ Mastic

____ Caulking

Estimated cost =                                          $150

APPLIANCES

____ Refrigerator/freezer

____ Garbage disposal

____ Washer

____ Dryer

____ Dishwasher

____ Other

Total estimated cost =                                    _____

GRAND TOTAL—Or how much needs to be added to the cost of the manufactured house package =                                   _____

---

ventilation, and electrical systems. Few people are qualified to make these cost assessments, so obtain rough estimates from local contractors in these trades. Residential electrical systems can often be estimated on a per-outlet basis or watts per square foot. Heating systems can be estimated on the size of the house or BTU's per square foot. You may not get accurate figures, but they should be good enough for preliminary estimates.

### Labor Costs

If you plan to have your house built and finished by a contractor, you should make an estimate of contracting costs too. This can be done by consulting with the contractor of your choice. If you don't plan to use a contractor, determine how much you can do with your own two hands, how much you can do with the help of friends and family, and how much skilled or unskilled labor you'll have to hire. Tally the outside man-hours you feel you'll need, and multiply them by the appropriate labor rates in your area.

There are a number of ways to determine the cost of labor and contracting help. Roughly, labor can be divided into general contractor, subcontractors, skilled labor, and unskilled labor. Depending on how you plan to get the job done, each of these categories must be estimated for the total amount of time involved, and then translated into an approximate cost. Estimate them on the high side, and you won't be surprised later. A rule of thumb is that labor will cost about as much as the materials.

### Adding It Up: What It Really Costs

At this point, you should have figures for all aspects of building a manufactured home: the kit or package price; everything the buyer must provide (except shipping and the foundation); the services of a general contractor if needed; subcontractor services; other labor; and anything else you can think of that would add to the cost of the house. Add these figures to your notes on each house you're considering, and determine the total for each house.

Now you can determine the

cost of the foundation for each of your house choices. There are several possibilities—crawl space, full basement, slab, or open piers—and all but the slab type can be made of concrete blocks as well as poured concrete. The cost of any of the types of foundations can be roughly estimated on a per-square-foot basis. You can find the approximate cost for a foundation in your area by contacting local building or foundation contractors, masonry contractors, and possibly the municipal building department. Multiply the per-square-foot figure for your foundation by the total area of each house; compute it by using the house's outside dimensions—not the living space area. Be sure to include such items as concrete stoops, garage floors, patios, or anything else that might be a part of the construction. Add this figure to the total for each house.

That leaves shipping costs. The first thing to determine, of course, is whether shipping costs are the responsibility of the buyer—they usually are. Ask the manufacturer how many trucks will be needed to transport the house, and the current approximate cost of trucking per loaded mile. Multiply the cost per mile by the number of truckloads by the number of miles you are from the company's manufacturing facility. Add that figure to the total for each house. At the same time, estimate the cost for unloading the house package at the building site, if that is required of you. If you'll have to provide a forklift and three or four men for half a day, for instance, add this cost to the total, too.

Now you should have a total estimated cost for each house, exclusive of the items that are always provided by the buyer and that will have approximately the same cost regardless of the house you buy. You can use this grand total to directly compare the houses you've selected for final consideration.

To get a somewhat different view of overall costs, divide your grand total for each house by the square footage of living area of that house; this will tell you which is the best buy of the group when it comes to getting the most living space. Of course, you should also take into consideration the value of the non-living space—a garage or porch—that may be the cause of a higher per-square-foot cost for one model over another.

There is another comparison that may prove interesting. It is often said that manufactured houses are the least expensive way to buy a home, but this isn't always true. Is it true in your case? Here's how you can find out. Check the real estate market in your area carefully. See what's available in existing houses that may be comparable in size, construction, and design. Are there houses on the market that might serve your needs for less money and without the hassle of building a new house? Do they have more space, better features, or lower taxes for a comparable cost?

Also check the new-house market. Can you buy a good, already-built new house for the same or less money? And last, check the local per-square-foot cost of having a new house of comparable size, style, and quality custom-built for you, and perhaps customer-designed as well. If the cost of a manufactured house is $75 a square foot, and you could have a similar house built locally for $60 a square foot, you may be looking in

the wrong direction.

After you've completed your preliminary cost estimate and made your initial comparisons, your next task is to decide on one or two houses and concentrate on them. Your rough cost estimates must be turned into well-defined statements of cost. This means obtaining any information from the manufacturers you don't already have, and going over all of the specific details, one by one. You'll also have to get firm figures from local contractors and subcontractors; often the house manufacturer or the local dealer can help with this. The result should be a definite figure for each completed structure, including *all* of the items on the "owner provides" list discussed earlier.

### How To Assess Quality

Making an accurate assessment of the quality of a manufactured house is a difficult job, especially if you're unfamiliar with residential construction and building materials. There are, however, a number of ways to reach some definitive conclusions.

First, you can determine whether a particular manufacturer is well-known and has a good reputation. The fact that Company X has been around for a long time may or may not have much meaning: there are plenty of relatively new firms that produce fine products. Most reputable companies offer references, which you can check; and contact with Chambers of Commerce, Better Business Bureaus, and similar organizations may prove helpful. The municipal building department, your bank, or even local contractors may have experience with some of the house manufacturers you're interested in.

You may be able to get a feel for the quality level of a company's products by examining its literature, although your conclusions could easily be wrong. Another possibility is to read as much as possible about manufactured houses. You can, however, find out whether or not the house designs comply with national building codes.

Virtually all manufactured houses comply with model building code standards that cover the design and construction of manufactured houses. These may be any one of three codes covering different regions of the country: The International Conference of Building Officials (ICBO) code covers the western United States, the Building Officials and Code Administrators (BOCA) code covers the midwest and the northeast, and the Southern Building Code International, Inc. (SBCC) code covers the southern states. Generally, if a manufacturer's house meets one of these three codes, they will be accepted by building officials anywhere in the country. However, do not assume that because the manufacturer's literature states compliance with one of these codes, that all house models have been approved. This will not always be the case. A check with the manufacturer should determine what standards are being met.

Where there are local building codes, manufactured houses usually require changes or modifications to comply. Discuss the plans and specifications with your local building department officials to determine what changes may be necessary. In most cases, it is reasonable to expect that some changes will be necessary. In a few cases, manufacturers may have already received various

state code approvals; this is another indicator that the house is of good quality.

Warranties are highly variable, and they should be checked carefully. Generally a manufacturer's warranty covers any combination of materials and any design and engineering work. Often the warranty covers only the materials, but does not cover house construction. When the house is assembled by the manufacturer's crew, the construction warranty is included in the construction contract. If you are unsure about a warranty and what it covers, consult the manufacturer, the dealer, or an attorney.

The fact that a company does not offer a written warranty—and some don't—is not necessarily cause to reject its product. What is more important is the company's reputation. No matter how extensive a warranty may appear, it is no better than the willingness of the company to stand behind it. Many companies have programs to cope with whatever difficulties might arise, and these may actually be more effective than written warranties.

The manufacturer's literature will sometimes mention brand names for some components in a house package, such as windows, doors, and roof coverings. If they are widely known brand names in which you can have confidence, their inclusion is an indication—though not a statement of fact—that probably other components are of good quality too. Brand name materials invariably are accompanied by their own warranties that are passed along to the buyer.

Although many avenues of investigation should be explored, it's best to inspect, in

person, a completed house made by the manufacturer. Preferably, the house should have been occupied for at least a year, but it shouldn't be so old that the manufacturer's new products are different. Some manufacturers maintain houses that can be visited; many manufacturers' representatives or dealers live in houses made by their companies. The best situation is to arrange to talk to people who have recently purchased a house from the manufacturer and possibly arrange a brief inspection tour of their home.

## How Design Changes Affect Cost

All house manufacturers offer a certain number of stock models, along with a standard package of components and materials for each one. In a few cases, the manufacturer will make no changes or modifications to those stock houses, although there's nothing to prevent you from making alterations you want during building and finishing, on your own. Some companies will make only a few minor modifications—the exclusion of a small section of interior non-load-bearing wall, for instance—at no extra charge, but the house package stays essentially as advertised. Many companies will make numerous design modifications in stock plans; and some companies offer custom design and engineering services. All of these changes have a bearing on the cost of the house package.

Some modifications can be made without adding at all to the cost of the house. Just what they are, and how extensive or

*Continued on page 49*

# The Unconventional Look of Kit House Living

Consider the solidity of log houses, the futuristic look of domes, or the beauty of timber houses for some new living ideas

*Log houses, like the log cabins they are based upon, seem to fit naturally into any wooded setting. (Green Mountain Cabins)*

33

1

2

34

3

4    5

The mass of the logs, heavy beaming, and the solid country feeling of log houses make them feel as if they'd last forever. The estimate isn't too far off—a well-built log house has a lifetime of at least 100 years. (1,2: Beaver Log Homes; 3–5: Boyne Falls Log Homes)

Log houses are all built the same solid way, but they don't all look alike—you'll find styles from greenhouse to country cabin, from family home to pace-setter. (1–3: Boyne Falls Log Homes; 4: Green Mountain Cabins)

**1**

**2**

3

4

**1**

Like old-time cabins, many log houses are built around a fireplace. Since the logs themselves form the interior walls, little finishing is needed. (1: New England Log Homes; 2: Lodge Logs; 3: Cabin Log Co. of America)

**2**

**1**

*Whatever the style, log houses go together the same way. You'll need few skills to build them, but make sure you're in good condition—lifting and moving the logs is strenuous work. (1,2,5: Ward Cabin Co.; 3,4: Real Log Homes; 6: Western Log Homes)*

**2**

**3**

**4**

5

6

The log houses currently available range from old-style log cabins to large modern houses that include solar features. (1: Western Log Homes; 2,3: Eureka Log Homes)

**1**

**2**

**3**

1

2

3

*Timber houses offer all of the advantages of log houses with a distinctively different look. Timbers are cut flat on all four sides, and look like wood siding on the outside. (1–4: Justus Homes)*

4

1

2

3

4

5  6

Timber houses have a more open design than log houses, and frequently have more and larger windows. Cathedral ceilings are quite common and often include exposed wood posts or beams. (1–6: Pan Abode Cedar Homes)

45

3

1

2

4

Extremely large airy interiors are characteristic of domes. The rounded structures have no right angles; even when partition walls are added, rooms don't have a rectangular shape. (1–3: The Big Outdoors People; 4: Domes and Homes; 5–7: Monterey Domes)

5

6

7

**1**

*A dome is the ideal house for you to build yourself; construction of the exterior shell is relatively easy. But the shell represents only 20–25% of the materials needed to complete a dome. (1,2: Monterey Domes)*

**2**

*Continued from page 32*

numerous they can be, depends on the manufacturer. And, of course, much also depends on the nature of the modifications themselves, and on the house design. For example, it may be feasible to move an interior non-load-bearing wall a few inches, or even feet, or to omit it; a door can be deleted, a window made a bit larger or smaller, or one type of trim substituted. If there's no additional cost to the manufacturer for making such changes, there will—as a rule—be none to the customer. Generally, with the possible exception of a small service fee, changes that don't involve making any alterations to the structure or framework itself, or require extra materials or architectural planning or engineering, will not raise the cost of the house package.

## Construction Options

Many manufacturers offer a list of available options, which are essentially nothing more than a series of preplanned modifications. These options almost always carry an extra cost. Sometimes, deletions, which result in a package price reduction, are also offered. Standard options consist of such things as double-glazed windows instead of single-glazed; one type of exterior door instead of another; or the addition of roof decking, cedar shakes, cabinetry, or appliances. Many options can be more extensive, and constitute major modifications, sometimes structural ones, to the house. These might include adding a garage, porch, or veranda; moving an exterior wall several feet; building one or more dormers; or including a complete floor or roof system.

Regardless of the modification or design change involved in an option, your cost will be increased. Deleting major items,

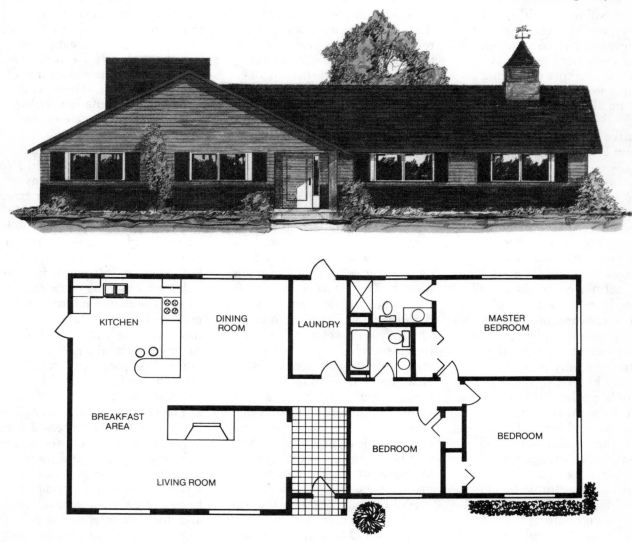

*Starting with a stock house model, it's relatively easy to make a variety of modifications.*

*Four different exteriors are possible for the house shown on page 49; the interior has remained the same.*

where possible, should result in a corresponding cost reduction. Whenever you're considering special options, you should determine the cost of buying the same items locally; you might be able to save money.

### Extensive Changes and Custom Design

Many house manufacturers permit substantial changes to be made in their standard house models. Most have many different sets of plans in their files, many more than the house packages they offer. Often, the manufacturer can make modifications from these stock plans, which means minimal or possibly no extra planning cost to you; except for a small service fee, the only additional cost may be that of the materials needed for the change.

But if the manufacturer doesn't have plans on file to cover your modifications, a custom design change must be made. This involves planning, perhaps architectural work, engineering, changes in the materials and cutting program for the house, possibly the substitution of materials, and

other changes in procedure. In this case, the buyer is usually required to pay a certain fee in advance for the design of the modifications and their incorporation into the structure. The plans are then submitted for approval, and the added cost is determined. It is also possible that the cost might be lowered, if the modification involves removing something significant from the house such as a porch or an attached garage.

Many companies also offer complete custom design and engineering services; some, in fact, prefer selling custom-made houses. They start with one of their stock or file plans, or a plan that you have discovered. Or, they will work with your rough sketches, or even by means of verbal descriptions, changing and refining and rearranging until the plans are complete, and exactly to your satisfaction. During the process they also offer practical advice and point out cost-cutting measures or possible design improvements.

As you might expect, the fees for this service are fairly substantial. There are only two basic restrictions on this kind of

custom design work. One is that companies will not release, or copy, custom designs that they have done for others. The other is that a manufacturer of log houses, for instance, will not design a dome house; the custom design work must be within the scope of the manufacturer's product line.

Many manufacturers will also work with complete designs or plans that you provide, or have your own architect prepare. In this case, the manufacturer will refine the plans as necessary to fit in with its own product line. For example, this might involve adjusting material specifications to suit the manufacturer's normal stock. Then, the manufacturer will work out material cutting and fabrication programs, complete with detailed instructions for putting the structure together.

The cost of making modifications or having a custom design made for a manufactured house is highly variable, and there is no rule of thumb to guide you. Often, a few minor modifications can be made without an additional charge, or for a slight fee, plus the cost of any additional materials required.

Options can usually be added or subtracted with specific, listed increases or decreases in the cost of the house package. Sometimes the manufacturer can give you a rough estimate of what the total cost of a more extensive modification might be; this helps you decide whether you want to go ahead before you're committed to paying an extra design fee.

Custom designs are another matter, and they are accompanied by custom prices. A custom rearrangement of an ex-isting design is likely to be the least costly, while a complete custom design done on the basis of the manufacturer's own building system, materials, and components will be more expensive. If you provide a set of plans for a manufacturer to convert and make up as a house package, the cost is likely to escalate a bit more.

### Working With the Dealer: How Much Help You Can Expect

When you're trying to decide whether to make design modifications, contract for a custom design, or even considering special options, you can usually get all the help you need from the manufacturer or a local dealer. It's easier if the manufacturer or the dealer is nearby; otherwise, you'll have to work by mail or telephone.

In any case, manufacturers who offer design modifications or custom design services are happy to offer advice, discuss design possibilities, and help you however they can to design a house that's right for you.

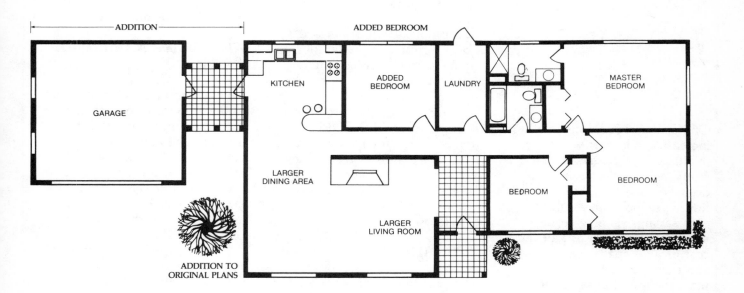

*Several extensions have been added to the house shown above to change both the exterior and interior.*

# Should You Build It Yourself?

One of the big reasons for the increasing popularity of manufactured houses is that many types can be bought as do-it-yourself kits. Building the house yourself can result in cash savings ranging from modest to as much as half the cost of a comparable contractor-built house. Every manufactured-house buyer should give serious attention to the money-saving possibilities of do-it-yourself construction,

and decide whether it's a wise choice.

Unfortunately, there is a tendency among manufactured-house buyers to underestimate the complexity of building a house—from site preparation to final decorating. Frequently, buyers overestimate their own resources and abilities. And although a manufactured house is easier to build than designing and building one from scratch, it's still a long way from being your average weekend project. Before you start counting all the money you will save, be sure you know what is involved.

## Savings Are Possible

The possibilities of some modest savings do exist when you have your manufactured house built by a contractor. But the oppor-

tunities to save money increase dramatically when you choose to assemble and finish the house personally. How much can be saved depends mostly on you.

### Where Savings Are Always Possible

Savings are in direct proportion to the amount of owner involvement in the construction project. The more you do yourself, and the less you hire others to do, the greater your savings will be. No matter what kind of house is involved, there are certain jobs that the buyer can always do.

By doing preliminary planning and design modifications yourself, with the help of the manufacturer's design staff, you'll probably save, even if the manufacturer charges a nominal design fee. If survey work must be done on your building site, make those arrangements yourself, and then oversee the job yourself instead of leaving it for the contractor to take care of. Once the survey is done, you can use the information to work up a plot plan. Even if you don't do the finished drawing yourself, you'll save a considerable amount by gathering the information and making up the rough drawings or sketches.

Then comes the siting and orientation of the house. This is an important job with any kind of house, and absolutely vital for solar models. This too is best committed to a plan or sketch, which can be a part of the plot plan in many instances. You might like to get some professional advice during the process of siting and orientation.

You can obtain the building permits, well permit, septic system permit, and take care of all similar preliminary work that has to be done. Although a contractor or an architect can do this too, you'll be charged for the time involved. And it does take time—sometimes lots of it. If you will require a septic system and can get the permission of the local health or building authorities, you might be able to run the percolation tests yourself, with an inspector on hand to check the results. This isn't a difficult job, but it takes time that you'd otherwise have to pay for.

Another area where you can spend your own time instead of someone else's is in making the arrangements for all of the utilities. You'll need electric and telephone service; start early on these, since frequently a lot of lead time is required. And you'll have to have electricity on the premises before construction can start. A pole or two may have to be set, or a trench dug

for underground service—you can arrange for contractors to take care of this, while you oversee the work.

You may need to have a well drilled, and you'll need a water supply line from either the well or the street water main to the house. You can contract for all of this work, or if you're really ambitious, you can hire someone to dig the water line trench with a backhoe, then lay the pipe yourself and do the backfilling by hand. Some buyers dig their own trenches, for an even greater saving.

And, of course, there's the sewer line. If the line will go to a municipal sewer main in the street, make arrangements for the tap, and for a trench to be dug to the house. The pipe itself will usually be installed by a licensed plumber, or possibly by a municipal crew. If a septic system is involved, you will need a tank, piping, fittings, and other associated gear, and someone to dig the tank hole and leach field trenches. In some areas you can do the pipework yourself, once the tank is set. There is a good potential for savings here that should be investigated. Again, you can probably do the backfilling yourself, by hand. You may need a natural gas line or an oil tank and line for your heating fuel supply, or a propane installation for heating and cooking. You can also take part in these arrangements, though you won't be able to do much, if any, of the actual work.

Before any construction can start, you'll have to provide access to the building site. In some cases this is as uncomplicated as a broad, 20-foot driveway, while in others it may consist of a road a mile or more long. In any case, the basic positioning of the

driveway or road should be lined out on the plot plan. Using that information, you can readily lay out the course with stakes, string, and measuring tape, and place the driveway exactly where you want it. This will result in savings, and allow you to make course changes, to save an old tree or to go around a boulder. At the same time, you can red-flag any trees or shrubbery that you might want to save—this is something that only you can or will bother to do. If there's usable firewood or transplantable shrubbery in the way, you can save that, too.

Then contract with an excavator to bulldoze out the driveway or road and the turnaround or parking area, rough grade it, and install a gravel base. If you are there to oversee the job from start to finish, this will usually produce better finished results. This is an intangible and inestimatable saving that is well worth the investment of your time.

In all cases there must be excavating work done for the house foundation. This can be as little as a few small holes for piers or posts, a medium-sized grading job for a poured concrete slab, or a major excavation for a full basement. Along with the excavation, some ground contouring might be necessary. You might be able to dig pier holes yourself, but the other kinds of work are best done by a backhoe or other earth-moving machinery. You can do the layout work to establish the location and boundaries of the contouring and excavation, then contract with an excavator to do the digging while you oversee the project.

In most cases the buyer of a manufactured house is required to take care of all foundation construction; there are a few ex-

ceptions where an All Weather Wood Foundation is provided as a part of the house package. In any event, a foundation must be built, and there are two choices. If the house plans include foundation plans you can arrange to have the foundation built, instead of turning the chore over to an architect. This will save you a few dollars. Or, you can build the entire foundation yourself and save a lot more money. This isn't an easy job and it requires some skills, but many home buyers do it themselves. But if you suspect any problems with soil conditions, this is a good time to forget saving money and to get professional help.

No masonry work of any kind is included with manufactured houses, so this provides another opportunity for an ambitious do-it-yourselfer to save. You can build your own chimney, retaining walls, patio, or stoop, and lay up your own stone or brick veneer house siding.

After construction has been completed, there are further opportunities for savings. Post-construction cleanup is one—instead of paying skilled workers to sweep up rubbish and pick up the grounds, take care of this yourself. Even if you have to hire a utility trailer or a small truck to haul rubbish to the dump, you'll save money.

It is also possible to save on the landscaping. You can work up your own landscaping plan and do the drawings even if you're not familiar with the subject. You don't really need a landscape architect, especially for an informal residential layout. It's not that difficult to do all of the planting, except for large shrubs or trees; at worst, you'll lose a few plants, but you'll save a lot of money.

These are the areas where there is a potential for saving some hard-earned cash by substituting your personal involvement. This is often referred to as "sweat equity." There are also many possibilities that can be taken advantage of during the construction process itself. How much you can save here depends entirely on what type of house is involved, how complete the house package is when it arrives, and how much on-site labor is provided by the manufacturer and included in the package price.

**Where Savings Are Sometimes Possible**

There is little chance for a do-it-yourselfer to save much money with a modular/sectional house. These houses are 95 percent or more complete when they arrive at the site; crews are on hand to move them onto the foundations and bolt them together, and that's that. Panelized houses offer more opportunities for buyer involvement during the construction process. The closed-wall types are little different than the modular/sectionals. The buyer is left with only some minor interior trim and decorating work to do, if that. But the open-wall panelized houses are a different story. These can be divided into two types. Those houses that have large factory-assembled floor, wall, and roof sections have to be erected with a crane and a trained crew. Those that are made up of small sections can be assembled by three or four men.

The large-panel houses have to be erected by professionals. This is not a job even for a local contractor, much less a gang of do-it-yourselfers. But in many cases, once the shell is

erected, the do-it-yourselfers can take over, and install the heating and ventilating system, the electrical system, and the plumbing system. Other possibilities include finishing stairways, putting down flooring, putting up and finishing the drywall, putting up ceilings, painting and wallpapering, installing appliances, and installing the interior trim. There's quite a list of things to do, and many manufactured house buyers do it all.

The situation is somewhat different with the small-panel houses. Here the do-it-yourselfer can start with the bare foundation walls and work up from there. The first floor panels can be put down, then the walls, the second floor if there is one, and then the roof can be put on. In such a way the whole house can be erected by the buyer with the help of a few friends or hired workers. Then the interior can be worked on, just like in the large-panel houses. This is an excellent choice for the capable do-it-yourselfer who isn't concerned with saving every last dime, but still wants to minimize the construction time and expense as much as possible. This is because small-panel houses go together easily, with relatively few components to handle. And much of the critical fitting and assembly work has been done at the factory.

The maximum amount of owner involvement is possible with the precut, log, timber, dome, and post-and-beam houses. These kits generally require similar construction skills, but a few log types provide random- or uniform-length logs and nothing is precut or fitted. This is where the experienced do-it-yourselfer with a large, willing, and able family, or a

*This panelized house from Helikon Design Corp. is relatively easy to assemble. A crew of four is all that is needed to put up this shell—but that's only about half the work. The interior and exterior will still require a lot of work before this house is ready to live in.*

lot of helpful friends, has the greatest opportunity to save construction dollars. The house package consists basically of a big stack of building materials and parts, and a set of plans and instructions. The builder must cut, fit, and trim everything and put it all together.

Because precut house packages are so much easier and faster to build, only a few uncut kits are still available. The precut kits include the conventional frame style houses, as well as timber houses, post-and-beam houses, domes, and log houses. All of the component parts for these houses are precut and fitted; in many cases sections of the building are actually assembled at the factory, then disassembled for shipping

and reassembly. A few manufacturers also preassemble some small sections or assemblies, and ship them ready to install. The amount of cutting, fitting, and trimming required on the job site is minimal. All the builder has to do is follow the plans and the directions.

While the chances for cash savings are not quite as substantial as those that can be realized with an uncut house kit, the relative ease of construction far outweighs the few extra dollars that must be spent. With this kind of house the ambitious do-it-yourselfer and crew can build the first floor, erect the walls, build the second floor, put on the roof, set all the exterior trim, and then proceed to the interior details. All

of this work is done with component parts that fit together with little difficulty. The entire job can be done by the owner, with no professional help at all.

## What It Takes

If you plan on buying a manufactured house that allows some owner involvement during construction, keep several factors in mind. You will need a certain amount of skill in building or do-it-yourself experience to be able to successfully complete the house. The level of skill will depend on the type of house and how much of the work you plan to do yourself. No matter how skilled you might be, you are also going to need help. Either

skilled labor to do those jobs you can't do on your own—plumbing, electrical, and heating/cooling installations—or unskilled labor to help you hold and carry.

It takes time to construct a house. Generally, no matter how much time you allow, you will probably end up needing more. Tools are another necessity. Having the right tools when you need them will make construction easier and faster. And, you need your health. Building a house on a do-it-yourself basis is not a good idea for anyone who isn't physically fit.

Putting together a house is a job full of potential problems. Manufacturers who sell their houses to the do-it-yourself market readily admit this. Many go to great lengths to make it easier by providing detailed plans and instructions. Some even provide on-site technical supervision. Other manufacturers are very straightforward in stating that they prefer not to sell to the do-it-yourself builder. They might insist that a contractor handle the construction. Such a position is based on experience. Manufacturers are aware that some buyers have not been able to complete the house. In some cases these buyers have ended up losing their investment.

But don't be discouraged. If your decision to buy a manufactured house is based on doing as much of the construction as you can, go ahead and do it. You can end up with a well-built house if you are careful, and the possibility of cost savings are greatest if you do some of the work yourself.

### You Can Learn If You Want

A rank beginner, who has never handled carpenter's tools before,

can actually assemble and finish a manufactured-house kit. The skills needed to build a shell are minimal, and can be easily learned by anyone of average manual dexterity and intelligence. The part of building a house that is generally thought by the uninitiated to be the easiest—finishing off the interior—is actually the hardest, and requires the higher level of skills. The skills required in some of the specialty trades—heating, plumbing, electrical, or masonry—require training, and in most cases this work is best left to professionals.

In order to erect a house shell, you'll first have to learn to read plans, blueprints, and construction details, and to follow a construction manual. Much of this material is aimed at do-it-yourselfers—steps have been simplified and everything is explained in detail.

You'll need a basic familiarity with carpenter's hand tools, a few power tools, and how to use them properly. For the most part the uses are self-evident, and the techniques, especially for the carpentry involved in erecting a house shell, are quite simple. Basically, you'll need to be able to drive nails and spikes with a hammer, a screw with a screwdriver, and to use a handsaw or power saw for cutting.

You can learn to use most of the tools in just a few minutes, and only a few hours of work will build your competence and confidence. Actually, you can learn right on the job, as you start constructing your house. Be sure to follow the assembly instructions exactly, and don't be too concerned if you make mistakes at the start. Most mistakes on the shell can be easily corrected.

One advantage of building the shell of the house yourself is that by the time you finish,

you'll have gained enough experience to understand what's involved in the interior finishing process. And those basic skills will probably be refined for you to tackle the more precise work that's required. Additional tools will be needed as well as more care, precision, and attention to small details. A few mistakes—bent-over nails, gouges, or hammer marks—on the shell of the house won't make much difference, and every house structure is full of them. But they do make a difference in finish work, where everything shows and must be neat, clean, and tight-fitting.

The added skills and tools that you'll need for interior finishing depends on the interior design of the house, and how much finishing material is required. With a standard frame house, for instance, you'll have to learn to use a miter box, and a table or radial-arm power saw to cut moldings. Hand chisels or a power router will be needed for setting door hinges. Taping plasterboard panel joints requires some simple hand tools and, above all, practice—mistakes are easily correctable. Wood finishing, painting, and papering are all ideal do-it-yourself procedures that involve mostly repetitive labor.

Completing the interior, for the most part, is an extension of the woodworking and carpentry skills needed to put the shell together. A few different skills are needed for finishing and decorating. Practice and experience will lead to faster and cleaner workmanship, but learning is not difficult.

There are a few areas in house construction where specialized equipment, knowledge, and expertise are important. This work is best left to professionals. Carpet or sheet vinyl laying, installing

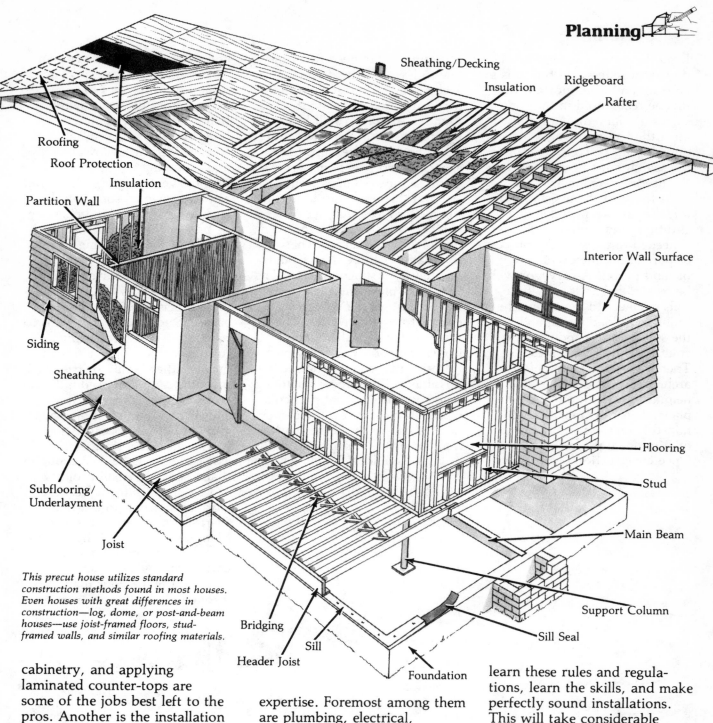

Roofing

Roof Protection

Insulation

Partition Wall

Siding

Sheathing

Subflooring/ Underlayment

Joist

Sheathing/Decking

Insulation

Ridgeboard

Rafter

Interior Wall Surface

Flooring

Stud

Main Beam

Support Column

Sill Seal

Bridging

Sill

Header Joist

Foundation

*This precut house utilizes standard construction methods found in most houses. Even houses with great differences in construction—log, dome, or post-and-beam houses—use joist-framed floors, stud-framed walls, and similar roofing materials.*

cabinetry, and applying laminated counter-tops are some of the jobs best left to the pros. Another is the installation of large pieces of stopped-in glass. This should generally be done by a glass company—if something goes wrong, it's their responsibility. There are bound to be some areas of construction that are beyond the ability of each do-it-yourselfer—that's the time to call for help.

The specialized building trades call for specialized tools and equipment, knowledge, and expertise. Foremost among them are plumbing, electrical, heating/ventilating/air conditioning, sheet-metal, and masonry trades. All of this work must be done correctly—there is little room for mistakes. In most areas these installations are covered by various rules and regulations, including those that specify that the work must be done by licensed tradesmen. It is possible for a do-it-yourselfer to learn these rules and regulations, learn the skills, and make perfectly sound installations. This will take considerable time, however, and is not recommended for everyone.

**Help You Will Need**

It is possible, but extremely difficult, for an experienced, versatile do-it-yourselfer to single-handedly assemble an entire manufactured house package. Outside help is usually needed to get the job done.

Even the most independent of do-it-yourselfers will find this to be true, and it's important that this be recognized in the early stages of planning. Not only must the fees and wages for outside help be considered, but the search must begin early for the needed personnel.

At the start the assistance of a real estate agent, a lending institution, and perhaps a lawyer is needed to assist in the process of purchasing the building lot or land parcel. A surveyor will be needed next, along with a soils engineer to determine the foundation loading capability of the soil, and to conduct percolation and drainage tests. Then there's the possibility of architectural and engineering help as you work out the house plans. This help might be obtained from the manufacturer, or from local professionals. Once construction begins, there

is an immediate need for someone to level off the driveway or access road, contour the site if necessary, and excavate the foundation hole. You'll have to get trenches dug for sewer and water lines, and perhaps for electrical and telephone service and a septic system as well.

From this point on, the do-it-yourselfer has a number of choices—much of the work can be done by the buyer. The foundation can be owner-built, or built by a subcontractor. The first floor platform might be built by either the owner, a contractor, or carpenter. The same is true of walls, second floor, and roof. For every part of residential construction it is possible to find subcontractors who specialize in that particular work. In most cases, the owner has the choice to do the work himself, or to let someone else do it. Where local building

codes prevent certain owner installations, even an experienced do-it-yourselfer uses outside help. Typically, most owner-builders have the foundation built by others, and usually subcontract the electrical and plumbing work, the heating/ventilating systems, and any extensive masonry work such as a fireplace and chimney or brick-veneer siding.

Any of the remaining construction jobs can be handled by a lone do-it-yourselfer, but in most instances the presence of a helper will make the work easier. Often the helper needs to have no skills except being able to follow directions. That means either family or friends, or both, can be pressed into service whenever a need arises. This is handy not only to save money, but also because no work scheduling is necessary. The situation is flexible enough that a series of small projects can be lined up for a weekend work session, or an old-time "barn-raising" can be arranged. Many an owner-built house has been helped along immeasurably with this approach.

As you make your plans, go through all of the construction

*A barn-raising party is a great way to get started on construction of a manufactured house.*

details in which you'll be directly involved, and determine just where you'll need help. As you set up your construction schedule, try to determine when the help will be needed. Then set about lining things up. You should try to obtain free help before hiring workers, but take care; it's unfair to expect too much from your friends and family. If the nature of the work requires lengthy labor, or help of a semiskilled or experienced type, it might be best to hire someone. You'll have to correlate your outside help schedule with your own work schedule, and relate both to whatever contracted work might be involved. Finally, make sure you set aside a healthy cost allowance for whatever labor you'll have to hire.

### Working Against the Clock

The most common problem for the do-it-yourself builder is time—there never seems to be enough. Building a complete house—or even just doing the interior finish work—can take far more time than an inexperienced builder would ever think possible. What's worse is that most people simply don't have much time to spare; they have too many other responsibilities and obligations. Often, they assume they'll have more time available for building than they really do; as a result, the project suffers.

There is no way to say exactly how much time is needed to build a house—there are just too many variables. But it's safe to assume that it will take at least several months, and it can easily take longer. For instance, with all of the work done by others, it can easily take a month to have the surveying done, driveway leveled, site

contoured, an excavation dug, and the foundation built. Add a couple of weeks at least for an owner-built foundation. Two do-it-yourself builders should be able to construct a rectangular first-floor platform in two weeks, assuming an area of about 1,500 square feet. Walls vary with their type and size. They could take anywhere from two weeks to two months for a couple of workers. Roofing also varies greatly. Interior finish work, except for most log and timber houses, takes a great deal of time; it can be a considerably longer job than putting up the shell and making it weathertight.

Whatever parts of the construction you want to undertake, figure that you'll need more time than you originally anticipate. One approach is to try to determine how much time you think you'll need for a given project, then double it. That's if you base your estimate on your own experience, or that of others who have done some do-it-yourself work. If you're working from the estimates of a professional, triple the time allowance. If you don't finish on time, problems can arise because the construction schedule will begin to fall behind. The money lenders don't like that, and subcontractors or other workers can get upset. If work gets too far behind schedule the situation can get worse—subcontractors can cancel, the bad weather season can suddenly arrive, or extra workers that weren't allowed for might be needed.

### The Complete Tool Kit

Assembling a manufactured house does require a fair number of tools. For the most part, none are specialized, none are overly expensive, and all

are easily obtainable. You can build up as complete and sophisticated a tool kit as you like, but this isn't really necessary. You can keep it

## Shell Erection Tool Kit

*Marking pencils*
*Measuring tape (50 foot)*
*Small spirit level, and 4-foot carpenter's level*
*Try square and carpenter's square*
*Chalk line*
*Plumb bob*
*Handsaw, circular saw, and keyhole saw*
*13- and 16-ounce claw hammers*
*20- or 22-ounce framing hammer*
*2-, 4-, or 8-pound sledge hammer*
*Electric drill ½-inch (preferably reversible)*
*Electric sander*
*½- or ¾-inch butt chisel*
*8-foot straightedge and saw guide*
*Nail apron*
*Prybar or utility bar*
*Caulking gun*
*Adjustable wrenches*
*Rope and pulleys*
*Extension cords*
*2 sawhorses*
*Stepladder*
*Extension ladder*
*Scaffolding*

## Interior Finishing Tool Kit

*Miter box*
*Back saw*
*Table saw*
*Nail sets*
*Putty knives (various sizes)*
*Staple gun or stapler*
*¼-, ⅜-, and ½-inch flat-tipped screwdrivers*
*No. 2, 3, and 4 Phillips screwdrivers*
*Awl*
*Power or hand plane*
*Power router*

simple too. The extent of your basic tool kit will vary with the type of house, and with the extent of the work you plan to do yourself.

There are many specialized tools as well, and a good rule is to buy the tools you need, as you need them. If a particular tool will save you some time and effort, it's well worth the expense. Good tools are a good investment for an active do-it-yourselfer, and will save their cost many times over. Buy only the best, and take good care of them.

### Physical Ability

It's important to realize that constructing a house is a tough job that requires physical strength and stamina. The bigger the house and the less preassembled it is, the greater the physical demands will be. If you plan to build your manufactured house as a do-it-yourself project, choose a type that involves a construction method within your physical abilities.

Most everyone is aware of their physical capabilities and is used to working around them. Your abilities should be taken into account before the job begins. This will keep you from suddenly finding yourself with unanticipated difficulties that might foul up your construction project. If the type of house you really want lies outside your abilities, you will have to settle for supervising the work being done by others.

The different types of manufactured houses require different levels of physical ability, strength, and stamina to construct. Here's how they stack up from the most to the least difficult: Log houses with logs more than 8-inches in diameter; traditional post-and-

beam houses; contemporary post-and-beam houses/log houses with smaller logs; timber houses; open-wall panelized houses with smaller sections; dome houses with panelized components; precut houses and dome houses.

Panelized houses employing large open- or closed-wall sections, and the modular/sectional houses are not included. These houses are always put up by professional crews.

As far as the interior work is concerned, there's little difference between any of the types, except the timber and log houses, where interior finishing is held to a minimum because of the way they are built. These houses are easier to finish. For the most part, interior finishing work depends neither on strength nor stamina—the work can be easily accomplished at the workers' own pace.

A related subject that deserves consideration is safety. Building a house is potentially dangerous. This is particularly true for shell erection, but also applies to interior finishing. Some accidents do happen, but most of the injuries that occur on construction jobs are due to carelessness. When working on a building job keep your mind on your work, and use safety equipment such as saw guards, safety goggles and hard hats. And be sure to keep a watchful eye on the other workers.

Another important factor that most buyers don't think about is health. If your health isn't good, the last thing you need is to become involved in a long-term do-it-yourself construction job. Even if you are healthy, you never know when you might suddenly become seriously ill. If you were halfway through the construction of your house and became seriously ill, what would become of

your house and family? To prepare for such an event—and it could happen to anyone—make sure that you have the proper insurance to cover any house-related financial obligations. Prepare plans for the completion of the house, whether you're around or not. And make sure that others know about those plans in advance.

The health, physical, and safety aspects of do-it-yourself house building are topics you will seldom hear mentioned. But they are very important. These factors are among the prime reasons why do-it-yourself house building projects are seriously disrupted or fail completely.

### How Much Can You Handle?

That's the big question, the one that a lot of owner-builders fail to adequately answer. How much time, care, thought, and patience can you really put into the job? How much skill can you bring to the job? If not that much, can you learn quickly? Can you successfully substitute your time, labor, and effort for your cash? There are a dozen questions of this sort, and they're all important. They have to be answered, and only you can.

For most people, building a house is the biggest project and the biggest investment they'll ever undertake. It makes no sense at all to go into it without making some in-depth assessments and evaluations. Then be guided by the conclusions, even if they aren't appealing. If you make an honest evaluation and take a down-to-earth approach, you might find that despite wanting to build your own house, you'd be better off paying someone else to do it.

# Section II
# Buying and Building

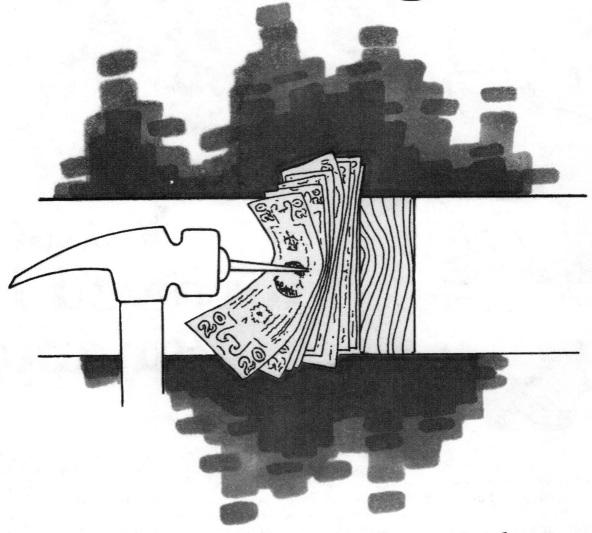

After you decide which house to buy
it still has to be built.
And even if you don't build it yourself,
there's lots of work involved—
but your house is worth it

CONSTRUCTION COSTS
INSURANCE
MORTGAGE
ASSESSMENTS
TAXES
INTEREST
DELIVERY
PLANNING

# What's Involved in Buying?

Buying a manufactured-house package and having it built is no more difficult than buying and building any other kind of house; in fact, it's usually easier. Even so, it can't be done over a weekend on the basis of a few snap decisions.

## Know Your Costs

After you've done your preliminary planning—selected a house manufacturer, a specific house design, laid out the plans and specifications—you'll have to delve more deeply into the costs. And, for most people, your house plans will have to be adjusted to mesh with your financial situation.

First, there's the matter of a building site. Unless you already have one, you'll have to consider how much you can afford to pay for a building lot or a parcel of land. Often, this will have a bearing on how much can be spent on the house itself, and over what period of time.

If you own property that you are still paying off, those figures enter into the picture, too.

No matter what kind of manufactured house you buy, site improvement costs will be about the same. The site may need a survey and a driveway or access road. Clearing— perhaps contouring—part of the land may be necessary. You'll also need trenches for water and sewer lines, maybe for a septic system, and perhaps for power, telephone, and gas too. And, there are the various permit and tap fees to be paid. Making an early assessment, as accurate as possible, of these figures will show you what's left for construction.

Foundation costs depend on the size and type of house you build, and on your preference as to foundation type. For example, pier or post-and-pedestal foundations are the least expensive; daylight basements most expensive. Once you decide on a specific house model, you can choose a foundation type and get an estimate of its cost.

### The Package Costs

The cost of the house package itself can't be determined until you decide on a final design and set of specifications, including all the changes and options you want—everything the manufacturer is to supply. Once that's done, you can obtain a firm house package price that is guaranteed in writing until the specified delivery date. You'll be required to pay a certain amount when you sign the contract, with the remainder probably due on delivery of the house package.

The cost of shipping the house package to your building site must be checked, too. In some cases, this cost may be included in the purchase price; some manufacturers offer free delivery within a certain radius of the factory. Usually, however, there is a charge per loaded mile from the nearest factory to the building site. The charge varies; have the manufacturer determine the total shipping charge before you sign the contract. This should be guaranteed in writing or made a part of the contract.

You should also determine offloading costs. If you have to hire a forklift, a trained operator, and three or four

laborers, the charges could surprise you. And, if you don't get the offloading done expeditiously, you may receive substantial hourly charges from the trucking company. Of course, some manufacturers may take care of offloading with a factory or a contractor crew; this is especially true of closed-wall panelized and modular/sectional houses.

Calculating construction costs is not easy, but it has to be done—by you, a contractor, or a number of subcontractors, and often all three. Naturally, these costs should be estimated at some point during the late planning stages, so that you don't find yourself in the position of buying a house package that you can't afford to assemble and finish. Included in these costs is everything you'll have to pay to erect the house, finish it, and make it ready for occupancy.

### Don't Forget Interest Charges

Interest rates are high, tend to move up and down a lot, and probably will never approach the relatively low rates of just a few years ago. And, different kinds of loan arrangements carry different rates. For example, construction loans, used to finance a house while it is being built, are frequently available at a lower rate than permanent mortgages that cover the completed house. Obviously, the less money you borrow, the lower your total interest charges will be. When you do have to borrow, shop around for the cheapest loan you can find, and try to borrow at a time when the rates are down.

If a construction loan is necessary, try to make the term as short as possible. This usually is feasible with a manufactured house because the house

can be built faster than a contractor-built house. Also, try to avoid using a loan to make the down payment for the house package. There can be a waiting period of up to 120 days between the contract signing and the delivery of the house package, and there's no point in paying four month's interest if you can avoid it.

## Financing

Financing is an accepted part of home ownership because few people can afford to pay cash for a possession as expensive as a house. But the financial arrangements for a manufactured house are somewhat different from what most home buyers—and many bankers—are used to. There are a number of possibilities, and all of them should be thoroughly investigated so you can choose the course that costs the least.

### Getting a Mortgage

The most straightforward financing situation occurs with the modular/sectional type of house. These packages are the most complete of any house type when they reach the building site. Purchase arrangements are almost invariably made through dealer/builders who take care of house assembly and finishing details. In effect, the buyer is purchasing a nearly complete house, which actually belongs to the manufacturer or the dealer until the work is done. Because the house is virtually complete, it qualifies for a mortgage, which goes into effect at the time of ownership transfer.

Similar financing is possible with all of the other types of manufactured houses, if all of the arrangements and the complete construction are taken care of by an architect or a general contractor, acting in your behalf. With this arrangement, you are merely someone's client ordering a finished house, and the house is eligible for a mortgage when you take possession. This arrangement depends entirely on the contracts entered into by the parties involved.

### Interim Financing

With the exception of modular/sectional houses, most manufactured houses require two kinds of financing—interim and permanent. A house package is not eligible for a mortgage because it's not a house yet; the house must be erected and finished before permanent financing can be obtained. And, the definition of "finished" can vary. The house doesn't have to necessarily be 100 percent complete. A house that has an unfinished basement or expandable attic, but is otherwise ready for occupancy, would be considered a finished house. Permanent financing is impossible when you buy a house package. Interim financing, or a "construction loan," must be arranged to pay for the package, and whatever materials and labor are needed to complete construction.

Manufactured houses are generally easy to finance. The designs and structures produced by many manufacturers have received formal finance approval from agencies like VA and FHA. This in itself is reassuring to many money-lenders. Also, many house manufacturers have developed good reputations; their houses are known nationally or regionally, by lending institutions who recognize them as a good lending risk. If the

manufacturer is not known or doesn't have finance approval from federal agencies, there is more hesitancy in loaning money. This isn't an insurmountable obstacle, but it can make matters more difficult.

Permanent financing, or mortgages, is generally no more difficult to arrange on manufactured houses than on any other kind of house. But interim financing can be a problem. Financial institutions tend to be conservative—they don't like to take chances. In addition to the quality and value of the package, they are concerned about who is going to construct the manufactured house, who's going to finish it, how good a job will be done, and how long the project will take. If the house is to be built and finished by a contractor of proven ability, obtaining interim financing shouldn't be a problem. But, if you are planning to do a good part of the assembly and finishing work yourself, without the continual presence of a trained construction supervisor, you'll have to do a lot of convincing. Do-it-yourselfers and amateur builders are not generally in high favor in money-lending circles because there are too many risks involved. But that doesn't mean that it can't be done.

### How to Get Started

You should make and confirm all of the financial arrangements before a purchase agreement for the house package is signed. There are many sources and approaches to consider. Check first with the house manufacturer to see what assistance might be available. A few companies offer their own financing program, although these are most often for interim financing. A number of companies

will give you advice and guidance in making the necessary arrangements through local sources. When such help isn't available you should discuss your proposed program with a banker or a financial advisor. If you are eligible for any federally-backed housing loan programs, be sure to investigate those, too.

The first hurdle is the down payment. No lender will advance 100 percent of the total amount needed, whether it's for interim financing or for a mortgage. A typical maximum for a conventional loan is 80 percent, which means you must put up 20 percent in cash. The lending institution will require a complete set of plans and specifications for the house with all of the details on who's going to do the work, a full breakdown of all costs, and other pertinent facts. You'll have to provide a personal financial disclosure, a business financial disclosure if that applies, personal and job history, and both business or credit and personal references.

There are several sources to which you can apply for either interim or permanent financing. Not all lenders necessarily make both kinds of loans, so you may have to deal with two lenders. Commercial banks are one possibility; savings and loan institutions are another. Finance companies might be appropriate in some circumstances, and for small loans a credit union might be the answer.

### Keeping Interest Costs Down

One approach is to put as much cash into the house as possible to keep the mortgage small and the term short. This is done because mortgages are expensive. For example, assume you need a total of $40,000 and can make a down payment of 25 percent. The loan proceeds are then $30,000; if the rate is 12 percent and the term is 10 years, the total amount of the note will be $51,650. The interest cost is $21,650. If the note is for 20 years at the same rate, the total is $79,279 with an interest cost of $49,279! By contrast, a $20,000 mortgage for 10 years at 12 percent would cost only $14,434.

There's another school of thought, however, that recommends a down payment that's as small as possible, and financing the maximum amount for the longest time period available. This is based on the fact that most people today never make that last mortgage payment and take title to the property. Instead, they pay a monthly "rent" to the bank and build up a small amount of equity for a short period, before moving on. Today, mortgages are only held for an average of seven to eight years. This is a useful ploy if you know that you'll only occupy the house for a few years at most, then sell for a profit that will allow you to buy a larger and better house. Meantime, your monthly payments are relatively small, because of the long-term mortgage.

For example, the payments on a 10-year, 12-percent, $30,000 note are $430 per month. On a 40-year note, they are $302. The total interest costs for the 40-year note are far greater, but that doesn't matter because the note will never go full term. In fact, the actual amount of interest paid during the first five years of each note are quite similar. That's because interest and principal are not paid on a straight-line basis. Instead, in the beginning each monthly payment is mostly interest, and

very little principal. The interest owed declines very slowly over the course of the note, and the principal paid in increases very slowly.

Thus, at the five-year mark of the two notes, the 10-year note-holder has paid back about $7,600 more than the 40-year note holder. The 40-year note holder has paid $2,700 more in interest. In the meantime, that $7,600 provided by the lower monthly payments has been available for use. And because the interest payments can be deducted from income tax, the 40-year note-holder may save money on tax payments over the short term.

On the other hand, the short-term note has developed good equity, but the long-term one none—except for what might accrue because of property appreciation. This can get complicated, but it points out that there are a lot of ways to set up a house financing plan.

## Alternative Choices

The dilemma of a would-be house buyer with time, ambition, and willingness, but no cash is a common one. But it can be resolved more easily with a manufactured house than in any other way. One excellent solution is to select a house package from a manufacturer who offers a financing program and whose building system is particularly geared to a do-it-yourselfer. This can be a good arrangement that allows a credit-worthy but cash-short buyer to own a house through the development of sweat equity.

The first step is to tie up a parcel of land or a house lot with as little cash outlay as possible. There are a number of ways to do this. A public land auction is one; outright pur-

chase on the open market is another. Land developers often sell lots for a very small down payment with monthly payments for several years. Sometimes it's possible to buy a building lot, but defer payment until after the house is built and permanent financing, which will cover both lot and house, has been secured.

The next step is to start improvements to make the site ready for house construction. Then select a small house. It should be a type that can be constructed with relative ease, and allows maximum buyer involvement in construction. It should also be readily expandable or of modular design (not the modular/sectional type, but one where two or more units can be connected). Low initial cost is important here, but so is good value. Over a period of time, equity develops as the land is paid off, site improvements are made, and construction is begun. You can borrow against this equity to further the construction. At the same time, additional small loans can help to keep the project going. This is a difficult route that may take a decade, but it works. The keys are perseverance, ingenuity, and a lot of careful financial planning.

# Insurance

Once your purchasing and construction plans have reached the final stages, you'll have to investigate insurance. There are several kinds of insurance coverage involved, but not all of them may be applicable.

If the house package is to be completed by a contractor, you should acquire a builder's risk insurance policy. During construction, materials, tools, equipment, and partial construction will be subject to storm damage, pilferage, vandalism, and fire. Appropriate coverages of reasonable dollar value must be obtained. Note that the value of the materials escalates as the house moves toward completion. If there is a mortgage on the property, builder's risk insurance is usually required. In any event, every manufactured house buyer should have this coverage.

This insurance package contains several different individual coverages; terms and conditions vary widely. Liability is a principal one, and the amount is best determined by your insurance agent. Fire coverage should be equal to the replacement value of the house. Comprehensive coverage for storm damage, vandalism, and the like can be included. Vandalism coverage is expensive and should have a deductible amount. A builder's risk policy can usually be converted to a homeowner's insurance policy when the house is finished.

If the house will be built by a contractor, you might also need liability insurance for protection against accident or injury to someone other than yourself at the building site or anywhere on the property either before or during construction. Both you and the contractor can be held liable, so make sure that all contractors and subcontractors have their own insurance as well. Discuss this subject with your insurance agent and your lawyer to be sure you are covered if there is any possibility of personal liability.

If the house will be at least partly owner-built, and persons other than owner and family and insured contractors or subcontractors are likely to be on the property, liability insurance is a must. This coverage may be separate and temporary, until a homeowner's policy can come into effect. It may be a rider attached to an existing policy. Again, discuss this with your insurance agent.

Life insurance is often overlooked, but even though not required, it's an excellent idea to have it. Anything can happen, especially where the owner is involved in the construction. A careful homeowner will determine the total amount of money that will be owed to others when the house is finished, and take out a decreasing-term life insurance policy in the same amount and for the same time period as the mortgage. The cost isn't high, and the protection is reassuring.

Title insurance is one other kind of insurance that may crop up during the process of purchasing the land parcel or house lot. In many areas, this is used in lieu of the more traditional abstract title. Both assure the buyer and the lender—if one is involved—that the title to the property is legally free and clear. Its use is a matter of local custom and often part of the requirements of lending institutions. If title insurance is required or advisable, you'll be made aware of the fact during purchase negotiations. In no case should you purchase a piece of property without a

*A house buyer with little cash could choose a smaller log cabin. The house allows for maximum buyer involvement in construction, and the initial investment can be small.*

favorable abstract or title insurance policy.

One further point: if you plan to hire tradesmen or laborers to help you, be sure to investigate the labor laws that apply in your state. Circumstances vary, but you could unknowingly become a full-fledged employer and subject to, among other things, contributions to a state unemployment insurance fund, or even the Federal Insurance Contributions Act.

# Taxes and Assessments

As you purchase a building site and a house package and begin construction, there are taxes and assessments for which you'll be liable. To save unwelcome surprises, it's a good idea to ascertain them as early as possible so that you'll be ready.

The building lot or land parcel is subject to property taxes. On unimproved land (that is, with no buildings) taxes are usually modest. You can determine the amount before

purchasing the property by asking the seller or tax assessor. When you purchase a piece of property, a certain amount of the current year's taxes is your responsibility. The amount is prorated to the number of months during the taxing year that you will own the property. Then when the next tax year arrives, the responsibility is entirely yours. If you have made some improvements by that time, the assessed valuation of the property may increase, depending on the nature of the improvements and the judgment of the assessor.

When you purchase the manufactured house package, you may also have to pay sales tax if you reside in the same state where the package was manufactured. Where this is the case, the amount depends on the price of the package and the state sales tax rate. You may also have to pay sales tax on additional building materials obtained locally. While this might not sound like much, it's a good idea to compare prices with tax included. It may pay to buy some options or extras from the manufacturer rather than locally, just to avoid that tax.

The major tax is, of course, the property tax assessed against the land and the improvements, which consist of the house and any other building you might erect. If the house package is assembled and finished within a taxing year, the assessment, and the ensuing tax, will be based on the completed value of the house. You can find out what that tax will be before you even contract for the house package by showing the tax assessor a set of the plans and specifications and noting the proposed building site. While the tax figure will not be exact, it will be close.

Then, if the tax liability is beyond your means, you can choose a lower-value house package, a different site, or both. If the house has not been completed by the end of the tax year, or whenever the assessor makes his yearly rounds, it will be assessed on its proportion of completeness in the judgment of the assessor. A completed shell with no interior work done, for instance, might be classed as 50 percent complete, and assessed at half the value the house would have if finished.

There is a possibility of another kind of property tax, too, and that's a special one due to an improvement bond issue or some similar matter in a neighborhood. For example, the residents of a town subdivision or addition might elect to impose an added tax in order to have all of the streets paved, or to join a sanitation district.

Assessments are another tax-like charge you might have to pay. Generally, assessments are a peculiarity of private subdivisions and similar housing developments, and work in much the same way as those for condominiums do. The affairs of the subdivision are handled by an association of resident homeowners, who oversee operation and maintenance of a water system, the roads, perhaps a sewer system, and similar items. The total cost of this work, together with legal and accounting fees, clerical costs, and the like, are divided among all subdivision homeowners in the form of a periodic assessment. If you buy a building lot in the subdivision, you immediately become liable for the assessments. Because they can be substantial, and will continue for the duration of your occupancy, it's wise to know about them in advance.

# Dealing With Codes and Regulations

The process of purchasing a building site and constructing a house is controlled by various ordinances, codes, regulations, and permit requirements. Not all are applicable in every area, and they vary considerably from place to place. Consult your local building officials or government personnel for more specific information.

## Zoning

Zoning refers to land-use regulations employed in town, city, or county planning that divide the governed locality into areas or zones. In each zone, only certain activities can take place, certain types of building occupancy are allowable, and certain kinds of construction are permitted. Along with the zone definitions, specific regulations govern many different aspects of each area, such as restricted building height and size. For example, a zone designated as Single-family Residential, and perhaps called R-1, can contain only single-family houses—nothing else. But, an R-2 zone might allow both single-family and duplex residences, and an R-3 zone might permit multiple-family buildings. An agricultural zone might be termed A-1 and allow only farming or ranching activities, with all their associated buildings.

Zoning is not in effect everywhere. There are plenty of places where anyone can build for whatever purposes. Where zoning is in effect, it can range from simple to complex, and from virtually unenforced to very strict. Before you purchase land to build on, be sure to obtain a copy of the zoning laws from your municipal building department or library and check them carefully for any restrictions that might interfere with your building plans. You also can check to see how much and what kind of protection the zoning might afford you against; for instance, the sudden appearance of a gravel pit or a pig farm next door. Depending on one's intent and point of view, zoning can be restrictive or protective. And, if there are zoning regulations that you don't understand, get a clear interpretation from a government official or a lawyer.

## Building Codes

In many parts of the country, houses must be designed and constructed according to various building codes. Like zoning laws, building codes are not in effect everywhere. The term "building codes" is a generic one that has come to mean not only the actual building codes, which govern the design and construction of structures, but also the mechanical codes for heating and ventilating, the plumbing codes, the fire codes, and the electrical codes, among others.

The so-called national codes are circulated on a nationwide basis, and include the different kinds of codes; they are not, however, enforced at a federal level. Instead, they are meant to be adopted by states, counties, cities, and towns.

There are several national codes, such as the Uniform Building Code published by the International Conference of Building Officials (ICBO); the companion codes to this are the Uniform Mechanical Code, the ICBO Plumbing Code, the Uniform Fire Code, and others. Although different national building codes are followed in different parts of the country, there is one code that governs electrical wiring and installations virtually everywhere—the National Electrical Code as published by the National Fire Protection Association.

State and local building codes are also used in many areas. Most of these use one national code or another as a basis. Various clauses are added to cover items not included in the national codes, or to make certain aspects more restrictive, more specific, or more detailed. These codes take precedence over the national code stipulations. For example, national codes allow the use of cedar shakes for roof shingles, but many municipal codes specifically prohibit them.

You can obtain copies of whatever building codes are in effect in your area from the library or the building department, but trying to wade through them is difficult and may be pointless. An exception to this is if you plan to start with a very basic house package and do most of the work without professional help or supervision. In this case, a familiarity with the appropriate codes is both helpful and wise.

Most house manufacturers design and build in compliance with at least one national building code, and many will make whatever alterations are required to conform to state and local codes. If there is any question, go over the house plans and specifications as originally proposed with a building inspector and determine what, if anything, does not meet local requirements. Then ask the manufacturer to make whatever changes are necessary. Note, too, that the business of building code compliance is an on going affair throughout the construction process. The foundation, house structure, plumbing, electrical wiring, and heating/ventilating system will be inspected several times, and whatever doesn't get official approval must be corrected before construction can proceed or occupancy is allowed.

## Covenants

If you elect to build your house in a private housing subdivision or some similar development, you may run into covenants, a set of regulations that apply only to residents of the subdivision. They are protective in nature and frequently are quite restrictive. In most cases, they take precedence over local building codes and zoning regulations whenever they are nonconflicting, more restrictive, or more definitive. In short, they must be followed. And, the property owner covered by such covenants must follow them whether or not the covenants were previously disclosed. Thus, it pays to find out whether any convenants exist, and if they do, get a copy. Usually they have been recorded as legal documents, and can be found on file at the municipal or county clerk's office.

Many covenants are simple. They may set a minimum square footage of a house's living area, limit the size of the garage, establish building setback distances from property lines, require service yards and clotheslines to be fenced in, prohibit the keeping of livestock, and so on. But they can also be very specific. They may regulate the kind of exterior siding a house may have, the color of the house's exterior, the specific place on a lot where the house must be built, the proportion of formal lawn to unimproved yard area, and even the kinds of shrubs and trees that can be planted.

## Permits

The term "building permit" is used loosely to include any or all of several permits that may be needed to carry out construction of a house. Not all may be required, and there are still a few places where none are needed, but the chances are good that you'll have to have a few permits.

The building permit is required for the house itself. It is issued by the municipal building department before construction can start. Usually, it must be posted prominently at the building site. To get a building permit, you must submit a full set of blueprints or construction drawings to the building department. Depending on the house,

they need not always be formal plans drawn by an architect; they can be informal, as long as they are complete and detailed. In some cases they must have an engineer's or architect's seal. The building department will tell you what the requirements are. In any event, most plans you receive from house manufacturers will be suitable.

Generally, the plan package must include a plot plan, floor plan, elevations, construction details, foundation plan, and mechanical plans, including electrical. A full set of specifications should accompany the plans. Building department personnel will review the plans, and if all is in order, you'll be issued the permit after paying a fee, usually nominal. If there are problems, you'll be notified and the details will be discussed with you; then whatever changes are necessary will have to be made and reviewed.

The other major permit almost always required is for the house electrical system. A set of electrical plans, usually consisting of a floor plan with the electrical system shown symbolically, specifications, and a materials schedule, may have to be supplied to the electrical inspector. Sometimes all that's needed is to make out a permit application, accompanied by a description of the work to be done and a check for the fee. Then the permit will be issued, and the inspector will make periodic inspections of the work. If a subcontractor will be doing the job, the permit will probably be taken care of for you.

Depending on the circumstances, other permits may be needed. If you must drill a well for your water supply, in some areas you must first apply for a domestic well permit, usually at a state office. You

can get the details from the municipal building department, though. Likewise, a septic system will probably require a permit, and this is usually handled through the municipal health and sanitation department. This process may be a bit more involved. It may require approval of a tank, piping, and leaching layout and materials; a set of plans showing the construction and installation of the system; percolation tests on the soil at the system location (with favorable results); and one or more inspections and tests of the installation.

In some places, a permit is required to make the plumbing installation; the situation is much the same as for an electrical permit. Plans and specifications may or may not be required for approval, but inspections almost certainly will be made. And again, the details may be taken care of by the plumbing contractor. It's also possible for separate permits to be required for installation of the heating/ventilating/cooling system, or even just for the foundation alone. Check with the municipal building department.

## Variances

Zoning laws and building code provisions are not always totally inflexible. Sometimes there is good reason to make an ex-

ception, or someone may feel that there's good reason to challenge an existing regulation.

Most communities have an established procedure to deal with challenges; it is called seeking or applying for a variance. After an application for a building permit has been turned down for some reason, or reasons, that the applicant feels is unreasonable, a variance can be sought.

There are many reasons for seeking a variance. There are times, for instance, when a quirk of topography might make a particular zoning regulation pointless. Or, a person might want to install polybutylene tubing for his water distribution system, but find it unmentioned and so disallowed in a local code, although it is perfectly acceptable elsewhere. Perhaps someone might want to build a garage only 10 feet from a property line instead of the regulated 15 feet, because there's no other place to put it.

Someone else might want to build a house that is 25 feet high instead of the allowable 22 feet and redesigning or repositioning would bring about an unsatisfactory appearance. In all such cases, variances can be granted and the applicant allowed to proceed with his plans.

The usual procedure is for the applicant to prepare a case for a variance. This should include all of the necessary facts and figures, plans and sketches if necessary, and proof that such-and-such a material or construction method is used in other areas or has proven to be superior in one way or another. Anything and everything that will support the applicant's contention that the variance should be granted can be included. All of this material is presented at a hearing before a planning and zoning board or similar group, usually by the applicant but often with professional help as well—a lawyer, architect, surveyor, or whoever can best

present the required details. Where a variance that might possibly affect neighbors is involved—the erection of a higher than normally allowed fence along a property line, for instance—a public hearing may be called as well, to give others an opportunity to voice either opposition or agreement. The board then deliberates on the arguments and, much like a court of law, hands down its decision.

If your building permit application is refused, the reasons should be carefully assessed, so that you can determine whether you should go ahead with the necessary changes, or seek a variance. Discuss it with the building officials or inspector, with a builder or architect, or anyone else who might be able to indicate whether or not a variance application is justifiable and reasonable. Many variances are almost automatically granted provided they aren't detrimental to the structure, the neighborhood, or whatever else is involved. Whether or not you decide to seek a variance the end result is likely to be added expenses. But a variance application may mean considerable extra time and effort on your part as well.

*Building in an out-of-the-way place will invariably require a septic system, permits, and approvals.*

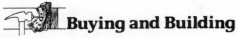 

Selecting and buying a manufactured-house package and bringing everything into compliance with the regulations that govern house construction are only part of the task of building a house. You'll also have to find a suitable building lot or land parcel, choose a particular site, and then prepare for construction.

## Choosing the Area

The first job is to choose the general area in which you'd like to live. For most people, the approximate geographical location is already established, and although it might be as broad an area as a particular state, it is most likely a certain county, or within or near a city or town. This narrows the choices to five different kinds of surroundings—urban, suburban, exurban, semirural, and rural. The one that is best for you is entirely a matter of preference and convenience. It's usually a compromise that depends upon such factors as lifestyle, social pressures or desires,

# Getting Ready to Build

finances, job, and health.

Urban or city areas, or even towns, have the highest population density and most concentrated social, cultural, commercial, and business amenities. They offer a full range of services like police and fire protection. Building sites are typically small and construction possibilities restrictive.

Suburban areas are near urban areas, and amenities and services are somewhat more limited and less convenient. The living, however, is quieter, building sites are usually larger, building tends to be less regulated and restricted, and taxes may be lower.

Exurban areas lie beyond the suburbs, farther from city amenities but still within a reasonable distance. Services and amenities are minimal. Property is usually available in parcels rather than lots and generally at modest cost. Building regulations are generally comparatively fewer, and taxes are not so burdensome.

Semirural and rural areas are mostly or completely countrified. Population density is lowest, there are no city amenities, and usually there are few, if any, services immediately available—you're largely on your own. But, parcels of land are available at the lowest cost, construction is apt to be the least regulated, and taxes are lowest.

In determining which is the best situation for you, you'll have to give plenty of thought to practical considerations. Transportation may be a major factor. You should also consider such things as trash pickup, snow removal, school bus routes, commuting time, shopping, health care, police and fire protection, entertainment and cultural activities, and water and sewage systems.

## Choosing a Lot

Once you've selected an area, you must pick a specific lot or land parcel. The site must have something that appeals to you; if there's no inner excitement, there may eventually be no interest.

There are practical considerations, too. If you plan to build on a lot, is it big enough? Sometimes two or even three town lots are needed to build one house. If you've selected a parcel, does it have at least one good building site? Two or three would be better. Check the property's access; there are two points to consider. One is legal access to the property itself; there has to be a clear right-of-way because a legally landlocked parcel does no one any good. And, there has to be a reasonable route for a driveway or a road to the homesite without building a bridge—unless you want one—or moving tons of earth. If you've already selected a house, would the lot or parcel be appropriate for it?

As a particular spot begins to look better, your questions should become more pointed. A site's features can be assets or hindrances that make building more difficult and expensive, or perhaps impossible. For example, check the terrain. You can't build in a swamp even if it's a seasonal one. You shouldn't build in a deep hollow, and building on a slope becomes more difficult as the angle increases. Check the drainage around the site; there should be good natural runoff.

A site that faces about 20 to 30 degrees to either side of due south will give you solar advantages; one that faces almost due south is best for either a passive or active solar system. Note the

sun track and the places on the site that are naturally shady in summer. Also, check into the storm and wind tracks. Is the location exposed, or is there some natural protection from the elements? A view might be very important to you. How close are the neighbors? Locate any noise-producing areas—a busy highway, airport or overhead airline route, school yard, factory—and determine whether the sounds will be carried on prevailing breezes, or if they'll be screened by topography, trees, or other buildings. Odors, as well as harmful gases and particulates, can also be carried by breezes from nearby feed lots or factories.

There are some terrain features that can affect construction, too. Check the ground in the site vicinity. If there is an underground rock ledge, digging a basement will be difficult. On the other hand, a slab foundation might be virtually immovable. A lot of rock or big boulders can be troublesome, especially for road-building. Check the soil, too; good topsoil and adequate ground moisture can mean good gardens and a nice lawn. If you'll need a septic system, there must be room for the leach field. And, the soil in the field area must have a good percolation rate to adequately absorb the effluent. Try to have percolation tests made before you buy, or include in the agreement that purchase is contingent upon a favorable percolation rate. If you can't get a septic system permit, which hinges on that rate, you won't be able to build your house.

The subsoil, at the level of the foundation bottom and over the entire building site area, must be solid enough to bear the weight of the house and foundation without sinking. You might want to have soil tests made by a soils engineer for this assurance. If you'll need a private water system, check for a natural spring, or try to get an idea of the feasibility of a well; not all properties have water under them, no matter how deep you go. And, if there is water, do you have a legal right to it? You might not.

Look for property assets, too. Good topsoil is one; trees and shrubbery that you can incorporate into the landscaping plan are another. Maybe there's a good supply of fieldstone for building stone walls or a foun-dation, or a nearby gravel pit or sandbank that you can make use of. A little pond or a creek, a large boulder or a rocky outcrop, an old apple orchard that can be rehabilitated can all become part of your design.

## Siting and Orientation

Once you own a lot or parcel, work can begin. If you don't have a recent survey, arrange for one so that you'll know just where your boundaries and various topographic features are.

The next step is to select the exact building site. On most small lots, there's not much leeway; but, even so, the positioning is important. On land parcels, there may be several potential sites, and choosing the right one may take some time and thought. The idea is to take maximum advantage of everything the site has to offer.

Once the approximate site has been chosen, the house

should be oriented on it. Orientation is a rather complex subject, one that is just now being commonly recognized as one of the most important aspects of a successful house. Actually, siting and orientation usually go hand in hand because one affects the other. A good site doesn't necessarily result in good orientation possibilities, and poor orientation may cause a site change.

Basically, house orientation involves coordinating the exact position of the house with the natural site features, such as seasonal sun tracks, sunrise and sunset directions, storm tracks, prevailing winds and breezes of the seasons, day/night air current shifts, existing shade pat-

terns, potential windbreaks, and turbulent areas. The idea is to gain maximum benefits and minimize any potential detriments. This process can only be done after careful research. For solar designed houses, it's absolutely essential. If you want the best housing results you can get, the importance of proper siting and orientation is something you should study further. Look for information that deals with solar, earth-sheltered, and so-called alternative housing styles, or talk to designers, architects, or builders who are familiar with this subject.

## Layout and Plot Plan

After you've finished with siting and orientation, and are satisfied that everything is to your liking, you can establish the general layout and make up the plot plan.

The position of the house itself can be easily marked with stakes and string; the positioning should be accurate within a few inches. Then you can locate the other elements that will be required, as well as those that you plan for in the future. Stake out the driveway or access road, the turnaround or parking area, and the garage if it's detached. Note the well location and the route of the power, water, and sewer lines. Look ahead and spot the vegetable garden, a storage shed, the studio, the workshop, the clothesline area or service yard—anything that will sooner or later be a part of your homesite. Then, analyze the arrangement to see if everything is satisfactory. If not, make whatever changes are necessary—this is virtually your last chance to do so.

Now is the time to have an improvement survey made if one is needed. Then, you can use the survey to make an accurate plot plan. You can make your own informal survey by measuring the relationships of various elements with a long tape and jotting down the figures on a rough map; indicate compass directions for a few major elements.

With this information, you can draw up the plot plan. If only a building lot is involved, it's small enough that everything can be included easily on one plan. If a parcel is involved, two plans usually give a better picture. The first plan covers the whole parcel or a substantial section of it that surrounds the building site. It should include major topographical features, at least some of the property boundaries, the access route, and the house location. The second plan, which is usually required in the plan package accompanying an application for a building permit, shows the building site and its immediate vicinity. It shows the house; property lines; well and septic system; power, water, sewer and telephone line routes; driveway or access road; and any other pertinent details. Major topographical features, contour lines, and elevations may be shown as well.

There are several approaches to making these plans. Such plans can be in the form of a relatively rough sketch, proportional but not done to scale; or they can be large and precise, complex and to scale. You can do the job yourself, or give your figures and notes—or a surveyor's—to an architect or a draftsman and have a formal plan drawn up. Choose whichever course is most practical.

*To be properly oriented a house should be positioned to get maximum benefit from natural site features. Because of its unique shape, proper orientation of a dome house is especially important.*

# Putting It All Together

The last phase before construction includes coordinating the house with the site, considering future plans, double-checking everything, and finalizing the details of the house plan and the plot layout. With many house packages, this is a job that must be done by you. Many manufacturers will provide some help; they'll go over the plan details with you to make sure that construction is correct, traffic patterns are functional, maximum use is made of living space, and so

on. Manufacturers that work through a dealer network can usually offer the most help.

Once the plans are finalized so that the house package can be manufactured, changes will be difficult and costly to make. Make sure that everything is as you want it to be. For example, if the nature of the building site suggests repositioning of some windows, now's the time to do it. Also consider what additions and improvements you might want to make in the future, and make sure that the present plans

allow for them or will not interfere when the time comes.

## Working With Outside Help

Unless you plan to build your house entirely on your own, you will have to work with outside contractors or laborers. This will involve getting estimates and bids, reaching a final decision, filling out contracts, and scheduling all of the various activities. If you hire a general contractor you'll have to go through this process only once; if not, you'll go through each of these steps for every subcontractor you use. Whichever way you choose to complete your house, be sure to shop around for the best deal.

## Handling Bids and Estimates

If you choose to have a contractor build your manufactured house, or have certain phases done by a subcontractor, getting bids or estimates is a part of the process. Estimates are used for determining approximate costs in the planning stages, and estimates or bids are used as various parts of the construction are undertaken. Which is best depends on the nature of the work, the policies of the contractor or supplier, and frequently, the size of the job.

An estimate is just that; the contractor gives you an educated guess of how much a job will cost, based on the information you've supplied. It's not legally binding, and the cost might actually be higher or lower. Small jobs, like hanging half a dozen doors, are often verbally contracted for on the basis of an estimate, with the understanding that whatever the final costs are, that's what the bill will be. Many contractors will undertake some kinds of jobs only on the basis of what they feel is a fair estimate. They're not interested in bidding, or giving a firm price, but if you want the work done, they'll do it. For example, a contractor could give you an hourly cost estimate to bulldoze an access road or dig a cellar hole. When the job is completed, the total cost will be based on the estimated rate that was given.

A bid, on the other hand, is a firm price to perform some specific service or supply some specific materials; generally it's made part of a legal contract. All the details, conditions, and specifications of the job must be in writing. The contractor considers them, allows for contingencies and a good profit, and arrives at a figure.

The bidding process can be competitive or negotiated. When they are competitive, invitations to bid with all of the pertinent details are sent to a number of contractors who might be interested. Bids that are returned are reviewed and one of them—not necessarily the lowest—is selected. With negotiated bids the price and sometimes some of the conditions and specifications of the job are negotiated with one or more contractors.

You can obtain an estimate for services or materials by contacting a contractor or supplier in person or by phone. You give him the details, and request a cost estimate. Since most contractors will also want to look at the job, you'll have to arrange that, too.

Getting bids is more complex and time-consuming. The best method is to use whatever standard forms and procedures are commonly used in your area—an architect, builder, or perhaps a lawyer can give you the details. You prepare the invitations to bid, select a number of contractors, send out the solicitations or conduct the negotiations, and make your choice.

## Choosing a Contractor

One of the most important steps in assembling and finishing a manufactured house is choosing contractors to do the work. Sometimes this is not a house buyer's responsibility;

many types of houses are partly or wholly completed by contractors of the manufacturer's choosing. The general contractor will usually choose whatever subcontractors might be needed. But if the buyer does a substantial part of the work, he will have to find several subcontractors to take care of certain jobs such as excavating, laying the foundation, or installing the electrical wiring, plumbing, or drywall.

Your local telephone directory is one source of information about contractors. It will list companies engaged in various construction activities. If you need a general or building contractor, look for those that specialize in residential construction. Subcontractors will be listed under their respective trades. You can also get suggestions and recommendations from your banker, the municipal building department, an architectural firm, or a building supplies dealer.

If you happen to know anyone who has just had a job completed by any one of the recommended companies, see if the job was satisfactorily done or if there were any problems. The Chamber of Commerce or the Better Business Bureau might have some information of value. Once you narrow the field to one or two names, investigate them more thoroughly. Request job and financial references and check them out with a few phone calls. If possible, inspect some of the work they've done.

Any contractors you choose should be financially sound, bondable, and have insurance. Honesty and integrity are important, and so is a good reputation for skill, know-how, and the ability to do a job quickly. If a company has been

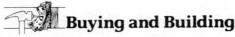 

in business for some time and is successful, that's often a good indicator, but a new company may be just as good or better. You'll have to use your judgment. If you'll be involved in the work, you'll want contractors you can get along with. Naturally, cost is an important factor, but remember that the lowest cost doesn't necessarily mean it's the best deal.

## Dealing With Contracts

When you purchase a manufactured house, you will have to deal with one or more contracts. The first will probably be a purchase agreement for a building lot or land parcel, or for a house, or both. The contract states that you have agreed to purchase the property or the house according to the conditions mentioned, and the seller has agreed to sell to you under those same conditions. The conditions include the price, perhaps a time limit, a specific description of the item, any requirements of the sale arrangement, and contingencies that might void the sale or change its conditions. The agreement is generally accompanied by an initial payment.

The time interval and the intent to buy statement in the purchase agreement allows the seller to prepare the sales contract, to ready the lot or parcel for transfer, or to begin manufacture of the house package. On the specified date, the documents required to transfer ownership of the property or house to the buyer are signed. At this point, final payment or some other predetermined arrangement is made or set into motion.

There may be a financial contract between you and a money lender. Basically, the lender agrees to lend a certain sum

under certain conditions for a period of time, and usually for a particular purpose, to be returned at a certain rate of interest in regular specified sums. You will have to agree to all of the conditions and details, and the loan is used to pay for the property, house package, or construction requirements.

In the case of a modular/sectional house, the sales contract will most likely include the construction work required to erect the house and complete it, and will probably include site preparation and foundation construction. All of this will be done by a dealer or builder. The same may be true of other types of houses where the manufacturer has the capability of arranging complete construction and finishing through a dealer or builder or by using an independent building contractor. If you request this kind of arrangement, it is made a part of the house sales contract.

Quite often the buyer of a manufactured house is on his own, although the manufacturer may offer some guidance on site preparation, foundation construction, house assembly, and finishing. There's a wide range of possibilities. For example, a buyer can have a general contractor do all of the work. Or the buyer can tackle certain parts of the job—foundation, the plumbing system, painting and papering, exterior siding—and hire a general contractor to do everything else. The buyer can act as his own general contractor, and have a building contractor do the construction and have various subcontractors do the electrical, plumbing, masonry, and other work. There are other possibilities as well, and in most cases, contracts are involved.

Building and construction contracts are used when a

general contractor or a building contractor and subcontractors are involved in the construction work. Contracts between a buyer and a general contractor are likely to be long and complex. Contracts used with subcontractors are usually shorter, but can also be complicated. An Agreement for Construction in long form can run easily to 15 pages. There are a number of standard forms that can be used and modified for each job; each contract is an individual one based on the particular job. And practically every clause of every contract is subject to negotiation by the parties involved.

To give you some idea of the items considered in such contracts, these are just a few of the points covered in a typical General Conditions of Agreement for Construction of Buildings: definitions of terms used; explanation of all contract documents; labor and materials; warranties; taxes; permits; fees; notices; duties of superintendent; progress schedule reports; subcontractors; separate contracts; progress and completion; payments; certificates for payment; withheld payments; completion and final payment; safety precautions; bonds and insurance; changes in work; change orders; contract price adjustments; correction of work; suspension of work; contract termination; and arbitration.

Before you sign any contract or other official legal document, you must understand what the document says. This can be difficult, because most contracts are complex. Do some reading on the basics of contracts so that you'll at least have a rudimentary understanding of the terminology and the fundamentals to protect yourself. Then discuss each detail of every contract with your attorney. If you are opposed to or uncomfortable with a clause, don't hesitate to attempt negotiation.

### Hiring Other Help

There are some circumstances when a buyer of a manufactured house doesn't need contractors, just some hired help—a skilled tradesman, some semiskilled labor, or some unskilled help. Where skilled help is needed, the same procedure used for selecting a contractor can be used. Usually, however, it depends on who might be available—and capable—to do the job. Semiskilled and unskilled help can usually be found in the same way. One good source for this kind of help is the local high school, or perhaps a nearby college or trade and vocational school. Hiring arrangements are nearly always verbal, at a rate mutually agreed upon; no contracts are involved.

# Keeping Tabs on Construction

The planning and the paperwork can take an inordinate amount of time, and it's natural to wonder if construction will ever begin, but eventually the time comes for that first step to get underway. If you've carefully prepared for the construction of your house, all of the details have been finalized by this time. And even if you won't be doing any of the construction yourself, you should still supervise or check the work while it is being done. This will further assure that the completed house meets your expectations.

### Site Preparation

The preparation of the building site usually starts with an accurate layout of all the building elements. The driveway or access road must be precisely staked out. The house site must be checked and all of the measurements verified, so that the foundation can be constructed in the right place, and to the right dimensions. Often the water and sewer line trenches are staked out, but sometimes this is done after the foundation has been built. Work on a septic system layout or drilling a well can start now, too. Sometimes it's necessary to clear brush or trees away from these locations, or to make an access route for a drilling rig to get to the well site.

As soon as the layout work is done and verified, the driveway or access road can be cut in, graded, and surfaced. Remember that for most manufactured house projects, the road surface must be firm and at least graveled, so that it will hold the weight of a 30-ton truck even in wet weather or during a spring thaw.

At the same time, the house site should be cleared. Trees and underbrush have to be cut down, but low vegetation and surface rocks will be removed by the excavating machinery.

*If you oversee the site preparation you can make sure trees, rocks, and other natural features are kept just as you want them.*

Then, any necessary contouring can be done and the foundation pit can be excavated; topsoil should be saved, and subsoil can be heaped wherever convenient. Excess soil remaining can be hauled off, or used for contouring, and the topsoil will later be used for landscaping. At the same time, any other required excavations can be made. Try to coordinate the movements of earth moving equipment as closely as possible so you don't have to bring them back to the job site repeatedly, because of the added expense.

In some cases, all of this work may take place under the supervision of a general contractor. In others, you may choose to do some of the work—for example, staking layouts or clearing brush and trees—while an excavating contractor does the rest. But either way, it's a good idea if you are on hand to oversee all of the site preparation work. If you are present, you can make minor decisions that often need to be made and answer any questions.

### Inspecting and Scheduling

Once the site preparation work is done, construction can begin. If the whole job is being done by a contractor, there's no essential need for any further involvement on your part. But it's still a good idea for you to keep an eye on things. Whether or not you participate in construction, you'll need some knowledge of how to read blueprints and specifications. Some of this can be learned during the planning stages. If a factory representative or a dealer is involved, ask for a short course on reading blueprints and understanding materials schedules, detail drawings, and specification

sheets. This will enable you to inspect the work as it progresses and have a reasonable understanding of what's going on. Many manufactured houses come with simplified drawings that are relatively easy for even an inexperienced do-it-yourselfer to understand; others may be more complex. If at any time you are unsure of just what you are seeing on a set of prints, ask someone.

As the job moves along, you should periodically inspect the work. Make sure that it is to your satisfaction. If the job is being run by a supervisor or a general contractor, you should still inspect the work but take care not to interfere with the workers; schedule your inspections when work is finished for the day. Questions or difficulties should always be taken to the supervisor of the job. If you're doing some work at the same time a contractor is, it might be best to ask questions or discuss problems during coffee or lunch breaks. In any event, as the owner of the house, it's your responsibility to oversee the job from start to finish and make sure that you get the quality of materials, construction, and workmanship that you are paying for.

If you plan to run the construction job yourself, you'll have to coordinate the different phases. This doesn't matter much if you're doing virtually everything yourself and have no particular deadline. But if there is a deadline, timing will be important, and various tradesmen engaged in plumbing, electrical, insulating, or other phases will have to be scheduled well in advance. Everyone should be able to get his job done in the proper sequence. That schedule must be followed; otherwise, various tradesmen will be interfering with each other, and

some may have to quit and come back later. This can be frustrating and costly. Sequencing is important, too; if the drywall is put up before the electrician comes in, you have problems.

### Cost-Cutting Ideas

If your house is to be completed by a contractor, any efforts at cutting the costs must be made before the contract is signed. You can reduce costs by weighing all the options and extras that are offered, and choosing only those that you need and can afford. Perhaps there are some items or materials that you can purchase locally more economically than from a house manufacturer, especially after shipping costs are considered. Shop around for prices, try to take advantage of sales, find good used materials, or substitute a less expensive—but equally satisfactory—product or material. It may also be possible to exclude on-site extras from the contract—a deck or patio, for instance. You might build such extras yourself later, or have them built when you can better afford it.

Negotiating the building contract and getting as favorable a price as you reasonably can is another way to keep costs down. And changes in design, construction, or specifications once the job has been started should be avoided, unless you discover one that will somehow save you money.

There is more opportunity for cost cutting with a buyer-built house, usually in direct proportion to the amount of buyer involvement. Doing as much work as possible yourself and hiring as little outside help as is reasonable is the most obvious cost-cutting measure.

# Buyers' Guide to Prefabs, Kits, and Manufactured Houses

Whether you want a log house
or a dome, a split-level or a ranch,
or any house in between,
it's listed here with all
the information you need
to make buying easier

Buying a house is a big investment, and choosing a manufacturer is not a decision to be made lightly. Investigate the market carefully—you'll need all the information you can get on as many manufacturers as you can reasonably choose from. You'll also need to decide which house type is right for you. Is an old style log cabin what you need, or are you better suited for a more conventional looking precut or panelized house? Maybe the futuristic look of a dome is what you had in mind, or perhaps the open interiors of a post-and-beam house would be best.

Whatever kind of manufactured house you're looking for, you'll find it listed in this buyers' guide. The guide is divided into seven sections, each containing information on a single type of manufactured house and profiles of the manufacturers that make it. There are two levels of profiles. Manufacturers covered in the longer, more detailed profiles have been chosen based on such factors as a wide selection of house plans, the completeness of materials provided, the availability of custom design and engineering services, or special options other manufacturers don't offer. The shorter profiles cover other manufacturers producing that same type of house. There are other companies that sell manufactured houses; don't rule them out of your search.

## How to Use This Guide

Read the introduction to each section. Consider the differences in construction, appearance, do-it-yourself opportunities, and other relevant factors to decide which house type is right for you. Once you decide on type, use the material lists, price ranges, degree of completeness, and other information in the profiles to compare the manufacturers.

If you're interested in more than one type of house, direct comparisons may be difficult. Some house types are, on the whole, considerably cheaper than others. In many cases this depends on how complete the houses are. Timber houses as a rule are more expensive than dome houses, but you would expect as much because timber houses are more complete than domes. In addition to the walls, roof, floor, and windows and doors that come with a dome, timber houses frequently include materials for partition walls, second floors, stairways, and kitchen cabinets and appliances. Timber houses are approximately 50% complete; domes only 25% complete. It will cost more to finish a dome house than a timber house.

Other types of houses are less expensive by type. Modular/sectional houses can be as much as 95% complete, and are often priced as low as other house types that are only 50% complete. But modular/sectional houses offer far fewer floor plan options than other house types, so they might not be the best buy. Before you decide on a house type make sure you understand the differences among them in terms of price, materials provided, features, or services.

When choosing a manufacturer be certain of what differentiates one from another. If one manufacturer's house is more expensive than another's try to see what is making the difference. The price may be higher because the house is more complete, or because more materials are provided, those materials are of better quality, or more manufacturer or dealer service is offered. Your own needs will determine what these differences mean to you.

## What the Profiles Cover

The information in the profiles covers the manufacturer's standard houses, and was accurate at the time of publication. Use these profiles to compare one house against another.

Before reading the profiles, read the sample profile below to understand what is covered. This sample profile covers a precut house package. For construction details on other types of houses see the introductions to the different sections of the buyers' guide.

## ABC Homes Co.

2700 North St.
Skokie, IL 60076
(000) 000-0000

This listing provides the name, address, and telephone number of the company providing the houses being reviewed. In a few cases, more than one company is listed in a single profile; when this occurs, both offer the same product, and you should contact the nearest manufacturer. Call or write asking for further information, the name of the nearest dealer or representative, and the price of their latest catalog. Very few complete information packets are free; prices range from $1 to $10, with most packets costing between $4 and $5.

**MODELS:** 15 stock models; modifications possible; approximately 30% of the houses are custom designed.

This listing gives the number of house models offered, whether modifications are possible, and the degree of custom design services offered. If custom design services are available, the manufacturer will design and engineer any changes, as long as the company's materials and building system are used. An additional charge is made for this service.

**SQUARE FOOTAGE:** 500 to 1,500 square feet.

This figure gives the range of house sizes offered, from the smallest to the largest stock models. It specifies the amount of interior space, and does not include non-living space such as garages and porches. In some instances, the area is computed on the outside dimensions of the house, not by the inside dimensions. This means that the actual living space will be slightly smaller than the figures indicate. This method of listing square footage is most common in log houses. Many manufacturers can also provide specific models larger than the square footage listed.

**PRICE: $17,000 to $55,000.**

Prices quoted are for the basic models without modifications or options. The range given covers the cost spread from the smallest to the largest houses offered. In fact, these basic houses are seldom purchased as is; in most cases modifications are made, which raise the price. If a price range is not listed, either the manufacturer provides custom-designed houses only—no stock models are available—or the manufacturer only sells through independent dealer/builders. The prices for these houses will vary from one dealer/builder to the next. Often these houses must be built by the same dealer/builder, with little or no opportunity for do-it-yourself construction.

Price ranges should be regarded as a comparative guide only; contact the manufacturer or dealer/builder to determine the exact price for a particular house.

**COMPLETENESS OF PACKAGE:** About 50% complete.

This figure gives the manufacturer's estimate. It describes how complete the package is, and gives an indication of the amount of additional materials that the buyer will have to provide. The house shown above is about 50% complete; you could expect to spend about double the package price to complete this house. If the package was 25% complete, it would cost four times the price shown to complete the house. These costs are based on having the house constructed by a contractor; if you do the construction yourself, the total cost will be less.

**CONSTRUCTION: Floors.** *First floor:* Joist framing • Plywood subflooring • Particle board underlayment • Flooring not provided
*Second floor/loft:* Same as first floor
**Walls.** *Exterior walls:* Stud framing • Fiberglass insulation • Exterior plywood sheathing • Exterior cedar siding • Interior wall surface not provided
*Partition walls:* Stud framing • Wall surface not provided
**Roof.** Rafter framing • Fiberglass insulation • Plywood decking • Roof protection and roofing not provided
**Windows/Doors.** Double-glazed, aluminum-framed sliding or double-hung windows • Stopped-in glass not provided • Prehung metal insulated exterior doors • Double-glazed, aluminum-framed sliding patio doors with screens • Interior doors not provided

This listing presents the basic construction system that the manufacturer uses in standard house models. It covers the basic house packages that are available, without options or modifications. In many cases,

specific dimensions of materials are noted; where they are not, this means that the dimensions vary according to the structural needs of the various house models. Components listed as "not provided" are not included in the house package, but are still necessary for construction.

The type of house listed here uses the platform framing method of construction that requires numerous small components such as studs, joists, and rafters. For details on the construction of other types of houses, see the introductions to those sections.

**MANUFACTURER PROVIDES:**
Structural plans (including foundation)    Specifications
Construction manual
First floor framing, subflooring, and underlayment
Second floor/loft framing, subflooring, and underlayment
Exterior walls    Partition walls
Roof rafters and decking    Windows    Exterior doors
Interior and exterior trim    Insulation
Some fasteners and builders' hardware

This lists the basic components that the manufacturer provides in each house package. There are some variables; for example, if the house is to be built on a concrete slab, usually a first-floor frame isn't necessary. Full details and materials lists for specific models can be obtained from the manufacturer. Items that are not noted as being provided are sometimes available as options or extras; see the "Options Available" section.

**BUYER PROVIDES:**
Foundation    First and second floor covering
Interior wall surfaces    Roof protection and roofing
Flashing    Guttering system    Interior doors
Garage doors if applicable    Stairways and railings
Vapor barriers    Interior and exterior applied finishes
Weatherstripping    Caulking
Some fasteners and builders' hardware
Electrical system    Plumbing systems and fixtures
Heating/cooling system    Ventilating system
Appliances    Cabinetry

This listing indicates what the buyer must supply. If an item does not appear in a profile, but has in others, the item is not required for that particular house model or building system.

All of the items listed here are normally used to construct a house, but you may choose not to include some of them. For example, gutters are not always necessary, and depending on where the house is located a furnace may not be needed. The exclusion of a number of items may be possible; you should consult with an architect, a contractor, or the house manufacturer to determine what can be left out.

**OPTIONS AVAILABLE:** Garages; choice of windows and doors; stairways and railings; choice of cabinetry; kitchen sinks; vent hoods; plumbing fixtures and

supplies; electrical fixtures and supplies; heating/cooling system; ventilating system; appliances; countertops; carpeting.

This listing indicates items not included with standard models that are available for an additional cost. Options listed are subject to change, and the listings are not necessarily complete—many manufacturers can offer items that they do not catalog, and many will supply custom features or materials.

**SPECIAL FEATURES:** Planning services available; manufacturer's representative will consult on initial phases of construction for an additional fee; financing and financial assistance available; passive solar designs and options.

This heading covers design features, services, and values that distinguish one manufacturer from another. Features of special interest, such as solar options, are also included.

**EASE OF CONSTRUCTION:** Oriented to do-it-yourselfer. Almost all parts are precut and premarked. No special tools or equipment needed; no special skills or previous experience necessary to construct shell. Plans are explicit and fully detailed. Some carpentry and trade skills helpful but not essential.

This listing provides information on the relative ease of construction of the house package. Any special skills or experience, tools, and equipment necessary

for construction are listed. If do-it-yourself construction is out of the question or extremely unlikely, this information is given as well.

**MANUFACTURER ASSISTANCE:** Manufacturer will consult on all aspects of design. Manufacturer or dealer/builder will consult during initial phases of construction. Financing is available.

All manufacturers offer assistance in selecting and purchasing a house package. Some will continue to offer assistance after purchase, but this depends on the individual company. For example, some manufacturers send a representative out to the building site to make sure that the package is complete as delivered, that the construction is started correctly, and that any construction questions are answered. In other cases the manufacturer or dealer may help in selecting a contractor or arranging for financing. The degree of assistance provided by the manufacturer or the dealer should be agreed upon and written into the contract.

**SALES AREA:** National.

This heading defines the geographic area where the manufacturer's houses are available.

# Log Houses

Log houses, the descendants of the frontier cabin, have become increasingly popular in recent years—and with good reason. Logs have a natural warmth and charm that few mass-produced building materials can equal; they look—and are—extremely permanent.

*Log house assembly goes quickly, but it's not necessarily easy. Logs are heavy, and manipulating them is strenuous work.*

Log houses offer a degree of solidity almost unheard-of by today's standards. A well-built log house has a lifetime of at least 100 years. It is massive, storm-resistant, and enduring.

The solidity of log construction gives it other advantages, too. Log structures have considerable thermal mass; they absorb heat gradually and release it slowly. The climate inside a log house is tempered by this thermal lag, and energy efficiency is high. Log houses are practically soundproof. And because logs are massive, they do not burn easily; a log house is usually more fire-safe than a frame house.

Visually, log houses can be classified by the final form of the logs. Two basic types of logs are used: hand-peeled, and machine-peeled. Hand-peeled logs are more rustic-looking, and usually the biggest. They are left in their natural shape, and may retain as much as 30% of their bark. These logs are usually cut flat on top and bottom so that they stack easier. Some machine-peeled logs are milled to a uniform diameter, with all bark removed and all logs the same size. Others are only roughly the same diameter, and some bark—as much as 30 percent—may remain. All machine-peeled logs are cut flat on two or three sides. Some manufacturers of both types of log houses cut their logs in half, producing two half-round timbers from each log.

## Log House Construction

Log houses are popular with do-it-yourselfers, because the logs are precut and fitting them together is not difficult. However, lifting logs into place is both strenuous and time consuming. The main advantage to log house construction is that little interior trim work is necessary; the logs themselves form the inside walls, and no plastering, drywall installation, or painting is necessary. This reduces the amount of extra money that will be needed to finish the house.

This method of construction has one corresponding disadvantage—because the exterior walls are not hollow, there is nowhere to hide electrical cable and piping, so plumbing and electricity must be carefully planned to avoid exposed wiring and piping. Logs can be bored, however, to accommodate wiring, and some manufacturers provide bored logs as standard.

Perhaps one of the biggest advantages in the construction of a log house is that it can go up quickly, because on-site cutting and trimming is often not necessary. But to say it could be quick does not necessarily mean it will be easy. The ease or difficulty of construction depends mostly on the diameter of the logs. Houses built with large logs demand considerable strength and at least two workers for assembly. A two-story house with large logs is the most physically demanding type of manufactured house for a do-it-yourself builder to construct. Smaller logs require less effort to move, but there are more of them to handle. The size of the logs has other impacts as well; the largest logs make the heaviest, strongest, and warmest structure.

Several construction methods are used to assemble and seal log houses. The methods are all about equal in their effectiveness; what is more important is adequate caulking and gasketing, and the fit of the logs. All reputable log house manufacturers offer houses with logs that fit together well.

Most manufacturers use tongue-and-groove joints, either single or double, to lock the logs together. Less widely used joining techniques are the Swedish cope, in which each log is cupped to fit the curve of the next one, and the splined joint, in which a separate spline is driven into both logs being joined. The joints between logs are sealed with caulking, or with foam or vinyl gaskets. Many manufacturers use extra splines at corners and at butt joints where logs meet end to end. Properly done, all three methods are effective in preventing air infiltration between the logs; a well-built log house is usually tighter than a conventional frame house.

During the first two years the walls of a log house settle from two to three inches, and construction must allow for this settling. All manufacturers allow for this in their plans, and the buyer doesn't have to worry about it. Log houses also experience the same settling and shifting that conventional houses do. Outside seams should be caulked after one or two years, and cracks should be caulked after four or five years. No other upkeep of the walls is required.

Although the mass of the logs themselves makes the house stable, most manufacturers secure the logs with spikes, dowels, or tie rods for extra strength. Spikes or spiral spikes, 6 to 12 inches long, are the most common fasteners used to hold stacked logs in place. Dowels are sometimes used with the spikes to maintain the proper alignment. Tie rods, usually used only at corners, provide the most stable structure; these are long steel rods, secured to the foundation, that extend completely through the wall logs.

## Log Selection

Several species of trees are used for log houses. The most common, depending on what is available locally, are: red and white cedar, Douglas fir, spruce, cypress, and pine. Cedar and cypress are naturally rot-, fungus-, and insect-resistant. Northern white cedar is considered the most durable and fire-resistant, but offers no significant practical advantage. Most manufacturers treat all other logs with preservative to prevent rot, fungus, and insect damage, and recommend additional coats of preservative at completion of the house, after two or three years, and after eight to ten years.

The logs should be dried, or cured, before they are used. A few manufacturers, in the West, cut their logs from dead standing timber; these logs need no further drying. Most logs, however, are cut green, and are dried to a uniform moisture content. Uncured green timber should not be used for log houses, and all reputable log home manufacturers use dry timber.

There are various methods for drying logs, but all

methods produce roughly the same results. Some logs are air-dried, some kiln-dried. Some manufacturers make a curing kerf—a deep saw cut the full length of each log—before the drying process; some bore out the center of each log. These techniques are used to allow the logs to cure from the inside out, without splitting. Neither kerf-cutting nor boring affects the performance or the durability of the logs, but kerf-cut and bored logs usually develop fewer splits and cracks. A few manufacturers of log houses use partially cured logs; when this is done, shrinkage caused by further air curing is allowed for in the house design.

## Choices Are Available

Log houses are built in several basic styles. Most common is the classic horizontal log-on-log construction. Some houses are built palisade-style, with logs set vertically; others are sectional, with short horizontal logs stacked between pairs of vertical logs. Some houses use a combination of styles. Vertical logs shed water more readily than horizontal ones, but they may tend to decay near the foundation. Large horizontal logs, with wide chinking—the fill used between the logs—may collect water at the chinking. But for the most part, there is no practical advantage to any particular style.

Log house packages, or kits, are available in varying stages of completion. Walls-only packages, sometimes called logs-only, include precut logs, perhaps some finished interior walls, spikes, dowels, splines, and sealants. Basic-shell packages also include log beams, rafters, trusses, and window and door frames. Complete-shell packages include all of the components of the basic shell plus flooring, roofing, insulation, doors and windows, interior partitions, second floor materials, and stairs. Complete-house packages include all of these components plus utility systems, interior wiring and plumbing, interior trim, and bath and kitchen fixtures. Of the four, the basic shell and the complete shell are the most common.

The log houses currently available range from old-style log cabins to large modern houses that include solar features and matching garages. They come in sizes from 300 to 3,500 square feet, at prices ranging from $3,400 to more than $75,000. Most log house manufacturers offer stock designs and allow modifications; many offer custom design services as well.

# Hand-Peeled Log Houses

Houses built with hand-peeled logs are the nearest modern equivalent to the frontier cabin; they are more massive and more cabin-like in appearance than machine-peeled log houses. They are available with logs up to 12 inches in diameter. Hand-peeled logs are quite individual; knots and branch bumps are plainly visible. As much as 30 percent of the bark may be left on the logs.

Most manufacturers cut hand-peeled logs flat at the top and bottom, and sometimes on the interior side as well, leaving only one or two rounded sides. Others, however, cut logs in half, or leave them fully rounded. Most hand-peeled log house packages require only a small amount of cutting, fitting, or trimming at the job site to assemble the house. But, some manufacturers provide random-length, uncut logs, which must be cut and fitted together during construction.

## Boyne Falls Log Homes, Inc.

Highway 131
Boyne Falls, MI 49713
(616) 549-2421

**MODELS:** 16 stock models; modifications possible; approximately 25% of the houses are custom designed.

**SQUARE FOOTAGE:** 868 to 3,310 square feet.

**PRICES:** Horizontal log—$28,610 to $60,655; vertical log—$28,815 to $51,380; sectional log—$23,625 to $54,375.

**COMPLETENESS OF PACKAGE:** About 80% complete.

*Photos Courtesy Boyne Falls Log Homes, Inc.*

**CONSTRUCTION: Floors.** *First floor*: Joist framing •
Plywood subflooring • Felt underlayment • Tongue-
and-groove oak strip or pine flooring
*Second floor/loft*: Joist framing • Plywood
subflooring • Tongue-and-groove oak strip or pine
flooring
**Walls.** *Exterior walls:* Northern white cedar logs,
3½-inch (vertical and sectional formats) or 5½-inch
(horizontal format) thickness, cut flat on three sides •
No preservative applied • Secured with eight-inch
screw spikes
*Partition walls:* Stud framing • 1×8 spruce or pine
paneling wall surface
**Roof.** Log rafter framing • Insulation • Decking •
Asphalt shingles • No roof protection needed
**Windows/Doors.** Double-glazed, wood-framed
double-hung windows with screens • Solid wood
exterior doors • Red cedar interior doors

**MANUFACTURER PROVIDES:**
Structural plans (including foundation)
Typical mechanical plans   Specifications
Construction manual
Complete first floor and second floor/loft
Ceiling materials   Exterior wall logs   Log spikes
Partition walls   Complete roof system   Flashing
Windows   Interior and exterior doors
Door thresholds   Stairways
Interior and exterior trim   Insulation   Caulking
Fasteners and builders' hardware
Closet rods and shelves

**BUYER PROVIDES:**
Formal mechanical plans if needed   Foundation
Guttering system   Interior and exterior applied finishes
Vapor barriers   Weatherstripping   Electrical system
Plumbing system and fixtures   Heating/cooling system
Ventilating system   Appliances   Cabinetry

**OPTIONS AVAILABLE:** Rough sawn log exterior;
red cedar exterior doors; cedar shake roofing;
porches; decks; garages; 6-inch pine logs can be
substituted for cedar logs in horizontal format, to
reduce cost.

**SPECIAL FEATURES:** One of the most complete
house packages. Availability of three log placement
formats—horizontal, vertical, sectional—alone or in
combination; vertical format wall sections delivered
25 percent preassembled, sectional wall sections
delivered 75 percent preassembled. 1×10 tongue-and-
groove pine ceilings. Boyne Falls personnel involved
in all stages, from manufacture to delivery.

**EASE OF CONSTRUCTION:** Designed for fast
assembly. Work physically demanding. Some sections
partly preassembled; all parts numbered and coded to
plans, accurately cut and fitted. No on-site cutting or
fitting is usually required.

**MANUFACTURER ASSISTANCE:** Advice and
estimates on planning, foundations, plumbing, and
heating, etc. Assistance from factory representatives
in finding contractors or skilled help. All materials

delivered by Boyne Falls personnel in Boyne Falls
trucks. Shell erection by Boyne Falls crew if desired.

**SALES AREA:** National.

# Eureka Log Homes, Inc.
Commercial Avenue
Berryville, AR 72616
(501) 423-3396

**MODELS:** 14 stock models; modifications possible;
approximately 70% of the houses are custom
designed.

**SQUARE FOOTAGE:** 1,200 to 2,400 square feet.

**PRICE:** $11,663 to $30,243.

**COMPLETENESS OF PACKAGE:** Withheld.

**CONSTRUCTION: Floors.** *First floor:* Joist framing •
Subflooring, underlayment, and flooring not provided
*Second floor/loft:* Log framing • Subflooring,
underlayment, and flooring not provided
**Walls.** *Exterior walls:* Pine logs, 6-inch average
thickness, cut flat on three sides • Preservative

*Photos Courtesy Eureka Log Homes, Inc.*

treated • Logs laid horizontally • Secured with
10-inch spikes
*Partition walls:* Stud framing • Wall surface not
provided
**Roof.** Cedar shake roofing • Framing,
decking/sheathing, and roof protection not provided
**Windows/Doors.** Not provided

MANUFACTURER PROVIDES:
Structural plans    Typical mechanical plans
Blueprints    Construction manual    First floor framing
Second floor/loft framing    Exterior wall logs
Log spikes    Partition wall framing    Roofing
Gable framing or siding on some models
Stairway halflogs (treads)
Porch floor framing and decking
Window and door exterior trim    Some interior trim

BUYER PROVIDES:
Foundation plans    Formal mechanical plans if needed
Foundation
First floor subflooring, underlayment, and flooring
Second floor/loft subflooring, underlayment, and
   flooring
Ceiling materials    Partition wall surface
Roof framing, roof protection, and decking
Flashing    Guttering system    Windows
Exterior and interior doors
Stair materials except treads    Porch roofing
Most interior trim    Some exterior trim
Interior and exterior applied finishes    Vapor barriers
Insulation    Weatherstripping    Caulking
All fasteners and builders' hardware except spikes
Electrical system    Plumbing system and fixtures
Heating/cooling system    Ventilating system
Appliances    Cabinetry

STANDARD OPTIONS: Caulking; exterior clear
wood finish; single- or double-glazed, wood-framed
double-hung windows; log gables; log sun deck;
rough-sawn lumber for gable interior or ceiling
covering; hand-peeled log accent railings; plank
doors.

SPECIAL FEATURES: Authentic frontier cabin
appearance. Duplex design available. Yellow pine logs
in all construction. Standard porch in all designs.
Accent half-log false beams for interior trim.
Extensive custom-design service. Free shipping in
continental U.S. for most models.

EASE OF CONSTRUCTION: Assembly can be
technically and physically demanding. Designed for
minor on-site modifications as desired; materials are
not precut or numbered; logs supplied in random
lengths. All parts must be cut, fitted, and trimmed.

MANUFACTURER ASSISTANCE: Manufacturers or
dealers will assist in design, selection, planning, and
all similar details associated with package purchase;
many dealers are equipped to erect shell and/or
complete the house.

SALES AREA: National.

# New England Log Homes, Inc.
2301 State Street
P.O. Box 5056
Hamden, CT 06518
(203) 562-9981

MODELS: 59 stock models; modifications possible;
approximately 30% of the houses are custom
designed.

SQUARE FOOTAGE: 704 to 3,552 square feet.

PRICE: $8,295 to $31,995.

COMPLETENESS OF PACKAGE: About 50% to 75%
complete.

CONSTRUCTION: Floors. *First floor:* Not provided
*Second floor/loft:* Log framing • Subflooring,
underlayment, and flooring not provided
**Walls.** *Exterior walls:* Pine logs, 8 to 11 inch
thickness, cut flat on top and bottom • Preservative
treated • Logs laid horizontally • Secured with
10-inch spikes

*Photos Courtesy New England Log Homes, Inc.*

*Partition walls:* Not provided
**Roof.** Log rafter or truss framing • Decking, underlayment, and roofing not provided
**Windows/Doors.** Single-glazed, wood-framed double-hung and picture windows • Prehung solid fir exterior doors • Interior doors not provided

## MANUFACTURER PROVIDES:
Structural plans (including foundation)
Typical mechanical plans    Blueprints
Construction manual    Second floor/loft log framing
Exterior wall logs    Log spikes
Roof framing    Gables on some models    Windows
Exterior doors    Porch plates, posts, and sills
Caulking    Additional wood preservative

## BUYER PROVIDES:
Formal mechanical plans if needed    Foundation
Complete first floor
Second floor/loft subflooring, underlayment, and flooring
Ceiling materials    Partition walls
Roof decking, roof protection, and roofing    Flashing
Guttering system    Interior doors    Stairways
Porch decking and roofing    Interior and exterior trim
Interior and exterior applied finishes
Vapor barriers    Insulation    Weatherstripping
All fasteners and builders' hardware except spikes
Electrical system    Plumbing system and fixtures
Heating/cooling system    Ventilating system
Appliances    Cabinetry

**OPTIONS AVAILABLE:** Dormers (8-foot, 12-foot, 16-foot, 20-foot, 24-foot, 28-foot, 32-foot, and 36-foot); front extensions; kitchen sidewall extensions; full second floor; 16-foot side porch; family room; two car garage; second floor/loft flooring package; roofing package; double-glazed windows; wood-framed combination screen/storm doors. Many options available only on specific models.

**SPECIAL FEATURES:** A large choice of dormer systems and house extensions. Standard porch with all packages. Accessory outbuildings for garage/stable/workshop. Optional log system with tongue-and-groove joints, using fully milled logs cut flat on three sides and milled to a curve on the outside. New England personnel on-site for first four hours of construction, to ensure proper delivery of materials, and to supervise initial construction.

**EASE OF CONSTRUCTION:** Assembly is technically simple, but physically demanding. Components are precut and coded to plans for ease of assembly. Some field trimming, cutting, or fitting may be required.

**MANUFACTURER ASSISTANCE:** Design, technical, and engineering help from the factory; dealer assistance ranging from selection and design to complete erection and finishing service. Four hours of initial on-site technical assistance at construction startup are included in the package price.

**SALES AREA:** National.

# Alpine Log Homes, Inc.
P.O. Box 85
Victor, MT 59875
(406) 642-3451

**MODELS:** 10 stock models; modifications possible; custom design specialty.

**SQUARE FOOTAGE:** 900 to 3,000 square feet.

**PRICE:** $15,000 to $75,000.

**COMPLETENESS OF PACKAGE:** About 25% to 33% complete.

**SPECIAL FEATURES:** 8½-inch diameter logs, entirely handcrafted; logs chinked inside and out with cement and insulating material; very authentic appearance.

**SALES AREA:** National.

# Custom Log Homes
P.O. Box 226
Stevensville, MT 59870
(406) 777-5202

**MODELS:** 20 stock models; modifications possible; custom design specialty.

**SQUARE FOOTAGE:** 432 to 2,304 square feet.

**PRICE:** $6,126 to $24,763.

**COMPLETENESS OF PACKAGE:** About 25% complete.

**SPECIAL FEATURES:** Fully-round logs with masonry chinking held by nails available; chinkless Swedish cope log-joining method; optional log stairways available; massive, authentic frontier cabin appearance.

**SALES AREA:** Indiana to the West Coast.

# Green Mountain Cabins, Inc.
P.O. Box 190
Chester, VT 05143
(802) 875-2163

**MODELS:** Mainly custom design work with 10 typical sample models.

**SQUARE FOOTAGE:** 1,000 to 2,200 square feet.

**PRICE:** $10,000 to $50,000.

**COMPLETENESS OF PACKAGE:** About 33% to 50% complete.

**SPECIAL FEATURES:** Unique vinyl spline log joining method; solar compatability; complete owner-design manual.

**SALES AREA:** National.

 **Buyers' Guide**

# Green River Trading Co.

Boston Corners Road
Millerton, NY 12546
(518) 789-3311

**MODELS:** 6 stock models; modifications possible; custom design available.

**SQUARE FOOTAGE:** 748 to 2,190 square feet.

**PRICE:** $6,315 to $10,260.

**COMPLETENESS OF PACKAGE:** About 20% complete.

**SPECIAL FEATURES:** Barns, stables, garages, and utility buildings available; rough-sawn timbers.

**SALES AREA:** National.

# Katahdin Forest Products

P.O. Box 145
Oakfield, ME 04763
(207) 757-8278

**MODELS:** 14 stock models; modifications possible; custom design available.

**SQUARE FOOTAGE:** 864 to 1,680 square feet.

**PRICE:** $7,623 to $35,946.

**COMPLETENESS OF PACKAGE:** About 45% complete.

**SPECIAL FEATURES:** Choice of either white pine (less expensive) or northern white cedar; starter, shell, and complete kits offered.

**SALES AREA:** National.

# L. C. Andrew, Inc.

28 Depot Street
South Windham, ME 04082
(207) 892-8561

**MODELS:** 13 standard models; modifications possible; custom design available.

**SQUARE FOOTAGE:** 384 to 2,058 square feet.

**PRICE:** $9,700 to $33,000.

**COMPLETENESS OF PACKAGE:** About 40% complete.

**SPECIAL FEATURES:** Garage available; combined half-log and insulated-frame wall construction. Logs made exclusively of northern white cedar.

**SALES AREA:** National.

# Lok-N-Logs, Inc.

Route 80
RD No. 2, Box 212
Sherburne, NY 13460
(607) 674-4447

**MODELS:** 13 stock models; modifications possible; custom design available.

**SQUARE FOOTAGE:** 768 to 3,168 square feet.

**PRICE:** $7,000 to $16,300.

**COMPLETENESS OF PACKAGE:** About 25% complete.

**SPECIAL FEATURES:** Garage available; Andersen windows; ¾-inch thick tongue and groove white pine ceiling; logs available with one or two rounded sides; uncut-log kits available. Four log profiles to choose from.

**SALES AREA:** Connecticut, Delaware, Indiana, Maryland, Massachusetts, Michigan, New Hampshire, New Jersey, New York, North Carolina, Ohio, Pennsylvania, Vermont, Virginia, West Virginia.

# R & L Log Buildings, Inc.

P.O. Box 237
Mt. Upton, NY 13809
(607) 764-8118 or -8145

**MODELS:** 21 stock models; modifications possible; custom design available.

**SQUARE FOOTAGE:** 640 to 1,536 square feet.

**PRICE:** $7,905 to $16,208.

**COMPLETENESS OF PACKAGE:** About 33% to 50% complete.

**SPECIAL FEATURES:** Log sealing system uses continuous urethane and butyl rubber insulators; garages; workshop addition; utility room option; porch and dormer packages available; all standard insulated windows.

**SALES AREA:** National.

# Rustic Log Structures

14000 Interurban Avenue South
Seattle (Tukwila), WA 98168
(206) 246-1332 or -1333

**MODELS:** 12 stock models; modifications possible; mainly custom design.

**SQUARE FOOTAGE:** 1,200 to 6,000 square feet.

**PRICE:** $8,400 to $45,000.

**COMPLETENESS OF PACKAGE:** About 33% complete.

**SPECIAL FEATURES:** 8- to 10-inch logs; variety of packages from logs-only to complete or finished home; majority custom designed.

**SALES AREA:** National and Japan.

## The Rustics of Lindbergh Lake, Inc.
Highway 83
Condon, MT 59825
(406) 754-2222

Southern Rustics
P.O. Box 296
Foley, AL 36536
(205) 943-1588

**MODELS:** Custom design only.

**SQUARE FOOTAGE:** 875 to 2,000 square feet.

**PRICE:** $10,000 to $15,000.

**COMPLETENESS OF PACKAGE:** About 20% complete.

**SPECIAL FEATURES:** Log railings and steps; logs preassembled in production yard, then numbered, disassembled and shipped to site; delivery within 3 to 6 weeks; no chinking necessary, only small bead of caulking because logs are preassembled and fit together extremely well.

**SALES AREA:** National (Western ⅔ of the United States, also Alaska and Canada; affiliate: Southern Rustics of Foley, Alabama, which manufactures and distributes in the Eastern ⅓ of the U.S.)

## Wilderness Log Homes
Route #2
Plymouth, WI 53073
(414) 893-8416

**MODELS:** 40 stock models; modifications possible; custom design available.

**SQUARE FOOTAGE:** 288 to 2,552 square feet.

**PRICE:** $5,900 to $42,000.

**COMPLETENESS OF PACKAGE:** About 75% complete.

**SPECIAL FEATURES:** Half-log kit for a new house or to convert existing home to appearance of log house; cedar shakes; knotty pine paneling, flooring, and roof boards are available. Northern white cedar logs, if preferred.

**SALES AREA:** National.

# Machine-Peeled Log Houses

Houses built with machine-peeled logs, sometimes called lathe-turned or milled logs, usually have a more formal appearance than those built with hand-peeled logs. For the most part, they are less massive and more contemporary looking than hand-peeled log houses. The logs are milled to a uniform diameter, and their visual impression is distinctly less rustic. Log surfaces are smooth, and the bark is normally totally removed. A few rough-milled log houses are available with logs up to 12 inches in diameter, with as much as 30 percent of the bark retained.

All manufacturers cut machine-peeled logs flat on the joining sides and sometimes the interior, leaving only one or two rounded sides. A few manufacturers cut logs in half. Because they are milled for a uniform fit, machine-peeled logs are sometimes slightly easier to seal than hand-peeled logs.

## Air Lock Log Homes
Air Lock Log Company, Inc.
P.O. Box 2506
Las Vegas, NM 87701
(505) 425-8888

National Log Construction Company, Inc.
P.O. Box 68
Thompson Falls, MT 59873
(406) 827-3521

**MODELS:** 55 stock models; modifications possible; approximately 50% of houses are custom designed.

**SQUARE FOOTAGE:** 288 to 2,903 square feet.

**PRICE:** $5,180 to $32,250.

**COMPLETENESS OF PACKAGE:** About 25% to 33% complete.

*Courtesy Air Lock Log Homes*

*Courtesy Air Lock Log Homes*

**CONSTRUCTION: Floors.** *First floor:* Not provided
*Second floor/loft:* Log framing • Subflooring,
underlayment, and flooring not provided
**Walls.** *Exterior walls:* Pine logs, 6-inch thickness,
round on all sides • Preservative treated • Secured by
threaded rods if required or desired
*Partition walls:* Logs for major partitions • Minor
partitions not provided
**Roof.** Log rafter or log truss framing • Decking/
sheathing, roof protection, and roofing not provided
**Windows/Doors.** Not provided

**MANUFACTURER PROVIDES:**
Structural plans (including foundation)   Blueprints
Specifications   Construction manual
Second floor/loft framing   Exterior wall logs
Some partition wall logs   Roof framing   Gables
Window and door frames with exterior trim
Stairways   Porch wall logs   Porch posts
Caulking

**BUYER PROVIDES:**
Formal mechanical plans   Foundation
Complete first floor
Second floor/loft subflooring, underlayment, and
   flooring
Ceiling materials   Minor partition walls
Roof decking/sheathing, roof protection, and roofing
Flashing   Guttering system   Windows
Interior and exterior doors   Porch decking
Some exterior trim   All interior trim
Interior and exterior applied finishes   Vapor barriers
Insulation   Weatherstripping
Fasteners and builders' hardware
Wall tie rods if required   Electrical system
Plumbing system and fixtures   Heating/cooling system
Ventilating system   Appliances   Cabinetry

**OPTIONS AVAILABLE:** Wall tie rods and hardware;
caulking for all interior walls and partitions; interior
half-log trim; special box window frames; 7-inch and
8-inch logs.

**SPECIAL FEATURES:** Centerbored, hollow logs for
easy installation of wiring; massive wood truss
assemblies in some models; combined Swedish cope
and tongue-and-groove log joints; standard porches in
most stock models; authentic log-cabin interior.

**EASE OF CONSTRUCTION:** Assembly is technically
simple but physically demanding, especially for larger
log diameters and placement of roof trusses. Parts are
precut and coded to plans for ease of assembly. Some
on-site cutting, fitting, and trimming may be required.

**MANUFACTURER ASSISTANCE:** Planning, design,
technical, and engineering advice from factory.

**SALES AREA:** National.

# Beaver Log Homes, Inc.
Box 1145
Claremore, OK 74017
(918) 341-5932

**MODELS:** 36 stock models; modifications possible;
approximately 80% of the houses are custom
designed.

**SQUARE FOOTAGE:** 512 to 2,793 square feet.

**PRICE:** $5,635 to $17,345.

**COMPLETENESS OF PACKAGE:** About 20%
complete.

**CONSTRUCTION: Floors.** *First floor:* Not provided
*Second floor/loft:* Not provided
**Walls.** *Exterior walls:* Pine logs, 8-inch and 10-inch
thickness, cut flat on top and bottom • Preservative
treated • Logs laid horizontally • Logs secured by
8½-foot threaded rods when required by buyer or
code
*Partition walls:* Logs for major partitions on some
models • Other partitions not provided

*Courtesy Beaver Log Homes, Inc.*

*Courtesy Beaver Log Homes, Inc.*

**Roof.** Not provided
**Windows/Doors.** Not provided

## MANUFACTURER PROVIDES:
Structural plans (including foundation)   Blueprints
Specifications   Construction manual
Exterior wall logs
Partition wall logs on some models   Caulking
Securing rods if desired

## BUYER PROVIDES:
Formal mechanical plans   Foundation
Complete first floor   Complete second floor/loft
Ceiling materials   Partition walls if applicable
Complete roof system   Flashing   Guttering system
Windows   Interior and exterior doors   Stairways
Interior and exterior trim
Interior and exterior applied finishes   Vapor barriers
Insulation   Weatherstripping
Fasteners and builders' hardware   Electrical system
Plumbing system and fixtures
Heating/cooling system   Ventilating system
Appliances   Cabinetry

**OPTIONS AVAILABLE:** Choice of 8-inch, 10-inch, or 12-inch logs; percentage of bark can be left on logs.

**SPECIAL FEATURES:** Large tongue-and-groove log joints provide an effective system of sealing joints against air infiltration; uniform log sizing for ease of handling and assembly. Basic walls-only package allows buyer to choose remaining materials. Extensive custom designing services.

**EASE OF CONSTRUCTION:** Assembly of the kit itself (walls only) is technically simple, but physically demanding. Logs are precut and labeled according to plans; only minor on-site cutting, fitting, and trimming is required.

**MANUFACTURER ASSISTANCE:** Planning, design, and engineering help available at extra cost; dealers will assist in finding local contractor, and some are equipped to erect the structure. Dealers will also guide an owner-assembly project where feasible, and can arrange for shipping of the package.

**SALES AREA:** National.

# Real Log Homes
National Information Center
Box 202
Hartland, VT 05048
(800) 451-4485

**MODELS:** 34 stock models; modifications possible; approximately 5% of the houses are custom designed.

**SQUARE FOOTAGE:** 748 to 2,938 square feet.

**PRICE:** $8,600 to $30,200.

**COMPLETENESS OF PACKAGE:** Withheld.

**CONSTRUCTION: Floors.** *First floor:* Not provided *Second floor/loft:* Log joist and beam framing • Subflooring, underlayment, and flooring not provided **Walls.** *Exterior walls:* Pine logs, 8-inch and 11-inch thickness cut flat on top and bottom • Preservative treated • Logs laid horizontally • Secured with 10-inch spiral spikes *Partition walls:* Not provided **Roof.** Conventional rafter or log rafter framing • Sheathing or decking, roof protection, and roofing not provided • Framing not provided on some models **Windows/Doors.** Prehung single-glazed, wood-framed double-hung or picture windows • Prehung fir exterior doors • Interior doors not provided

*Photos Courtesy Real Log Homes*

**MANUFACTURER PROVIDES:**
Structural plans (including foundation)
Typical mechanical plans   Blueprints   Specifications
Construction manual   Second floor/loft framing
Exterior wall logs   Roof framing on some models
Windows   Exterior doors
Porch framing on some models
Log dormer framing on some models   Spikes

**BUYER PROVIDES:**
Formal mechanical plans if needed   Foundation
Complete first floor
Second floor/loft subflooring, underlayment, and
   flooring
Ceiling materials   Partition walls
Roof sheathing/decking, roof protection, and roofing
Roof framing if applicable   Flashing
Guttering system   Interior doors   Stairways
Porch and dormer decking and roofing if applicable
Interior and exterior trim
Interior and exterior applied finishes   Vapor barriers
Insulation   Weatherstripping   Caulking
Fasteners and builders' hardware   Electrical system
Plumbing system and fixtures   Heating/cooling system
Ventilating system   Appliances   Cabinetry

**OPTIONS AVAILABLE:** Double-glazed windows;
prehung interior pine doors; storm doors.

**SPECIAL FEATURES:** Passive solar model available;
undimensioned logs for more rustic appearance;
exposed log ceiling joists and roof rafters; matching
log outbuildings and garages available.

**EASE OF CONSTRUCTION:** Assembly is technically
simple, but physically demanding. Logs precut,
numbered, and coded to plans; some on-site cutting,
fitting, and trimming required.

**MANUFACTURER ASSISTANCE:** Manufacturer or
dealer will consult on financing, siting, foundations,
construction techniques, heating, etc. At least four
hours of on-site assistance and guidance when
construction begins.

**SALES AREA:** National.

# Rocky Mountain Log Homes
3353 Highway 93 South
Hamilton, MT 59840
(406) 363-5680

**MODELS:** 32 stock models; modifications possible;
approximately 50% of the houses are custom
designed.

**SQUARE FOOTAGE:** 440 to 3,064 square feet.

**PRICE:** $6,500 to $26,000.

**COMPLETENESS OF PACKAGE:** About 25% to
50% complete.

**CONSTRUCTION: Floors.** *First floor:* Not provided
*Second floor/loft:* Log and beam framing •

Subflooring, underlayment, and flooring not provided
**Walls.** *Exterior walls:* Pine logs, 7-inch thickness,
round on three sides and cupped on the bottom
(Swedish cope) • No preservative applied • Logs laid
horizontally • Secured with spikes
*Partition walls:* Not provided
**Roof.** Log or beam rafter framing • Decking,
roof protection, and roofing not provided
**Windows/Doors.** Not provided

**MANUFACTURER PROVIDES:**
Structural plans (including foundation)
Typical mechanical plans   Blueprints   Specifications
Construction manual   Second floor/loft framing
Exterior wall logs   Roof framing
Porch rafters, posts, and headers on some models  Spikes

**BUYER PROVIDES:**
Formal mechanical plans   Foundation
Complete first floor
Second floor/loft subflooring, underlayment, and
   flooring
Ceiling materials   Preservative for log walls
Partition walls
Roof decking, roof protection, and roofing
Flashing   Guttering system   Windows
Interior and exterior doors   Stairways
Porch flooring and roofing if applicable
Interior and exterior trim
Interior and exterior applied finishes
Vapor barriers   Insulation   Weatherstripping

*Photos Courtesy Rocky Mountain Log Homes*

Caulking  Fasteners and builders' hardware
Electrical system  Plumbing system and fixtures
Heating/cooling system  Ventilating system
Appliances  Cabinetry

**OPTIONS AVAILABLE:** Logs in 8-inch, 9-inch, 10-inch, 11-inch, and 12-inch diameters; second floor/loft arrangements; porches; decks; railings; stairways; active solar heating system; solar water heating system; tongue-and-groove floor or roof decking; 2×4 or 2×6 partition wall studs; double- or triple-glazed wood-framed windows.

**SPECIAL FEATURES:** Wide range of log diameters; Swedish cope log-joining method; traditional log cabin construction and appearance; on-site design-change flexibility; active solar model. Wide range of options; six different manufacturing locations, which may reduce shipping costs.

**EASE OF CONSTRUCTION:** Work can be both technically difficult and physically demanding, especially in two-story structures of 12-inch logs. No parts are precut. Logs must be cut to fit on-site, windows are cut in after wall assembly; full range of cutting, fitting, and trimming skills necessary.

**MANUFACTURER ASSISTANCE:** Dealers will assist in all phases from site selection to construction details, and from kit selection to finished house. Shell assembly can be done by trained factory crew.

**SALES AREA:** National.

# Authentic Homes Corporation
Laramie, WY 82070
(307) 742-3786

**MODELS:** 40 stock models; modifications possible on most models; custom design available.

**SQUARE FOOTAGE:** 404 to 2,842 square feet.

**PRICE:** $5,300 to $26,000.

**COMPLETENESS OF PACKAGE:** About 20% complete.

**SPECIAL FEATURES:** Garage, stable, and compact cabin kits available; passive solar models available.

**SALES AREA:** National except New England.

# Bellaire Log Cabin Manufacturing Company
Box 322 G
Bellaire, MI 49615
(616) 533-8633

**MODELS:** 15 stock models; modifications possible; custom design available.

**SQUARE FOOTAGE:** 396 to 2,184 square feet.

**PRICE:** $6,000 to $40,000.

**COMPLETENESS OF PACKAGE:** About 50% complete.

**SPECIAL FEATURES:** Cedar logs; half-log and spline construction, vertical log format; optional roof and exterior wall insulation; knotty pine paneling.

**SALES AREA:** Georgia, Illinois, Indiana, Iowa, Kentucky, Michigan, Minnesota, New York, Ohio, Pennsylvania, Tennessee, Virginia, West Virginia.

# Cabin Log Company of America, Inc.
2809 Highway 167 North
Lafayette, LA 70507
(318) 232-9568

**MODELS:** 4 stock models; modifications possible; custom design available.

**SQUARE FOOTAGE:** 768 to 1,632 square feet.

**PRICE:** $8,000 to $24,000.

**COMPLETENESS OF PACKAGE:** About 35% to 40% complete.

**SPECIAL FEATURES:** Cypress or fir logs; cypress log siding package; 1×8 cypress lap siding package; cypress tongue-and-groove decking; double insulated windows.

**SALES AREA:** National.

# Finlandia Log Homes
4515 Lake Avenue
Glenview, IL 60025
(312) 635-7711

**MODELS:** 40 stock models; modifications possible; custom design available.

**SQUARE FOOTAGE:** 500 to 2,000 square feet.

**PRICE:** $12,500 to $70,000.

**COMPLETENESS OF PACKAGE:** About 50% complete.

**SPECIAL FEATURES:** Arctic pine logs from Finland, diameters from 4 to 12 inches; choice of round or squared logs; copper nails; tongue-and-groove floors and ceilings; wood dowels in the walls; patented cross-corner bolts; double ceilings and floors; all visible joints finger glued; optional sauna.

**SALES AREA:** National.

# Heritage Log Homes

P.O. Box 610
Gatlinburg, TN 37738
(615) 436-9331

**MODELS:** 30 stock models; modifications possible; custom design available.

**SQUARE FOOTAGE:** 70 to 4,177 square feet.

**PRICE:** $1,950 to $21,200.

**COMPLETENESS OF PACKAGE:** About 20% to 25% complete.

**SPECIAL FEATURES:** Cathedral ceilings with exposed beams; country kitchens; simple interchangeable-log numbering system; 8-inch diameter logs; garages available; manufacturer's own shipping service.

**SALES AREA:** National.

# Lincoln Logs Ltd.

Riverside Drive
Chestertown, NY 12817
(518) 494-2426

**MODELS:** 20 stock models; modifications possible; custom design available.

**SQUARE FOOTAGE:** 560 to 2,530 square feet.

**PRICE:** $8,500 to $30,000.

**COMPLETENESS OF PACKAGE:** About 33% to 50% complete.

**SPECIAL FEATURES:** Logs are not precut; complete roof system is part of standard package; vented roof ridge; 100-year limited warranty covering materials.

**SALES AREA:** National.

# Lodge Logs

3200 Gowen Road
Boise, ID 83705
(208) 336-2450

**MODELS:** 52 stock models; modifications possible; custom design available.

**SQUARE FOOTAGE:** 520 to 2,603 square feet.

**PRICE:** $5,100 to $20,000.

**COMPLETENESS OF PACKAGE:** About 20% to 25% complete.

**SPECIAL FEATURES:** Wall logs secured with full-height ready rods; massive log trusses and rafters; window, door, and cabinetry packages; 6- to 10-inch diameter logs.

**SALES AREA:** Midwest and West.

# Lok-Log Homes

P.O. Box 300
Gunnison, CO 81230
(303) 641-1844

**MODELS:** 33 stock models; modifications possible; custom design available.

**SQUARE FOOTAGE:** 453 to 2,148 square feet.

**PRICE:** $11,606 to $45,282.

**COMPLETENESS OF PACKAGE:** About 70% to 75% complete.

**SPECIAL FEATURES:** Walls aligned with dowels, secured with floor-to-ceiling tie rods; logs predrilled every 12 inches for dowels, tie rods, and electrical wiring; partition framing included.

**SALES AREA:** National.

# Model-Log Homes

Lumber Enterprises, Inc.
75777 Gallatin Road
Bozeman, MT 59715
(406) 763-4411

**MODELS:** Custom design only.

**SQUARE FOOTAGE:** 400 to 2,500 square feet.

**PRICE:** $8,600 to $43,000.

**COMPLETENESS OF PACKAGE:** About 33% to 40% complete.

**SPECIAL FEATURES:** Choice of frame trusses, scissor trusses, or custom log trusses; full-round, triple tongue-and-groove logs; 6- to 10-inch diameter logs.

**SALES AREA:** National.

# Northeastern Log Homes, Inc.

P.O. Box 46
Kenduskeag, ME 04450
(207) 884-7000

**MODELS:** 39 stock models; modifications possible; custom design available.

**SQUARE FOOTAGE:** 672 to 3,740 square feet.

**PRICE:** $12,790 to $58,390.

**COMPLETENESS OF PACKAGE:** About 40% complete.

**SPECIAL FEATURES:** Scaled floor plan drawing and itemized price quotation at no cost or obligation; open timber roof trusses; double roof construction.

**SALES AREA:** National.

# Northern Products Log Homes, Inc.

P.O. Box 616
Bomarc Road
Bangor, ME 04401
(207) 945-6413

**MODELS:** 20 stock models; modifications possible; custom design available.

**SQUARE FOOTAGE:** 425 to 4,829 square feet.

**PRICE:** $9,150 to $172,859.

**COMPLETENESS OF PACKAGE:** About 40% complete.

**SPECIAL FEATURES:** Garages and breezeways available; triple-glazed windows; double roof construction; solar options; PVC log-joint gasket; solar designs available.

**SALES AREA:** Connecticut, Illinois, Indiana, Kentucky, Maine, Maryland, Massachusetts, Michigan, Minnesota, Missouri, New Hampshire, New Jersey, New York, Pennsylvania, South Carolina, Vermont, West Virginia, Wisconsin.

# Northern Industries, Inc.

P.O. Box 236
LaPorte, MN 56461
(218) 224-2659

**MODELS:** 6 stock models; modifications possible; custom design available.

**SQUARE FOOTAGE:** 924 to 1,488 square feet.

**PRICE:** $14,754 to $17,332 (Prices up 15% to 20% by June, 1981).

**COMPLETENESS OF PACKAGE:** About 50% complete.

**SPECIAL FEATURES:** Log staircases, railings, and balusters; porch and deck packages; fresh air fireplace/furnace unit with blowers included in package price; cathedral ceilings with round-log exposed rafters; lofts.

**SALES AREA:** National.

# Northwoods Log Homes, Inc.

LaPorte, MN 56461
(218) 224-2251

**MODELS:** 100+ stock models; modifications possible; mainly custom design.

**SQUARE FOOTAGE:** 700 to 4,000 square feet.

**PRICE:** Withheld (about $28 to $32 per square foot).

**COMPLETENESS OF PACKAGE:** About 60% complete.

**SPECIAL FEATURES:** Fireplace-furnace unit with blowers included; logs bolted together and neoprene-sealed; log staircases, railings, and balusters; porch and deck packages; logs up to 40 feet long.

**SALES AREA:** Georgia, Illinois, Indiana, Iowa, Kansas, Maryland, Michigan, Minnesota, Missouri, Nebraska, New Jersey, North Dakota, Ohio, Pennsylvania, South Dakota, West Virginia, Wisconsin, Wyoming.

# Rustic Log Homes

1207 Grover Road, Highway 216
Kings Mountain, NC 28086
(704) 739-3613

**MODELS:** 34 stock models; modifications possible; custom design available.

**SQUARE FOOTAGE:** 512 to 3,456 square feet.

**PRICE:** $8,000 to $21,000.

**COMPLETENESS OF PACKAGE:** About 33% complete.

**SPECIAL FEATURES:** Storage buildings and garages available; log porches; beams; 6×8-inch logs; flat interior finish, if desired.

**SALES AREA:** National.

# Ward Cabin Company

Box 72
Houlton, ME 04730
(207) 532-6531

**MODELS:** 33 stock models; modifications possible; custom design available.

**SQUARE FOOTAGE:** 600 to 2,185 square feet.

**PRICE:** $28,950 to $83,220.

**COMPLETENESS OF PACKAGE:** About 40% complete.

**SPECIAL FEATURES:** Northern white cedar logs; very complete packages; optional oak flooring; variety of roof options; dormers, garages, and small cabin kits available; log doors.

**SALES AREA:** National.

# Western Log Homes

5297 West 48th Ave.
Denver, CO 80212
(303) 455-0993

**MODELS:** 21 stock models; modifications

possible; custom design available.

**SQUARE FOOTAGE:** 600 to 2,652 square feet.

**PRICE:** $13,650 to $43,200.

**COMPLETENESS OF PACKAGE:** About 30% to 40% complete.

**SPECIAL FEATURES:** Decks and porches included in stock designs; energy efficient walls optional; shake shingles optional; five solar designed models.

**SALES AREA:** National.

## Youngstrom Log Homes

P.O. Box 385
Blackfoot, ID 83221
(208) 785-0632

**MODELS:** 22 stock models; modifications possible; mostly custom designs.

**SQUARE FOOTAGE:** 480 to 2,700 square feet.

**PRICE:** $5,193 to $32,883.

**COMPLETENESS OF PACKAGE:** About 33% complete.

**SPECIAL FEATURES:** Swedish cope log joints glued together; log diameters available from 7 to 12 inches; optional log gables and log interior walls; split log wraparounds available for trailers or other homes.

**SALES AREA:** National and Canada.

# Timber Houses

If you like the idea of a solid wood house, but a house that looks like a log cabin isn't your style, then why not try a timber house. Timber houses, also called solid-wood, solid-wall, or flat-milled log houses, offer many of the advantages of log houses—in fact, in many respects they are the same—but timber houses present a distinctively different appearance.

The wall pieces, or timbers, are solid-wood beams generally three or four inches thick, that have been milled flat on all four sides. When assembled, exterior walls look like wood siding on the outside, and like they are tongue-and-groove wood paneled on the inside. A few manufacturers offer houses with timbers that are slightly rounded on the outside face to simulate a log house in appearance. Even in these cases, however, the walls look more like siding or paneling than individual logs.

Both traditional and contemporary house designs are available in this type of manufactured house. Ex-

teriors range from those with a cabin-like appearance to ones that look much like a conventional paneled house. Interiors range from rustic to modern, with both types featuring a considerable amount of exposed wood. Many manufacturers continue that exposed wood theme outdoors by offering—as standard or optional—a wide selection of porches, decks, and sundecks.

The timber beams that make up the walls of a timber house are generally less massive than the logs used in hand- or machine-peeled log houses. The smaller size of the timbers makes possible more open designs, and timber houses frequently have more and larger windows than log houses. Cathedral or vaulted ceilings are also quite common, and frequently these include exposed wood posts or beams.

With all of that wood, it's no surprise that timber houses offer many of the same advantages that log houses do. Like log houses, timber houses are solid and well-built. Walls are typically constructed with interlocking tongue-and-groove timbers, and can be further secured with spikes or cables. Corner and butt joints frequently interlock as well, and sometimes dovetailed joints are used. The end result is an exceptionally solid wall. And timber houses offer the same fire resistance that log houses do; they are more fire-safe than a frame house.

## The Benefits of Wood Construction

Interlocking timber construction has other benefits as well. In almost all cases, logs are accurately milled for a very tight fit, so little or no caulking is required. That tight fit ensures that air infiltration is kept very low. And like log houses, thermal efficiency is high. The large quantity of solid wood acts as a thermal mass, tempering the interior climate; the walls absorb large quantities of heat that is released back into the interior of the house as needed.

Because the thermal mass—the solid wood—is contained within the insulation envelope, it creates a thermal flywheel effect. The timbers release heat slowly, over a 12 to 14 hour period. By the time the house walls begin to cool down after a day of absorbing heat, the low nighttime temperatures have already passed and are on the rise again. A number of manufacturers take advantage of this built-in thermal mass by incorporating it in passive solar heating systems. The end result is that timber house walls, combined with the thermal efficiency of the timbers, make timber houses one of the most energy efficient of all manufactured house types.

In wall construction, timbers are placed either horizontally or vertically, depending on the manufacturer's construction system; in some cases a combination of the two styles is used. Oftentimes load-bearing interior partition walls are built from the same timbers. Some settling of the walls is normal after construction, and is allowed for by the manufacturer

*Construction of timber walls is simple, repetitive, and nearly foolproof. Only modest skills are needed, and these can be learned on the job.*

in the house plans. Like log houses, little interior finishing work is necessary; the timbers themselves form the inside walls in most cases, and no plastering, drywall installation, or painting is necessary.

Variations in construction include the use of a sandwich wall, where a layer of rigid insulation is placed between an exterior timber wall and an interior wall covering of wood paneling. Another is the method of double-wall construction, where exterior and interior timber walls run parallel and are separated with an air space of several inches. With double-wall construction, wall thickness increases to about nine inches. Where higher than normal thermal efficiency is desired, additional insulation can be added with either the double-wall or the sandwich wall construction method.

Either cedar or pine is used to manufacture the timbers. Cedar is naturally resistant to decay, insects, and dry rot, and treating the timbers with preservative is not necessary. However, many manufacturers recommend treatment to preserve the natural beauty of the wood; left untreated the wood ages to a silvery gray color. Cedar timbers can also be stained. Pine timbers should be treated with preservative for protection, and can be finished with paint or varnish. In some cases, timbers are not single slabs of wood, but are laminated, having three or more layers of wood glued together to form the solid timber.

# Packages Are More Complete

Timber house packages include the typical range, but generally come with more materials than some other manufactured houses. Complete shell packages containing walls and roof assembly, floors, windows and doors, second floors frames, non-load-bearing interior walls, and stairs are the most common package. Complete houses with all of the above plus utility systems, wiring, plumbing, kitchen and bathroom fixtures, and appliances are also common. At least one manufacturer will supply nearly everything, including carpeting and decorating.

Construction of a timber house is similar to log house construction, but they are much easier to assemble. Packages are precut, pieces don't have to be trimmed before they are connected, and the interlocking tongue-and-groove, dovetail, and saddle-notch joints go together easily. Wall construction is simple, repetitive, and nearly foolproof; only modest skills are necessary and they can be learned on the job. Timber houses are one of the easier types of manufactured houses to construct.

Long wall timbers can be heavy, and moving and lifting them can be physically demanding. But because the timbers are less massive than the logs used in most log houses, construction is not quite as strenuous. Timbers are lighter, easier to handle, and require much less strength to maneuver. Once the outside shell is up, a good deal of the interior finish work is complete. What remains, typically, is flooring work and finish work on any stud-framed partition walls. And timber houses offer ample opportunity for do-it-yourself involvement; construction work on all parts of the house can be done by the owner.

Timber houses are available in styles ranging from small, log cabin type houses to large, open, luxurious models including active and passive solar heating

systems. They are available in sizes from around 300 to more than 3,000 square feet with prices ranging from about $8,000 to more than $75,000. Manufacturers of timber houses are prepared to make minor modifications in stock models, and custom design and engineering services are usually available.

# Justus Homes

P.O. Box 98300
Tacoma, WA 98499
(206) 582-3404

**MODELS:** 64 stock models; modifications possible; approximately 66% of the houses are custom designed.

**SQUARE FOOTAGE:** 785 to 5,000 square feet.

**PRICE:** $21,900 to $73,400; some custom-designed houses over $100,000.

**COMPLETENESS OF PACKAGE:** About 50% complete.

*Photos Courtesy Justus Homes*

**CONSTRUCTION: Floors.** *First floor:* Joist or beam framing • Plywood subflooring • Underlayment • Flooring not provided
*Second floor/loft:* Same materials as first floor
**Walls.** *Exterior walls:* Western red cedar timbers, four inches thick and eight inches wide, milled flat on four sides • No preservative applied • Timbers driven together and not secured with fasteners • Stud-framed second floor exterior walls on some models • Plywood sheathing • Cedar siding • Blanket insulation • Interior wall surface not provided
*Partition walls:* Same as exterior walls on most models • Some stud-framed partition walls • Partition wall surface not provided
**Roof:** Beam or truss framing • Furring strips (for shakes) or plywood sheathing (for shingles) • Felt roof protection • Insulation • Cedar shakes or shingles
**Windows/Doors.** Prehung anodized bronze double-glazed, aluminum-framed windows • Double-glazed picture windows and gable glass in preassembled wood frames • Prehung wood panel exterior doors • Prehung flush hollow-core interior doors

**MANUFACTURER PROVIDES:**
Structural plans (including foundation)
Typical mechanical plans   Blueprints   Specifications
Construction manual
First floor framing, subflooring, and underlayment
Second-floor/loft framing, subflooring, and
   underlayment
Exterior wall timbers
Stud-framing for exterior walls on some models
Partition wall timbers
Stud framing for some partition walls
Complete roof system   Flashing   Windows
Interior and exterior doors
Garage doors where applicable   Stairways
Balusters and railings   Interior and exterior trim
Closet rods and shelves   Insulation
Weatherstripping   Caulking
Fasteners and builders' hardware   Locks

**BUYER PROVIDES:**
Formal mechanical plans if needed   Foundation
Flooring   Ceiling materials
Partition wall surface, if applicable
Some interior trim   Guttering system
Interior and exterior applied finishes
Vapor barriers   Electrical system
Plumbing system and fixtures
Heating/cooling system   Ventilating system
Appliances   Cabinetry·

**OPTIONS AVAILABLE:** Double-glazed, wood-framed sliding or awning windows; interior cedar wall planking; interior wall paneling; special energy-efficient wall construction; extra insulation; several kinds of exterior doors; basement package; garage package; deck kits; skylights; solar water heating; solar heating.

**SPECIAL FEATURES:** Active solar model available; solar water heating components available; basement and deck packages; energy-efficient wall and roof constructions available.

**EASE OF CONSTRUCTION:** Assembly technically simple, and only moderately demanding physically. Designed for easy assembly; walls individually bundled, all parts precut, labeled, and coded to plans. Some on-site cutting, fitting, and trimming may be required.

**MANUFACTURER ASSISTANCE:** Factory can provide technical, design, and engineering help. Dealers can assist in all phases, including site selection, inventorying materials at offloading, finding qualified contractors, and advising during construction.

**SALES AREA:** National.

## Pan Abode, Inc.

4350 Lake Washington Blvd. North
Renton, WA 98055
(206) 255-8260

---

**MODELS:** 30 stock models, modifications possible; approximately 50% of the houses are custom designed.

**SQUARE FOOTAGE:** 320 to 2,900 square feet.

**PRICE:** $8,500 to $78,500.

**COMPLETENESS OF PACKAGE:** About 50% complete.

**CONSTRUCTION: Floors.** *First floor:* Joist framing • Plywood subflooring • Plywood or particle board underlayment as required • Flooring not provided
*Second floor/loft:* Beam framing • Plywood subflooring • Plywood or particle board underlayment as required • Flooring not provided
**Walls.** *Exterior walls:* Western red cedar timber, three inches thick and six inches wide, milled flat on four sides • Preservative supplied • Timbers laid horizontally • Secured with spikes
*Partition walls:* Same as exterior walls
**Roof.** Hemlock beam framing • Tongue-and-groove fir sheathing • Rigid insulation • Felt roof protection • Asphalt shingles
**Windows/Doors.** Prehung double-glazed, wood-framed sliding windows • Frame only for stopped-in glass • Prehung solid cedar panel or slab exterior doors • Double-glazed, wood-framed sliding glass doors with screens • Prehung wood hollow-core flush, or solid cedar interior doors • Full-louvered bifold closet doors

**MANUFACTURER PROVIDES:**
Structural plans Blueprints Specifications
Construction manual
First floor framing, subflooring, and underlayment
Second floor/loft framing
Second floor subflooring and underlayment
Ceiling materials Exterior wall timbers
Partition walls Complete roof system
Roof cable anchoring Windows
Interior and exterior doors
Frames for stopped-in glass Exterior trim
Most interior trim Some insulation
Weatherstripping Caulking
Interior and exterior wood sealing and waterproofing package
Most fasteners and builders' hardware
Weatherstripping Caulk

**BUYER PROVIDES:**
Foundation plan Formal mechanical plans
Foundation Flooring Flashing
Guttering system Stopped-in glass Stairways
Some interior trim
Interior and exterior applied finishes Vapor barriers
Some insulation Electrical system
Plumbing system and fixtures Heating/cooling system
Ventilating system Appliances Cabinetry

**OPTIONS AVAILABLE:** Inside insulated and planked exterior wall system; double exterior wall system; 4-inch-thick wall logs; porches; decks; garages; skylights; cedar roofing shakes; cedar roof sheathing; tongue-and-groove cedar wall planking; rigid foam insulation; fiberglass batt insulation; Andersen windows and/or sliding doors; stopped-in glass; solid cedar exterior doors; insulated metal exterior doors;

*Photos Courtesy Pan Abode Inc.*

basement components; custom interior decorating; custom kitchen package; carpeting; appliances; sinks; countertops; solarium windows; whirlpool bath; freestanding fireplace.

**SPECIAL FEATURES:** Very complete packages; choice of two different energy-efficient wall constructions; wide range of options; timber interior partition walls; roof cable anchoring system.

**EASE OF CONSTRUCTION:** Assembly technically simple, and only moderately demanding physically. All parts precut, numbered, and coded to plans. Some on-site cutting, fitting, and trimming may be required.

**MANUFACTURER ASSISTANCE:** Assistance is available through all phases of site and house selection and construction; extra charge services include basement plans, site plan, heating or engineering calculations. Dealers can assist in offloading house package and inventorying parts; on-site supervisory and/or technical assistance. Pan Abode crews will construct the house, if desired.

**SALES AREA:** National.

# Solid Wall Building, Inc.

P.O. Box 41
Newport, NH 03773
(603) 863-3107

**MODELS:** 14 stock models; modifications possible; 98% of the houses are custom designed.

**SQUARE FOOTAGE:** 768 to 3,220 square feet.

**PRICE:** $11,500 to $33,600.

**COMPLETENESS OF PACKAGE:** About 33% complete.

**CONSTRUCTION: Floors.** *First floor:* Joist framing •

Plywood subflooring • Underlayment and flooring not provided
*Second floor/loft:* Beam framing • Subflooring, underlayment, and flooring not provided
**Walls.** *Exterior walls:* Pine timbers, four inches wide and six inches thick, milled flat on the inside, clapboard milled on the outside • Preservative not supplied • Secured with ringed pole-barn spikes
*Partition walls:* Not provided
**Roof.** Rafter framing (truss frame on one model) • Plywood sheathing • Felt roof protection • Asphalt shingles
**Windows/Doors.** Double-glazed, wood-framed double-hung windows with removable sash • Prehung fir exterior doors • Interior doors not provided

**MANUFACTURER PROVIDES:**
Structural plans (including foundation)   Blueprints
Specifications   Construction manual   Sills
First floor framing and subflooring
Second floor/loft framing   Ceiling joists
Exterior wall timbers   Roof rafter or truss framing
Roof sheathing, underlayment, and roofing
Guttering system   Windows   Exterior doors
Exterior trim   Soffit material   Vent louvers
Some fasteners and builders' hardware

**BUYER PROVIDES:**
Formal mechanical plans   Foundation
First floor underlayment and flooring
Second floor/loft subflooring, underlayment, and
   flooring
Ceiling materials   Wood preservative   Partition walls
Flashing   Interior doors   Stairways   Interior trim
Interior and exterior applied finishes   Vapor barriers
Insulation   Weatherstripping
Some fasteners and builders' hardware
Electrical system   Plumbing system and fixtures
Heating/cooling system
Ventilating system (except louvers)   Appliances
Cabinetry

*Courtesy Solid Wall Building, Inc.*

*Courtesy Solid Wall Building, Inc.*

**OPTIONS AVAILABLE:** Variety of windows and doors; double-glazed entry-door sidelights; 4×6 beams; 6×6 ceiling joists; lauan or pine thermal shutters; exterior wall rigid insulation covering; porches and decks; tongue-and-groove ceilings; tongue-and-groove subflooring; solar greenhouse; solariums.

**SPECIAL FEATURES:** Exceptionally heavy solid-wall construction; traditional beam-type second floor/loft frame; timbers milled for clapboard effect; special model line incorporating outside envelope of rigid insulation covered by exterior siding; insulating shutters available for special model line.

**EASE OF CONSTRUCTION:** Assembly is technically simple but fairly demanding physically. Shell components milled, precut, and coded to assembly plans; shell can be assembled rapidly.

**MANUFACTURER ASSISTANCE:** A complete buying and planning guide is available; manufacturer will offer advice through the processes of siting and planning, and offer counsel on construction problems; on-site help at construction startup in New England area only.

**SALES AREA:** National.

## Alta Industries
P.O. Box 88
Halcottsville, NY 12438
(914) 586-3336

**MODELS:** 29 stock models; modifications possible; custom design available.

**SQUARE FOOTAGE:** 576 to 1,860 square feet.

**PRICE:** $8,050 to $28,900.

**COMPLETENESS OF PACKAGE:** About 40% complete.

**SPECIAL FEATURES:** Complete packages; detailed plans; special roof trusses; garage available.

**SALES AREA:** East of the Rockies.

## Cedar Forest Products Company
107 W. Colden St.
Polo, IL 61064
(815) 946-2331

**MODELS:** 15 stock models; modifications possible; custom design available.

**SQUARE FOOTAGE:** 750 to 3,000 square feet.

**PRICE:** $15,500 to $57,000.

**COMPLETENESS OF PACKAGE:** About 75% complete.

**SPECIAL FEATURES:** Detailed plans; manufacturer

can provide supervision or contracting services; 5×8 red cedar timbers.

**SALES AREA:** East of the Rockies.

## Cedar Homes, Inc.
555 116th NE, Suite 150
Bellevue, WA 98004
(206) 454-3966

**MODELS:** Custom design only.

**SQUARE FOOTAGE:** 670 to 3,600 square feet.

**PRICE:** $20,000 to $60,000 precut materials; $75,000 to $200,000 finished.

**COMPLETENESS OF PACKAGE:** About 33% complete.

**SPECIAL FEATURES:** Solid-wall plus post and beam construction; red cedar wall timbers; complete personalized home planning and custom design/engineering service; optional floor and wall coverings; very attractive house designs; individualized construction training to buyer or contractor at no extra cost.

**SALES AREA:** Alaska, Arizona, California, Colorado, Hawaii, Idaho, Montana, Nevada, New Mexico, Oregon, Utah, Washington, Wyoming.

## Laurentien Log Homes USA
4961 Karls Gate Drive
Marietta, GA 30067
(404) 992-4559

**MODELS:** 20 stock models; modifications possible; mainly custom design.

**SQUARE FOOTAGE:** 624 to 2,604 square feet.

**PRICE:** $5,000 to $22,000.

**COMPLETENESS OF PACKAGE:** Withheld.

**SPECIAL FEATURES:** Triple tongue-and-groove timber joints; timbers milled to curve, for log-look inside and out.

**SALES AREA:** National.

## Lok-Log
Dayton, WY 82836
(307) 655-2226

**MODELS:** Custom design only.

**SQUARE FOOTAGE:** 600 to 3,800 square feet.

**PRICE:** $11,100 to $66,500.

**COMPLETENESS OF PACKAGE:** About 33% to 40% complete.

**SPECIAL FEATURES:** 3-part laminated, double tongue-and-groove 6×6 timbers; milled to curve for log-look on outside; special drip lip; basic line not recommended for do-it-yourself builders; optional line of old, dry timbers for do-it-yourself applications.

**SALES AREA:** 500 mile radius of Dayton, Wyoming.

## National Beauti-Log Cedar Homes, Inc.

1250 S. Wilson Way
Stockton, CA 95205
(209) 465-3437

**MODELS:** 31 stock models; modifications possible; custom design available.

**SQUARE FOOTAGE:** 400 to 3,042 square feet.

**PRICE:** $10,995 to $65,870.

**COMPLETENESS OF PACKAGE:** About 50% complete.

**SPECIAL FEATURES:** Double tongue-and-groove timbers; optional cedar shakes; optional double-glazed aluminum slider windows; optional Pella windows.

**SALES AREA:** National.

## Pacific Frontier Homes, Inc.

17975 North Highway I
P.O. Box 1247
Fort Bragg, CA 95437
(707) 964-0204

**MODELS:** 27 stock models; modifications possible; custom design available.

**SQUARE FOOTAGE:** 400 to 1,824 square feet.

**PRICE:** $11,038 to $36,610.

**COMPLETENESS OF PACKAGE:** About 50% complete.

**SPECIAL FEATURES:** Post-and-beam frame; foam-sandwich wall construction; tongue-and-groove redwood exterior; interior redwood paneling; pre-glazed patio doors.

**SALES AREA:** National.

## Pre-Cut International Homes

P.O. Box 97
Woodinville, WA 98072
(206) 568-8511

**MODELS:** 42 stock models; modifications possible; custom design available.

**SQUARE FOOTAGE:** 272 to 2,718 square feet.

**PRICE:** $7,039 to $74,620.

**COMPLETENESS OF PACKAGE:** About 60% to 70% complete.

**SPECIAL FEATURES:** Laminated, kiln-dried, 2¾-inch ponderosa pine walls standard; 2¾-inch or 5-inch western red cedar, or special foam-insulated wall systems optional; patented tongue-and-groove interlocking construction; passive solar possibilities; solid pine or cedar interior walls.

**SALES AREA:** National.

# Dome Houses

Are you looking for the unusual in a house? If so, a dome house presents an unmistakably different appearance. On the outside a dome looks like a sphere cut in half and placed open-side down on the ground. Because the dome structure is self-supporting, interiors can be left open to allow extremely large airy spaces impossible in any other house type. And the rounded structure has no right angles; even when partition walls are added, rooms don't have a rectangular shape.

To some the dome's unique shapes present an unlivable environment, with odd-shaped rooms, no straight walls, and wide open spaces. For the more adventurous, however, the interior design possibilities are virtually unlimited. With a little imagination and a dash of creativity, domes can be decorated in any number of ways. Even antique furnishings can be worked into a dome house.

In its purest and simplest form the dome house is part of a sphere made up of a series of triangular sections. Most dome houses, in fact, are classed in fractions of a whole sphere, such as ⅝, ½, and ⅜. The design is based on the geodesic dome configuration devised by R. Buckminster Fuller. Most dome houses, however, modify or expand the pure dome form to provide a more livable environment.

Riser walls are a common modification. These are walls about three feet high constructed of standard lumber—usually 2×4's—that attach to the foundation and raise the dome. The added height at the base of the dome results in more usable interior space. These walls eliminate the sharp angles where the dome meets the foundation, and extend the second floor living area. Two or more domes can be clustered together and interconnected, and garages or other structures can be attached. Extensions that incorporate windows, doorways, dormers, or passageways between domes can be added.

Despite alterations made to the basic dome structure, the look retains a futuristic appearance. For this reason, domes may not work well in every setting. Selection of a building site, and the orientation of the dome on that site, contribute to the visual impression

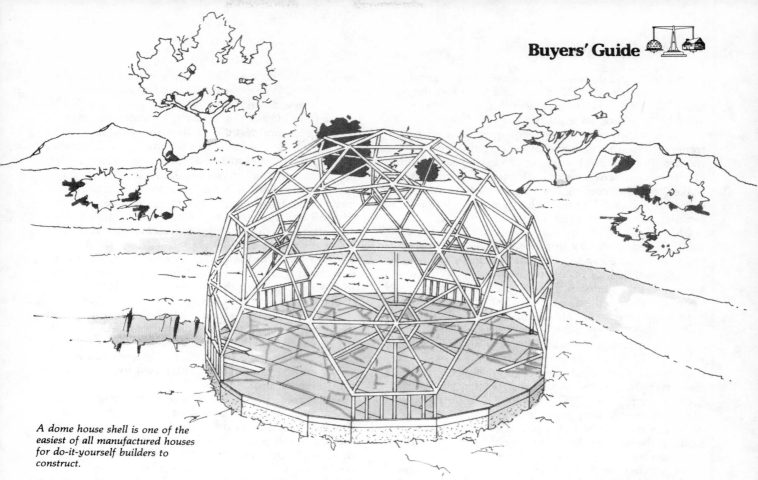

*A dome house shell is one of the easiest of all manufactured houses for do-it-yourself builders to construct.*

the dome house makes. Proper siting is important for any type of house, but is most crucial with a dome.

# An Advantageous Design

The geometric design of dome houses produces numerous advantages not available in conventional houses. The spherical dome shape covers the largest amount of floor space with the least amount of exterior surface of any house type. A dome covering 1,500 square feet of space has approximately 30 percent less surface area than a 1,500 square foot rectangular house. Because of this, about 30 percent less material is required to construct a dome shell.

Doubling the size of a conventional rectangular house doubles the square footage, volume, exposed exterior, and nearly doubles the cost. But doubling the size of a dome quadruples the square footage, quadruples the exposed surface area, and results in a structure with eight times the volume. The cost, however, will probably only double. As a result of these mathematical relationships the cost per square foot is generally lower for domes than other house types.

The geometric design offers more advantages. The strength of the triangular sections combined with the spherical shape results in an incredibly strong building. For its weight, the dome is the strongest structure known. The larger the dome gets, the stronger it becomes. Because of its shape winds just slip around it, rain runs right off, and snow rarely accumulates. Domes are very resistant to strong winds,

snow loads, earthquakes, and other natural disasters.

Domes are also very energy efficient. Because they present less surface area to the outside, the opportunities for outside air infiltration are reduced. As long as the interior is left open airflow and circulation are freer and more natural than in any other house design. This makes heating, cooling, and ventilating much easier. With the exception of sections that have been partitioned off, the air temperature in a dome remains pretty much the same from the top to the bottom. It is common for heating and cooling costs for a dome to be reduced by 30 percent below those for a conventional house, and with additional insulation costs can be reduced by as much as 50 percent.

# Dome Construction

Domes can be placed on almost any foundation—perimeter piers or posts, concrete slab, crawl space, full basement, and even an All Weather Wood Foundation. Some manufacturers offer a wood foundation, either as a standard component or as an option. Once the foundation is complete, riser walls—if they are included in the plans—are built with conventional building materials.

The dome itself is usually constructed of triangular sections that are bolted together. Assembly can proceed in a number of different ways. Preassembled triangles are either put in place and bolted together one at a time or are first assembled in groups of five and put up as a unit. Other domes go up one 2×4 frame piece at a time. Once the frame is up, sheathing

is applied. Some domes are panelized. The triangular sections have the sheathing, and in some cases the exterior covering, already preassembled. All of these assembly methods are equally effective. Floor construction is conventional, employing either a joist frame or a beam frame and plywood subflooring.

There is no exterior siding in the usual sense. With no distinction between sidewalls and roof, shingles, shakes, or other roofing material cover the entire outside of the dome. To be weathertight the exterior covering needs to be carefully applied.

Chimneys, soil stacks, and vents must be located and installed according to the manufacturer's instructions. In no case can the structural members or panels be cut, modified, or disturbed in any way. Windows and doors are framed in and installed in the conventional manner, and must be fully sealed and insulated.

Windows and skylights can be placed anywhere, and the variety of possible window treatments is one of the main design modifications possible with dome exteriors. When windows are placed on extensions or dormers they are usually rectangular, but anywhere else, triangular, round, or other geometric shapes are used. Triangular windows or skylights are often combined together in groups of three or five. Because windows can go anywhere it is possible to position them to track the sun, so the dome is kept light, without using electricity, all day long. Often solar panels can be substituted for skylights to take further advantage of the light collecting possibilities.

Dome interiors offer a good deal of design flexibility. A dome house doesn't require support walls, so partitions can be placed almost anywhere. Often interiors are left open, with no more than one or two partition walls. While such open layouts improve heating and cooling efficiency, without any interior walls to absorb noise, sounds travel quite easily. In the case of first-floor bathrooms, partition walls and a ceiling are necessary. The usual compromise between some walls and no walls is to partition off one side of the interior and to keep the other side open. If a second floor/loft is included either the post-and-beam method of framing, or conventional stud-framed walls and joists can be used. Second floors can also be added at some later date providing the dome is large enough.

## Domes Are Easy to Build

Domes are ideal for do-it-yourselfers. A dome house shell is the most easily assembled of all manufactured house types. It is not at all unusual for an inexperienced crew of three or four to put up a complete shell in two or three days. Some special equipment is usually necessary. A crane or boom truck is not always needed for setting the upper sections, but with larger domes with preassembled components they are a necessity. Scaffolding is recommended for both shell assembly and interior work.

Shell assembly is simple and repetitive, and usually involves bolting the sections or pieces together. With panelized domes once this bolting is finished the shell is complete. Where sheathing is attached after the frame is assembled the work can be strenuous. With as many as 60 individual triangles commonly making up a dome—and more than that are possible—putting up the sheathing can be physically demanding.

Finishing the interior of a dome is no different than for a conventional house. Insulation and vapor barriers are installed with the same procedures used in any house, and the framing can be covered with drywall and paneling or plastering. Only the shapes are different, which can become somewhat vexing when the owner does all the cutting on a do-it-yourself basis. In the case of drywall installations, the numerous triangular shapes that must be cut, placed in position, and taped, can be very physically demanding.

Applying the siding and roofing can also be strenuous. Ladders and other equipment are needed and the use of ropes or safety slings is advised. For both roof and drywall installations, where the work can be tricky and demanding, it is often best to leave these jobs for professionals.

Some dome packages are precut and must be fully assembled; others are panelized to a certain degree. The vast majority of dome house manufacturers provide materials just for the basic shell framework; this often represents less than 25 percent of the finished cost of the house. Often windows, doors, and skylights are options that cost extra.

The dome house packages offered today are fully engineered and available in a good range of sizes with a number of varying architectural features. Domes can be designed for passive solar heating, or can be fitted with the necessary solar collectors and associated hardware for active solar heating. They are available in sizes from 300 to about 3,000 square feet with prices ranging from about $4,000 to $40,000. Because the design and engineering of the dome structure is a complicated and precise mathematical process, dome buyers rarely have the opportunity to design their own house. Modifications and custom design and engineering services are available, but are far less common with domes than most other manufactured house types.

## The Big Outdoors People

26600 Fallbrook Avenue
Wyoming Industrial Park
Wyoming, MN 55092
(612) 462-1011

**MODELS:** 8 stock models; modifications possible; 30% to 35% of the houses are custom designed.

**SQUARE FOOTAGE:** 475 to 3,200 square feet.

**PRICE:** $4,000 to $66,000.

**COMPLETENESS OF PACKAGE:** About 15% (shell) to 70% (finished house) complete.

*Photos Courtesy The Big Outdoors People*

**CONSTRUCTION: Foundation:** Panelized All Weather Wood Foundation system

**Floors.** *First floor:* Plywood I-beam with support posts and beams • Plywood subflooring • Flooring not provided

*Second floor/loft:* Not provided

**Walls.** 2×8 stud-framed riser walls • Particle board sheathing • Asphalt shingle exterior siding • Particle board interior wall paneling

*Partition walls:* Not provided

**Shell:** 2×8 triangle frames • Particle board sheathing • Felt shell protection • Asphalt shingles • Particle board interior paneling • Vapor barrier • Interior venting system

**Windows/Doors.** Triangular or hexagonal-shaped stopped-in, double-insulated custom windows • Operable double-glazed awning or casement windows with screens • Prehung steel insulated exterior doors • Prehung aluminum- or wood-framed, double-glazed sliding patio doors • Interior doors not provided

**MANUFACTURER PROVIDES:**
Structural plans    Typical mechanical plans
Blueprints    Construction manual
All Weather Wood Foundation system
First floor framing and subflooring    Riser walls
Complete dome shell    Flashing
Windows and stopped-in glass    Exterior doors
Exterior trim    Vapor barriers    Insulation
Weatherstripping    Caulking
Some fasteners and builders' hardware
Ventilating system

**BUYER PROVIDES:**
Formal mechanical plans if needed    Flooring
Complete second floor/loft    Partition walls
Interior doors    Stairways    Interior trim
Interior and exterior applied finishes
Some fasteners and builders' hardware
Electrical system    Plumbing system and fixtures
Heating/cooling system    Appliances    Cabinetry

**OPTIONS AVAILABLE:** Six of the eight standard models can be purchased as "complete kits," which are about 70% complete. Complete kit prices range from $23,000 to $66,000. Specific options include: cedar shakes; tongue-and-groove pine or cedar interior shell panels; bathroom and kitchen packages; second floor/loft system; partition walls; electrical package; plumbing package; heating/cooling package; solar water heating; passive and active solar heating systems; freestanding fireplaces and woodstoves; custom oak spiral stairway; carpeting; vinyl flooring; 2×10 framing; 2×14 truss-strut framing; domes to 100-foot diameter and 6000 square feet.

**SPECIAL FEATURES:** One of the most complete dome packages. Standard framing heavier than normal, even heavier framing available. Wide range of options. Plumbing, electrical, and heating/cooling systems and custom plans available; both passive and active solar equipment available; offers a two-day seminar in geodesic dome construction for owner-builders.

**EASE OF CONSTRUCTION:** Assembly is technically simple and only moderately demanding physically. Most components are precut, color coded, and keyed to construction manual for ease of assembly. Construction process is simple, using mostly standard framing techniques and procedures. Shell can be quickly and easily erected by an inexperienced crew. Some on-site cutting and trimming required.

**MANUFACTURER ASSISTANCE:** Factory or dealer help in developing floor plan and interior design, and

in making modifications; construction superintendents available at a nominal fee to periodically inspect work and give advice; qualified builders/dealers available to build complete home; offers a dome building school to teach owner-builders.

**SALES AREA:** National.

# Cathedralite Domes

820 Bay Avenue, Suite 302
Capitola, CA 95010
(408) 462-2210

**MODELS:** 10 stock models; modifications possible; approximately 75% of the houses are custom designed.

**SQUARE FOOTAGE:** 426 to 2,896 square feet.

**PRICE:** $5,000 to $28,000.

**COMPLETENESS OF PACKAGE:** About 20% to 25% complete.

*Photos Courtesy Cathedralite Domes*

**CONSTRUCTION: Floors.** *First floor:* Not provided
*Second floor/loft:* Not provided
**Walls.** *Exterior walls:* Stud framed riser walls • Exterior plywood sheathing • Exterior siding and interior wall surface not provided
*Partition walls:* Stud framing • Wall surface not provided
**Shell.** 2×4 or 2×6 stud framing • Plywood sheathing • Exterior siding/roofing and interior surface not provided
**Windows/Doors.** Skylights • Other windows and all doors not provided

**MANUFACTURER PROVIDES:**
Structural plans (including foundation)  Blueprints
Specifications  Construction manual
Riser wall framing and sheathing
Partition wall framing
Complete shell framing and sheathing  Flashing
Some fasteners and builders' hardware

**BUYER PROVIDES:**
Formal mechanical plans  Foundation
Complete first floor  Complete second floor/loft
Ceiling materials
Riser wall siding and interior wall surface
Partition wall surface
Shell protection and siding/roofing
Most windows  Interior and exterior doors
Stairways  Interior and exterior trim
Interior and exterior applied finishes
Vapor barriers  Insulation  Weatherstripping
Caulking  Some fasteners and builders' hardware
Electrical system  Plumbing system and fixtures
Heating/cooling system  Ventilation system
Appliances  Cabinetry

**OPTIONS AVAILABLE:** Pre-panelized cedar or redwood interior wall system; skylights; extensions; cupula; dormers; extended sloping canopy; solar hot water system; passive solarium; 2 or 3 bedroom modular wings; garage; interior highlight design kit using cedar or redwood; "Vista" series provides first and second floor/loft framing and subflooring.

**EASE OF CONSTRUCTION:** Aimed at the do-it-yourselfer. 75% of buyers do some of the work themselves; 25% of those do all of the construction work. Most components are panelized or precut; all shell components are framed and sheathed. Manufacturer will recommend contractors to construct the dome, if desired.

**MANUFACTURER ASSISTANCE:** Assists in all phases of design and selection of the dome. Offers preconstruction reports, in which a manufacturer's representative inspects the building site, discusses financing, and recommends foundation size, dome type, and placement. Financing arrangements possible. Manufacturer will also inspect the final construction, if desired.

**SALES AREA:** National; will export.

# Monterey Domes, Inc.
1855-BF Iowa Avenue
P.O. Box 55166-BF
Riverside, CA 92517
(714) 684-2601

**MODELS:** 12 stock models; modifications possible; custom design available.

**SQUARE FOOTAGE:** 300 to 4,500 square feet.

**PRICE:** $3,995 to $12,850.

**COMPLETENESS OF PACKAGE:** About 20% complete.

**CONSTRUCTION: Floors.** *First floor:* Not provided
*Second floor/loft:* Not provided
**Walls:** 2×4 stud framed riser walls on some models • Plywood sheathing on riser walls • Exterior underlayment and siding and interior wall surface not provided
*Partition walls:* Not provided
**Shell:** 2×4 stud framing • Steel connecting hubs • Plywood sheathing • Exterior underlayment and siding/roofing and interior wall surface not provided
**Windows/Doors.** Not provided

**MANUFACTURER PROVIDES:**
Structural plans   Typical mechanical plans
Blueprints   Construction manual
Riser wall framing and sheathing for some models
Complete shell framing and sheathing
All hardware for shell and wall assembly

**BUYER PROVIDES:**
Foundation plans   Formal mechanical plans if needed
Foundation   Complete first and second floor/loft
Ceiling materials
Riser wall underlayment and siding if applicable
Interior wall and shell surface   Partition walls
Shell underlayment and siding/roofing   Flashing
Doors and windows   Interior and exterior trim
Interior and exterior applied finishes   Vapor barriers
Insulation   Weatherstripping   Caulking
Fasteners and builders' hardware   Electrical system
Plumbing system and fixtures   Heating/cooling system
Ventilating system   Appliances   Cabinetry

**OPTIONS AVAILABLE:** 2×6 framing system; riser wall packages; opening extension packages; skylights in triangular, hexagonal, and pentagonal shapes; skylight frame-in packages; dormer frame-in packages; rigid foam insulation; roofing system with either precut or uncut vinyl/fiberglass shakes; special solar collectors.

**SPECIAL FEATURES:** Good range of designs and options; special roofing option; availability of special active solar collectors; simple and lightweight component construction system.

**EASE OF CONSTRUCTION:** Most buyers assemble the shell themselves. Technically and physically

*Photos Courtesy Monterey Domes, Inc.*

simple. All shell components precut and color coded, and keyed to assembly manual. No on-site cutting, fitting, or trimming required for shell assembly.

**MANUFACTURER ASSISTANCE:** Dealer and/or manufacturer assists in selecting dome and floor plan, and in modifications or redesign as necessary; assists with and checks necessary prebuilding paperwork; provides full instructions, specifications, and documentation for each design package.

**SALES AREA:** National.

# Domes America, Inc.
6 S. 771 Western Ave.
Clarendon Hills, IL 60514
(312) 986-5060

**MODELS:** 16 stock models in 64 different sizes; modifications possible; custom design available.

**SQUARE FOOTAGE:** 500 to 44,000 square feet.

**PRICE:** $7,200 to $175,000.

**COMPLETENESS OF PACKAGE:** About 15% (shell) to 100% (finished house) complete.

**SPECIAL FEATURES:** Full scale testing for snow, wind, and seismic load; design flexibility; energy savings average 30% to 50% over conventional construction; dealer/builder supervises roofing application, foundation laying, and dome erection.

**SALES AREA:** National and Caribbean Islands.

# Domes and Homes, Inc.
P.O. Box 365
Brielle, NJ 08730
(215) 825-8290

**MODELS:** 9 stock models; modifications possible; custom design available.

**SQUARE FOOTAGE:** 485 to 6,000 square feet.

**PRICE:** $12,000 to over $200,000.

**COMPLETENESS OF PACKAGE:** About 20% to 25% complete.

**SPECIAL FEATURES:** Preassembled space-frame panels; rapid assembly; polygonal models available.

**SALES AREA:** National.

# Dome Home Systems, Inc.
Route 2, Box 247A
Reedsburg, WI 53959
(608) 524-4555

**MODELS:** 6 stock models; modifications possible; custom design available.

**SQUARE FOOTAGE:** 1,000 to 4,000 square feet.

**PRICE:** $8,000 to $15,000.

**COMPLETENESS OF PACKAGE:** About 30% to 40% complete.

**SPECIAL FEATURES:** Rustproofed steel frame connectors come 50% preassembled; 2×8 framing members contribute to structure strength, added insulation allowance, and elimination of furring strips; interior panels come in one piece which eliminates drywall splicing and taping at job site; manufacturer supplies expert supervision at construction site.

**SALES AREA:** National.

# Free-Space Geodesics
7094 N. Harrison Ave., Suite 165
Pinedale, CA 93650
(209) 431-8670

**MODELS:** 6 stock models.

**SQUARE FOOTAGE:** 450 to 2,700 square feet.

**PRICE:** $3,800 to $9,100.

**COMPLETENESS OF PACKAGE:** About 15% complete.

**SPECIAL FEATURES:** Packages available as complete shells, frame kits, shell assembly, or frame assembly; 2×6 frame members standard.

**SALES AREA:** National.

# Geodesic Domes, Inc.
10290 Davison Road
Davison, MI
(313) 653-2383

**MODELS:** 5 stock models; modifications possible; custom design available.

**SQUARE FOOTAGE:** 485 to 2,500 square feet.

**PRICE:** $3,600 to $8,400.

**COMPLETENESS OF PACKAGE:** About 20% to 25% complete.

**SPECIAL FEATURES:** Space-frame panels preassembled; several riser, extension, dormer, and canopy options; uses extra-strong stress-rated lumber.

**SALES AREA:** National.

# Polydome
3020 North Park Way
San Diego, CA 92104
(714) 574-1400

**MODELS:** 4 stock models; modifications possible; custom design available.

**SQUARE FOOTAGE:** 600 to 1,125 square feet (shell only).

**PRICE:** $3,750 to $6,795.

**COMPLETENESS OF PACKAGE:** About 33% complete.

**SPECIAL FEATURES:** Adaptable for solar heating; modified geodesic design (polygonal); fewer components to assemble than a true geodesic.

**SALES AREA:** National.

# Synapse Domes
P.O. Box 554
Lander, WY 82520
(307) 332-5773, -4117

**MODELS:** 12 stock models; modifications possible; custom design available.

**SQUARE FOOTAGE:** 100 to 4,000 square feet.

**PRICE:** $1,750 to $24,000.

**COMPLETENESS OF PACKAGE:** About 15% to 20% complete.

**SPECIAL FEATURES:** Complete engineering and architectural services; large selection of skylights and windows in various designs; polyurethane foam insulation for high R factors; extension and dormer options; cedar shake and shingle options; manufacturer shipping services; manufacturer construction services available in Rocky Mountain area only.

**SALES AREA:** National and Canada.

## Timberline Geodesics

2015 Blake St.
Berkeley, CA 94704
(415) 849-4481

**MODELS:** 8 stock models; modifications possible; custom design available.

**SQUARE FOOTAGE:** 238 to 1,564 square feet (shell only).

**PRICE:** $3,950 to $11,450.

**COMPLETENESS OF PACKAGE:** About 15% complete.

**SPECIAL FEATURES:** Will sell parts of a kit (plans, hardware, etc.); ½" plywood skin; struts and hubs color coded for easy assembly.

**SALES AREA:** National.

# Post-and-Beam Houses

A post-and-beam house looks much the same as a conventionally built frame house from the outside, but the similarity ends there. Because they use a construction method that is quite unlike ordinary framed houses, the interior appearance of post-and-beam houses is quite different.

The post-and-beam concept makes use of a series of heavy timber beams supported by timber posts in the form of a large, sturdy skeleton. This framework defines the shape of the house. The building sections that enclose the structure and make up the interior partitions are simply attached to it.

This skeleton bears the entire load of the house and accounts for much of its strength and rigidity. The added building sections bear little if any weight except their own, and are essentially nonstructural. By contrast, a great many of the smaller and lighter framing members of a conventionally built frame house each bears a small part of the weight, and each plays a part in the strength and rigidity of the finished structure—most of them are structural essentials.

From the outside, there is often no way to tell if a house is constructed using the post-and-beam method, but on the inside, the difference is immediately apparent. Usually the beams are left exposed and form an integral part of the interior design; they may be support beams for the second floor/loft, roof rafter beams or roof purlin beams, or open beam roof trusses. In some designs, all of the different types may be present. In addition, the heavy support posts may be partially or wholly visible. In smaller structures, they are found in the outside-wall constructions, while in larger buildings there may be individual, wholly exposed support posts located within the interior of the house. These form part of the interior design, and can be left in a natural state, or can be stained or painted and treated with various kinds of trimwork.

## Two Types Are Available

Post-and-beam houses can be separated into two general categories: traditional and contemporary. The traditional type retains the familiar appearance of New England rural architecture. It is based upon the massive, A-frame type of post-and-beam skeleton used for centuries in the construction of barns and houses. The system is deceptively simple but extremely rugged; because of the liberal use of 45-degree brace beams to strengthen the structure, this method is sometimes referred to as braced-beam construction.

Main girders are huge—8×12, for example—while the posts are often 8×8 or larger. Smaller framing members are typically 6×8 or 6×6; support beams and braces are no smaller than 4×4. If fully traditional procedures are followed, all of the structural members are joined with mortise-and-tenon joints and hardwood pegs; no nails or spikes are used. Some post-and-beam framing methods, however, do use simpler joints and liberal spiking.

Modern versions of these structures are currently being produced in three different ways. The first is by sawing out new posts and beams from logs, and fashioning them into a brand-new skeleton. The second is by salvaging old prime timbers from abandoned buildings, and recycling them into the skeletons for new houses. These old timbers are often of better quality and are hardened and toughened by age; old chestnut timbers are a real prize, since chestnut can no longer be bought at any price. The third method consists of actually dismantling old barns or carriage houses and then reassembling them and rebuilding them into houses on the buyer's site. With all of these methods, nearly all of the posts and beams are left exposed. Rough sawn wooden timbers are a part of the interior decor.

The contemporary category of post-and-beam houses is both more common and more popular. It uses mostly modern and spacious designs both inside and out. Although a timber framework is used, the

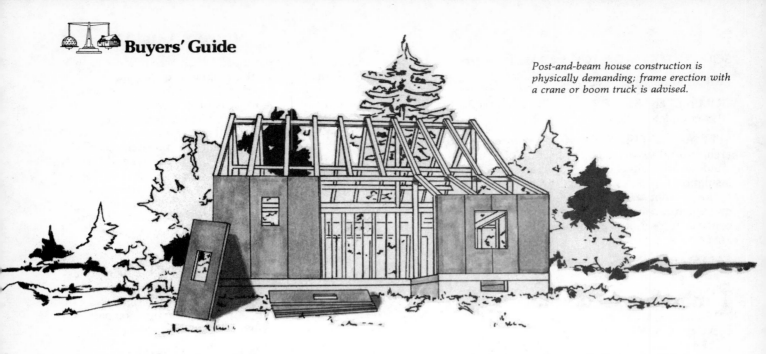

*Post-and-beam house construction is physically demanding; frame erection with a crane or boom truck is advised.*

posts and beams are typically somewhat smaller, and the framework is usually bolted together—often with special heavy steel saddles, plates, and similar hardware. The frame design is also a bit different. It is comprised of considerably fewer members, and presents an appearance unlike that of the traditional framework.

The timber materials are all new, taken from stock supplies and sizes available from most lumber mills; some special purpose beams may be laminated from smaller pieces. Frequently, posts and beams are covered by partition walls. When they are exposed, the texture of the wood is smooth, and the finish is usually glossy.

## A Different Method of Construction

Post-and-beam houses can be built upon any kind of foundation, but a poured concrete slab or full daylight basement are the most popular. Although traditional frame designs included a heavily framed floor system, today's post-and-beam building systems generally employ a conventional joist-type first floor frame covered with plywood and tongue-and-groove planks. The exterior wall sections that fill in the spaces between the posts are generally framed with 2 × 4's; in some instances the exterior wall sections are panelized. Second floor/loft systems are supported by heavy beam frames but the floor itself is put down in the usual manner.

Interior wall partitions can be standard stud frames covered with paneling or drywall, or made up of heavy timbers. Posts can be exposed or covered, and the interior covering of the exterior walls is usually conventional. The roof system can be applied over exposed beams, or a conventional joist-type frame. In some cases roof sections are panelized.

Because the post-and-beam house skeleton is en-

tirely self-supporting, there is no need for any load-bearing partition walls. This in turn leads to a great amount of flexibility in laying out the floor plans of post-and-beam houses. The plan can be as open as desired, and non-load-bearing partition walls can be erected anywhere. Most post-and-beam houses have open and spacious interior layouts with cathedral or vaulted ceilings, and partially or wholly open second floor/loft arrangements. Some larger houses incorporate two- or even three-tiered loft levels.

Because exterior walls are non-load-bearing, windows can be put in at any point. Post-and-beam houses often include large windows, and whole walls are sometimes made up entirely of windows. The ability to freely install windows makes post-and-beam houses readily adaptable to either active or passive solar systems, and some manufacturers offer solar designs. The non-load-bearing exterior walls make a number of modifications easy to achieve. Houses can be enlarged, additions can be put on at any time, or entire wings can be added without any structural changes in the original house plans.

The great flexibility of interior designs and the range of construction options are just two advantages of post-and-beam houses. With a choice of either traditional or contemporary designs, and options for expanding, moving around, or adding sections with little difficulty, post-and-beam houses offer a tremendous variety of designs.

The post-and-beam framework results in a structure with great strength and rigidity. They are generally more stable than conventional frame houses. Exterior wall sections can be made thicker to improve energy efficiency, and those post-and-beam houses with panelized wall and roof sections can be especially energy efficient.

*Continued on page 129*

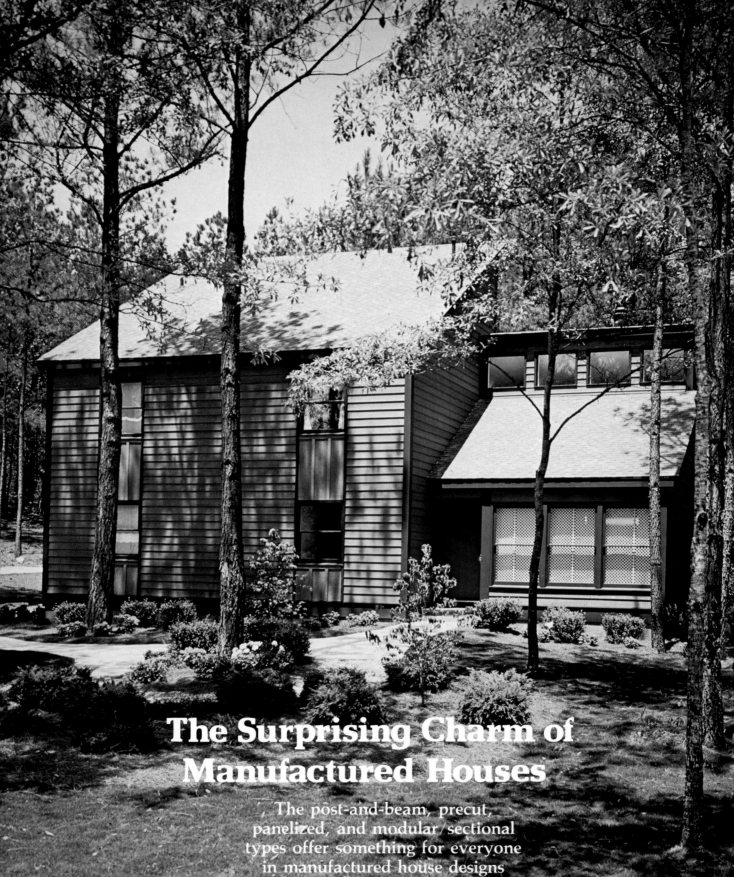

# The Surprising Charm of Manufactured Houses

The post-and-beam, precut,
panelized, and modular/sectional
types offer something for everyone
in manufactured house designs

*Panelized houses fit
easily on any site in
any community.
(Boise Cascade Corp.)*

1

2

**3**

Spacious interiors are characteristic of contemporary post-and-beam houses, because interior walls aren't necessary for structural support. The look is modern, but firmly founded in the past. (1–5: Deck House)

**4**

**5**

1

Because the exterior walls of a post-and-beam house are self-supporting, windows can be placed anywhere—bring the outside in with a whole wall of windows. (1–5: Deck House)

2

3

4

5

1

2

3

**4**

**5**  **6**

The post-and-beam frame isn't limited to one style. It's used in a wide range of houses from gambrel-roofed colonials to contemporary split-levels. (1,2: Deck House; 3–6: Lindal Cedar Homes)

119

The decorating potential of a post-and-beam house is unbeatable—without partition walls, the interiors can be left open for vaulted ceilings, or partially divided into lofts or balconies. (1,2: New England-Techbuilt; 3,4: Timberpeg)

1

2

3

4

*Panelized Houses go up quickly—the shells can be made weather tight in a day or less. You'd never know it to look at them! (5: American Timber Homes; 6: Affordable Luxury Homes)*

5

6

1

2    3

There's more to a panelized house than the basic box—solar features, vaulted ceilings, and unexpectedly well-designed windows are all used in this type of construction. (1,2: Acorn Structures; 3: American Timber Homes; 4–6 Boise Cascade Corp.)

122

4

5

6

1

2

3

4

5

6    7

*Panelized houses offer the largest choice of styles around in manufac-
tured houses—choose from traditional, circular-plan, Tudor, ranch,
split-level, and more. (1: Northern Homes; 2: Rondesics Homes; 3:
Topsider Homes; 4–7: Scholz Homes)*

125

**1**

**2**

**3** **4**

*Wherever you live, whatever style you're aiming at, you can probably find it in a panelized house—from small town to city and back again! (1: Scholz Homes; 2–4: Wausau Homes)*

126

5

6

Precut houses, the closest to traditional construction, go together like jigsaw puzzles. Construction is easy, but it's quite time-consuming because of the number of separate pieces involved. (5,6: Capp Homes; 7: Shelter-Kit; 8: Wickes Lumber)

7

8

The most complete house packages are often the simplest. While some precut houses are available in two-story models, modular/sectional houses—as much as 95% complete when you move into them—are almost always single-story. (1,2: Wickes Lumber; 3: Dynamic Homes; 4: Rodacorp)

1

2

3

4

Continued from page 112

## Do-It-Yourself Opportunities Vary

Post-and-beam house packages are available as frame assembly only, a basic shell with or without a first floor, as a complete shell with some interior components, or as a complete house lacking utility systems and finishing. Construction is not technically difficult, but it can be extremely physically demanding, especially with traditional houses using larger posts and beams. These houses, with larger framing pieces, are among the most physically difficult of all manufactured houses to construct.

The amount of do-it-yourself opportunity depends on the type of house selected. The traditional style post-and-beam house offers the greatest opportunity for owner involvement. It is possible to construct these houses from frame erection to final finishing. Construction is more demanding on this type; frame erection, with a crane or boom truck is advisable. For the most part these traditional post-and-beam houses are available only in the New England area. Contemporary post-and-beam houses offer far fewer opportunities for the do-it-yourselfer; most manufacturers recommend that buyers use a professional builder. A few of the contemporary houses, however, can be owner-built from the ground up. The contemporary houses are available nationally, and are a more popular selection with house buyers.

A large selection of houses from small to large is available. Custom designs are very common, and many post-and-beam houses require a considerable amount of custom building to complete. Numerous modifications are possible with this house type. Package prices vary tremendously, ranging from just a few thousand dollars for a traditional frame only package, to well over a quarter of a million dollars for a complete custom-designed contemporary house. Houses in this category offer the greatest variety of designs of any manufactured house type.

## Deck House

930 Main Street
Acton, MA 01720
(617) 259-9450

**MODELS:** 50 stock models; modifications possible; approximately 20% of the houses are custom designed.

**SQUARE FOOTAGE:** 1,200 to 6,030 square feet.

**PRICE:** $22,000 to $60,000.

**COMPLETENESS OF PACKAGE:** About 35% complete.

**CONSTRUCTION: Floors.** *First floor:* Beam framing • Tongue-and-groove decking • Underlayment and flooring not provided
*Second floor/loft:* Same as first floor
**Walls.** *Exterior walls:* Post and beam framing • Panelized stud fill-in framing • Plywood sheathing • Exterior white cedar siding • Interior wall surface not provided
*Partition walls:* Stud framing • Wall surface not provided
**Roof.** Beam framing • Laminated decking with red cedar interior face • Rigid insulation • Felt roof protection • Asphalt shingles or roll roofing
**Windows/Doors.** Prehung wood, solid-core exterior doors • Aluminum-framed, double-glazed sliding patio doors with screens • Prehung solid or hollow-core interior doors • Custom-made double-glazed, wood-framed stopped-in and operable casement windows with screens • Aluminum-framed, double-glazed skylights

### MANUFACTURER PROVIDES:
Structural plans (including foundation) Blueprints
Specifications Construction manual
First floor framing and decking
Second floor/loft framing and decking
Ceiling materials
Exterior wall framing, sheathing, and siding
Partition wall framing Complete roof system
Windows and skylights Exterior doors

*Photos Courtesy Deck House*

Porch and balcony system   Stairways and railings
Garage on some models   Interior and exterior trim
Insulation   Weatherstripping   Caulking
Most fasteners and builders' hardware

**BUYER PROVIDES:**
Formal mechanical plans   Foundation
First floor underlayment and flooring
Second floor/loft underlayment and flooring
Interior wall surface   Partition wall surface
Flashing   Guttering system   Interior doors
Interior and exterior applied finishes   Vapor barriers
Some fasteners and builders' hardware
Electrical system   Plumbing system and fixtures
Heating/cooling system   Ventilating system
Appliances   Cabinetry

**OPTIONS AVAILABLE:** Lighting fixtures; cabinetry;
carports; garages; screen and storm doors; storm
windows; wood paneling; waffle-pattern wood
entrance doors; wood light fixtures; patio blocks for
landscaping; wood king- and queen-sized beds.

**SPECIAL FEATURES:** Extensive design possibilities;
exceptional square footage range; solar model
available; precut frame components and preassembled
wall sections; extensive use of wood throughout
including trim and detailing; white cedar exterior
siding; weatherproof and energy-efficient design and
construction; unusual attention to small architectural
and construction details; luxurious estate-class house
to 12,000 + square feet.

**EASE OF CONSTRUCTION:** Assembly of frame not
technically difficult, but a fairly demanding job
physically. Not normally considered a project for the
average do-it-yourselfer, but some houses have been
successfully completed by wholly inexperienced
owner-builders. Frame components precut and wall
sections preassembled to reduce on-site labor;
complete construction details provided. Carpentry
skills advisable for assembly of the shell; meticulous
workmanship required for successful completion of
the house.

**MANUFACTURER ASSISTANCE:** Manufacturer
and/or representative will provide full counseling
through the entire house-building process from site
selection to design concept, planning and
implementation, through shell assembly, to house
completion and detailing.

**SALES AREA:** National.

# Lindal Cedar Homes

P.O. Box 24426
Seattle, WA 98124
(206) 725-0900

**MODELS:** 57 stock models; modifications possible;
approximately 10% of the houses are custom
designed.

*Photos Courtesy Lindal Cedar Homes*

**SQUARE FOOTAGE:** 726 to 2,646 square feet.

**PRICE:** $20,064 to $53,602.

**COMPLETENESS OF PACKAGE:** About 45% to
50% complete.

**CONSTRUCTION: Floors.** *First floor:* Beam framing •
2-inch plank decking • Particle board underlayment •
Flooring not provided
*Second floor/loft:* Same as first floor
**Walls.** *Exterior walls:* Post and beam framing • Stud
fill-in framing • Fiberglass insulation • Exterior
plywood sheathing • Exterior double tongue-and-
groove cedar plank siding • Interior wallboard or pine
panel wall surface
*Partition walls:* Stud framing • Wallboard or pine
panel wall surface
**Roof.** Beam and rafter framing • Fiberglass
insulation • Vapor barrier • Plywood sheathing • Felt
roof protection • Asphalt shingles • Wallboard or
pine panel interior surface on some models
**Windows/Doors.** Double-glazed, cedar-framed
casement windows • Prehung steel insulated exterior
doors • Single-glazed, aluminum-framed sliding patio
doors • Prehung, hollow-core, oak veneer interior
doors

**MANUFACTURER PROVIDES:**
Structural plans (including foundation)   Blueprints
Specifications
First floor framing, decking, and underlayment
Second floor/loft framing, decking, and underlayment

Ceiling materials  Exterior walls  Partition walls
Complete roof system  Flashing  Windows
Interior and exterior doors  Stairways and railings
Balconies (with railings) on some models
Interior and exterior trim  Vapor barriers
Insulation  Caulking
Most fasteners and builders' hardware

**BUYER PROVIDES:**
Formal mechanical plans  Foundation
First and second floor/loft flooring
Guttering system
Interior and exterior applied finishes
Weatherstripping
Some fasteners and builders' hardware
Electrical system  Plumbing system and fixtures
Heating/cooling system  Ventilating system
Appliances  Cabinetry

**OPTIONS AVAILABLE:** Double seal windows; triple-glazed windows; additional insulation; decks; various balcony rails; double-glazed patio doors; cedar or pine interior wall/roof covering; cedar roofing shingles; hand-split cedar roofing shakes; special highly energy-efficient roof and wall systems.

**SPECIAL FEATURES:** Use of 2-inch cedar exterior siding; particularly close attention to thermal efficiency; special wall and roof constructions allowing extremely high thermal efficiency; active and passive solar designs available.

**EASE OF CONSTRUCTION:** Shell assembly can be accomplished by an owner-builder with an understanding of residential construction and modest skills. All components precision-precut and numbered, coded to plans for ease of assembly.

**MANUFACTURER ASSISTANCE:** Distributors will offer all reasonable help in planning, design selection, choosing options, siting, construction, finishing—the whole gamut of house building; free cost and feasibility analysis on plan modifications or custom plans; model homes available for inspection in many areas.

**SALES AREA:** National.

# Sawmill River Post & Beam, Inc.
P.O. Box 227
Leverett, MA 01054
(413) 367-9969

**MODELS:** 10 stock models; modifications possible; approximately 60% of the houses are custom designed.

**SQUARE FOOTAGE:** 1,086 to 2,496 square feet.

**PRICE:** $17,900 to $33,900.

**COMPLETENESS OF PACKAGE:** About 33% to 40% complete.

*Photos Courtesy Sawmill River Post & Beam, Inc.*

**CONSTRUCTION: Floors.** *First floor:* Pine tongue-and-groove flooring • Framing, subflooring, and underlayment not provided
*Second floor/loft:* Beam framing • Pine tongue-and-groove board decking • Pine tongue-and-groove flooring • Underlayment not provided
**Walls.** *Exterior walls:* Post and beam framing • Stud fill-in framing or 2×4 blocking and spacers • Exterior rough-sawn pine siding • Interior rough-sawn pine wall surface • Exterior sheathing not provided
*Partition walls:* Not provided.
**Roof.** 2×12 rafter framing or 4×6 beam framing • Pine rough-sawn tongue-and-groove decking on beam framing • Decking on rafter framing, roof protection, and roofing not provided

**Windows/Doors.** Andersen double-glazed, wood-framed windows with screens • Marvin double-glazed, wood-framed windows with screens • Double-glazed stopped-in glass • Velux double-glazed, wood-framed skylights • Prehung solid pine and three-inch plank pine exterior doors • Double-glazed, wood-framed sliding patio doors with screens • Interior doors not provided

## MANUFACTURER PROVIDES:
Structural plans (including foundation)   Blueprints
Specifications   First floor flooring
Second floor/loft framing, subflooring, and flooring
Ceiling materials
Exterior wall framing and fill-in framing
Exterior wall siding   Interior wall surface
Roof framing   Roof decking on some models
Windows   Exterior doors

## BUYER PROVIDES:
Formal mechanical plans   Foundation
First floor framing, subflooring, and underlayment
Second floor/loft underlayment
Exterior wall sheathing   Partition walls
Roof sheathing/decking on some models
Roof protection and roofing on all models
Flashing   Guttering system   Interior doors
Stairways   Interior and exterior trim
Interior and exterior applied finishes   Vapor barriers
Insulation   Weatherstripping   Caulking
Fasteners and builders' hardware   Electrical system
Plumbing system and fixtures
Heating/cooling system   Ventilating system
Appliances   Cabinetry

**OPTIONS AVAILABLE:** 3-inch laminated pine door with hardware; precut pine stairway; pine clapboards; pine trimstock; custom millwork, including French doors and round-top windows; special window and door groups.

**SPECIAL FEATURES:** Construction system allows fully exposed posts and beams in interior; high thermal efficiency; shed and ell packages available; traditional styling and appearance; special passive solar model available; national first place winner in Single Family Passive Solar category at the 1980 Passive Solar Conference at the University of Massachusetts.

**EASE OF CONSTRUCTION:** Designed for do-it-yourself assembly. Frame components are precut, notched, and labeled; all timber lengths are relatively short for ease of handling. Packages are particularly good for maximum owner-involvement of relatively adept do-it-yourselfers.

**MANUFACTURER ASSISTANCE:** Manufacturer will assist in choosing frame and house design, or in making modifications or custom-designing; will provide a technical advisor to assist with questions or problems during shell assembly.

**SALES AREA:** National.

# Timberpeg
P.O. Box 1500
Claremont, NH 03743
(603) 542-7762

**MODELS:** 27 stock models; modifications possible; approximately 90% of the houses are custom designed.

**SQUARE FOOTAGE:** 192 to 3,584 square feet.

**PRICE:** $5,372 to $69,666.

**COMPLETENESS OF PACKAGE:** About 50% complete.

**CONSTRUCTION: Floor.** *First floor:* Not provided *Second floor/loft:* Beam and joist framing • Pine tongue-and-groove decking • Underlayment and flooring not provided
**Walls.** *Exterior walls:* Post and beam framing • Rigid insulation • Exterior sheathing not needed • Exterior resawn pine siding • Interior pine tongue-and-groove plank or white vinyl-faced wall surface *Partition walls:* Not provided
**Roof.** Beam and rafter framing • Pine tongue-and-groove decking • Rigid insulation • Roof protection not needed • Hand-split red cedar shakes
**Windows/Doors.** Andersen double-glazed casement, awning, picture, and double-hung windows with screens • Double-glazed, wood-framed roof windows on most models • Prehung pine exterior doors •

*Courtesy Timberpeg*

*Courtesy Timberpeg*

Double-glazed, wood-framed patio doors with screens • Interior doors not provided

**MANUFACTURER PROVIDES:**
Structural plans (including foundation)
Typical mechanical plans   Blueprints   Specifications
Second floor/loft framing and decking   Exterior walls
Complete roof system   Windows   Exterior doors
Some interior trim   Some insulation
Some fasteners and builders' hardware

**BUYER PROVIDES:**
Formal mechanical plans if needed   Foundation
Complete first floor
Second floor/loft underlayment and flooring
Ceiling materials   Partition walls   Flashing
Guttering system   Interior doors   Stairways
Most interior trim   Exterior trim
Interior and exterior applied finishes
Vapor barriers   Some insulation   Weatherstripping
Caulking   Some fasteners and builders' hardware
Electrical system   Plumbing system and fixtures
Heating/cooling system   Ventilating system
Appliances   Cabinetry

**OPTIONS AVAILABLE:** Cedar clapboard exterior siding; tongue-and-groove board exterior siding; contemporary trim/decor; wings and garages available; some models can be extended and/or widened; full dormers on some models.

**SPECIAL FEATURES:** Reversible interior paneling and exterior siding; Andersen windows standard; hand-split red cedar roofing shakes standard; stock models can be incrementally lengthened; several small structures can be combined; energy-efficient construction.

**EASE OF CONSTRUCTION:** Most buyers contract out for construction. Timber framing components precut and joints formed; parts numbered and coded to assembly plans. Substantial amount of on-site cutting, fitting, and trimming required. No special skills needed for frame assembly; carpentry skills advised for completion of house.

**MANUFACTURER ASSISTANCE:** Help in design selection, planning, and modifications; independent sales representatives will assist in planning and construction process, and will give technical advice and help for four to six hours during construction startup, and throughout construction as needed.

**SALES AREA:** National.

## Barn Homes Ltd.
P.O. Box 579
Woodstock, NY 12498
(914) 679-7322

**MODELS:** 40 stock models; modifications possible; custom design available.

**SQUARE FOOTAGE:** 864 to 5,760 square feet.

**PRICE:** $27,400 to $65,700.

**COMPLETENESS OF PACKAGE:** About 40% to 50% complete.

**SPECIAL FEATURES:** Classic barn with wood-pegged mortise and tenon joints; solar designs available; skylights available; garages available; great variety of doors, windows, and stairs; great flexibility of design; passive solar capability.

**SALES AREA:** National.

## The Barn People
Box 4
South Woodstock, VT 05071
(802) 457-3943

**MODELS:** Custom design only.

**SQUARE FOOTAGE:** 288 to 3,200 square feet.

**PRICE:** $15,840 to $176,000.

**COMPLETENESS OF PACKAGE:** About 15% (frame only) to 100% (finished house) complete.

**SPECIAL FEATURES:** Antique post-and-beam barn structures taken down and reassembled on buyer's lot; some beams 48' long; authentic barn-board ceiling materials; hayloft ladders; additional lofts/levels; sheds; wings; ells; yellow pine flooring; custom barn doors available; buildings used as homes, barns, studios, and pool shelters.

**SALES AREA:** National.

## David Howard, Inc.
P.O. Box 295
Alstead, NH 03602
(603) 835-6356

**MODELS:** Custom design only.

**SQUARE FOOTAGE:** 600 to 3,800 square feet.

**PRICE:** $6,600 to $57,000.

**COMPLETENESS OF PACKAGE:** About 20% complete.

**SPECIAL FEATURES:** All-oak frame; full planning service; construction supervision service; frames erected by manufacturer; extensive design possibilities; also imports from England and rebuilds antique timber-frames and buildings.

**SALES AREA:** National.

# Green Mountain Homes
Waterman Road
Royalton, VT 05068
(802) 763-8384

**MODELS:** 18 stock models; modifications possible; custom design available.

**SQUARE FOOTAGE:** 576 to 2,520 square feet.

**PRICE:** $7,960 to $29,920.

**COMPLETENESS OF PACKAGE:** About 33% to 40% complete.

**SPECIAL FEATURES:** All models have passive solar heating capability; patented thermal-mass heat exchange system; uses rough-sawn timbers; module models can be mixed and/or matched; custom-designed interiors.

**SALES AREA:** National.

# Habitat
123 Elm Street
Deerfield, MA 01373
(413) 665-4006

**MODELS:** 20 stock models; modifications possible; custom design available.

**SQUARE FOOTAGE:** 1,428 to 3,152 square feet.

**PRICE:** $23,632 to $57,245.

**COMPLETENESS OF PACKAGE:** About 40% complete.

**SPECIAL FEATURES:** Highly energy efficient; no-obligation estimating service; all homes use exposed wood ceilings; passive solar heating possible; exterior walls panelized; special solar room available.

**SALES AREA:** Eastern United States.

# Haida Hide, Inc.
19237 Aurora Avenue North
Seattle, WA 98133
(206) 546-4183

**MODELS:** 36 stock models; modifications possible; custom design available.

**SQUARE FOOTAGE:** 640 to 2,000 square feet.

**PRICE:** $14,140 to $45,000.

**COMPLETENESS OF PACKAGE:** About 50% complete, based on do-it-yourself construction.

**SPECIAL FEATURES:** Double wall construction; free standing prefab carport available; will meet FHA heat-loss requirement to suit any climate; package contains fully insulated walls and roof; custom models available in 4-foot multiples; free architectural service.

**SALES AREA:** National.

# New England-Techbuilt
585 State Road
North Dartmouth, MA 02747
(617) 993-9944

**MODELS:** 6 stock models; modifications possible; mainly custom design.

**SQUARE FOOTAGE:** 900 to 3,500 square feet.

**PRICE:** $12,000 to $200,000.

**COMPLETENESS OF PACKAGE:** About 40% to 50% complete.

**SPECIAL FEATURES:** Complete flexibility, interchangeability, and variety of design, including curvilinear and geometric forms.

**SALES AREA:** National.

# Timber Kit
P.O. Box 704
Amherst, MA 01002
(413) 665-2210

**MODELS:** 14 stock models; modifications possible; custom design available.

**SQUARE FOOTAGE:** 900 to 1,900 square feet.

**PRICE:** $19,374 to $29,715.

**COMPLETENESS OF PACKAGE:** About 40% complete.

**SPECIAL FEATURES:** Passive solar features; flexible and expandable designs; both traditional and contemporary styling; heavy-timber frame; solar room available; potential for do-it-yourself building.

**SALES AREA:** National.

# Yankee Barn Homes, Inc.
Star Route 3, Box 2
Grantham, NH 03753
(603) 863-4545

**MODELS:** 21 stock models; modifications possible; custom design available.

**SQUARE FOOTAGE:** 1,100 to 3,500 square feet.

**PRICE:** $26,000 to $75,000.

**COMPLETENESS OF PACKAGE:** About 40% to 45% complete.

**SPECIAL FEATURES:** Recycled old yellow pine beams from mills and factories; panelized double wall, floor, and roof sections; massive trimwork; special antique-patterncut nails and spikes.

**SALES AREA:** National.

# Precut Houses

Precut houses are what normally comes to mind when most people hear "manufactured" or "prefabricated." This category includes houses built with conventional frame construction techniques, with familiar designs and styling. They look like the ranch houses, split-levels, and tri-levels that can be seen in subdivisions, developments, and suburbs all around the country.

House packages consist mostly of unassembled and precut components. There are a few exceptions. Sometimes a post-and-beam type of framing is combined with the conventional construction. In a few cases the packages may include panelized sections or subassemblies that have been partly preassembled; these instances, however, are in the minority.

There is a fair amount of flexibility built into precut house designs. First, there is ample opportunity to make design changes, either in floor plans or in the designs themselves. Houses can be modified by flip-flopping all or part of the floor plan, adding an extension, or actually extending the house frame itself. Garages and porches can also be added. As with other kinds of manufactured houses, many manufacturers offer custom design services. And second, there is wide latitude in choosing materials and settling upon the ultimate appearance of the house, both inside and out. On the outside, different kinds of exterior siding, including brick or stone veneer, might be used. The roof color can be varied, and there are assorted window and exterior door options. Interiors can be decorated in a variety of ways.

Most precut houses are not only conventionally framed, but are also of very straightforward and simple construction. The main component parts are cut to fit together with little need for fitting or trimming and with as little waste as possible. Some manufacturers premark the components to show where, and how, they join. But not every part is precut—some items, like sheets of drywall or long strips of trim molding, are bundled in bulk and then fitted at the job site.

## Most Packages Are Complete

Although some precut house packages are only shells—floors, walls, and roof—most are quite complete as "standard" packages. A great range of options and additional materials is offered as well. This can be a considerable advantage to any buyer. With a precut house it's possible to order up a package that includes heating, electrical, and plumbing systems; appliances; paint; floor coverings; trim; kitchen cabinets; and even bathroom accessories.

Those parts and materials that are not actually produced by the house manufacturer, but are supplied as part of the house package, are usually recognizable name brands. The standard warranty for each of these parts or appliances is passed along to the house buyer. In effect, many precut house manufacturers act as one-stop shopping centers for the buyer, where just about everything needed to complete the house can be bought and assembled in one big package.

But, the buyer doesn't have to purchase all of these items if they're not wanted. Even if the manufacturer offers everything that's needed to finish the house, the buyer can choose to buy only a shell package, add other materials that seem desirable, and purchase the remaining items locally. But this course of action can create problems. Often the financing for a complete house package is easier to obtain than for just the shell. And, if all of the necessary materials to complete the house are on hand, chances are the house will be finished quicker.

## Houses for the Do-It-Yourselfer

These kits are designed for do-it-yourself erection and finishing. Complete instructions are usually included detailing how all parts must be assembled and installed. Some manufacturers offer tips on how the owner, his family, and friends can get the job done with a minimum of outside professional help.

Assembly of most precut house shells, especially smaller ones, is not a difficult job. Larger models with two stories and steep roof pitches are more difficult. Assembly does take time, because in a conventionally framed house there are many more components that have to be put together, one by one. Trimming and finishing the house also takes time—longer than the shell assembly—because nothing is prefinished.

In most instances, floors are built over conventional joist type frames, but beams may sometimes be used. Walls are stud-framed and covered with sheathing, exterior siding, and drywall. Roofs are generally rafter or conventional-truss framed, with sheathing and shingles. Heavy, open roof trusses or beams may sometimes be used along with cathedral ceilings, but most ceilings are of the usual flat, drywall variety. Trimwork and interior finishing are the same as in any conventional house.

Precut houses are available in sizes from very small to more than 3,000 square feet; most houses, however, are smaller than 2,000 square feet. Some houses are modular and can be arranged in groups or clusters to provide more living space. Prices are competitive, especially for smaller houses that are nearly complete. Many precut house manufacturers offer

*Assembly of a precut house isn't difficult, but it does take time. There are a great many separate components that have to be put together one piece at a time.*

financing on land purchases, house packages, and for buying materials, such as the foundation, that are not included in the package.

# Evans Products Co.

Capp Homes
Dublin Hall, Suite 200
177 Walton Road
Blue Bell, PA 19422
(215) 628-4800

Ridge Homes
200 Lakeside Drive
Horsham, PA 19044
(215) 443-7200

**MODELS:** 51 stock models (Capp), 58 stock models (Ridge); modifications possible; custom design available.

**SQUARE FOOTAGE:** 832 to 3,085 square feet (Capp); 1,056 to 2,893 square feet (Ridge).

**PRICE:** $28,420 to $82,310 (Capp); $29,000 to $75,200 (Ridge).

**COMPLETENESS OF PACKAGE:** About 80% complete.

**CONSTRUCTION: Floors.** *First floor:* Joist framing • Plywood subflooring • Hardboard underlayment • Tongue-and-groove oak and vinyl flooring
*Second floor/loft:* Same as first floor
**Walls.** *Exterior walls:* Stud framing • Plywood sheathing • Exterior aluminum siding on Ridge homes; hardboard siding on Capp homes • Interior drywall wall surface
*Partition walls:* Stud framing • Interior drywall wall surface

**Roof.** Rafter framing • Plywood sheathing • Felt roof protection • Fiberglass shingles
**Windows/Doors.** Double-glazed, wood-framed double-hung windows • Double-glazed, wood-framed picture and sliding windows on some models • Pre-hung metal insulated exterior doors • Hollow-core wood interior doors

**MANUFACTURER PROVIDES:**
Structural plans (including foundation)

*Photos Courtesy Evans Co. Products*

Formal mechanical plans   Blueprints   Specifications
Construction manual   Complete first floor
Complete second floor/loft   Ceiling materials
Exterior walls   Partition walls   Complete roof system
Flashing   Guttering system   Windows
Interior and exterior doors   Stairways
Garages on some models   Interior and exterior trim
Vapor barriers   Insulation   Weatherstripping
Caulking   Some fasteners and builders' hardware
Electrical system   Plumbing system and fixtures
Heating/cooling system   Ventilating system
Appliances   Cabinetry

## BUYER PROVIDES:
Foundation   Interior and exterior applied finishes
Some fasteners and builders' hardware

## OPTIONS AVAILABLE:
Additional choices in cabinetry and appliances; cedar and redwood siding; asphalt shingles; bathroom fixtures; energy-saving options; different flooring materials; bay and bow windows; patio doors; garages; bi-fold closet doors; heating/cooling system options; solar hot water system; lighting options; fireplaces.

## SPECIAL FEATURES:
Unusually complete package, especially within this category of homes. Evans Products provides just about everything necessary to finish the house. Special do-it-yourself program allows inexperienced owner-builders maximum involvement in construction. Wide range of options. Aluminum siding standard on all Ridge Homes. Many standard and optional energy features.

## EASE OF CONSTRUCTION:
Shell is usually erected by manufacturer. Ridge Homes construction crews will make the shell weathertight; Capp Homes crews construct up to the weathertight features (shingles, siding, etc.). Remaining materials are delivered to site by manufacturer. The finishing of the house is within the capabilities of the do-it-yourselfer, and many buyers choose to do this work.

## MANUFACTURER ASSISTANCE:
Manufacturer assists in all stages of buying and building, from design selection to completed house. Shell usually erected by manufacturer. All materials delivered to building site by manufacturer's trucks. Ridge Homes will construct foundation, if desired. Financing is available through Evans Financial Corp.

## SALES AREA:
Ridge Homes—eastern United States; Capp Homes—remaining United States. Only states excluded are Florida and Alabama.

# Miles Homes
4700 Nathan Lane
P.O. Box 41310
Minneapolis, MN 55442
(612) 553-8300

**MODELS:** 57 stock models; modifications possible;

approximately 5% to 10% of the houses are custom designed.

**SQUARE FOOTAGE:** 768 to 1800+ square feet.

**PRICE:** $19,300 to $36,300.

**COMPLETENESS OF PACKAGE:** About 50% complete.

**CONSTRUCTION: Floors.** *First floor:* Joist framing • Plywood subflooring • Particle board underlayment • Flooring not provided
*Second floor/loft:* Same as first floor
**Walls.** *Exterior walls:* Stud framing • Fiberglass insulation • Exterior sheathing • Exterior hardboard siding • Interior wallboard
*Partition walls:* Stud framing • Wallboard wall surface
**Roof.** Rafter framing • Fiberglass insulation • Plywood sheathing • Felt roof protection • Asphalt shingles
**Windows/Doors.** Double-glazed, wood- or aluminum-framed sliding, picture, double-hung, and bay windows • Prehung metal insulated exterior doors • Double-glazed, aluminum-framed sliding patio doors with screens • Hollow-core swinging, bi-fold, and sliding bypass interior doors

## MANUFACTURER PROVIDES:
Structural plans (including foundation)   Specifications
Construction manual
First floor framing, subflooring, and underlayment
Second floor/loft framing, subflooring, and
     underlayment
Ceiling materials   Exterior walls   Partition walls
Complete roof system   Windows
Interior and exterior doors   Stairways and railings
Garages on some models   Interior and exterior trim
Vapor barriers   Insulation
Fasteners and builders' hardware
Part of the ventilating system   Kitchen cabinetry
Closet rods and shelves

## BUYER PROVIDES:
Formal mechanical plans   Foundation
First and second floor flooring   Flashing
Guttering system   Garage doors if applicable
Interior and exterior applied finishes

*Courtesy Miles Homes*

*Courtesy Miles Homes*

Weatherstripping  Caulking  Electrical system
Plumbing system and fixtures
Heating/cooling system
Part of the ventilating system  Appliances
Additional cabinetry

**OPTIONS AVAILABLE:** Choice of doors and
windows; choice of cabinetry and additional
cabinetry; kitchen sinks; vent hoods; plumbing
fixtures and supplies; water heaters; electrical fixtures;
heating/cooling system; flooring; interior and exterior
applied finishes; additional insulation.

**SPECIAL FEATURES:** Planning services available;
electrical and heating packages and plumbing supplies;
wide range of options; no down payment financing
and financial assistance available; passive solar
models available.

**EASE OF CONSTRUCTION:** Oriented to do-it-
yourselfers. Almost all parts precut; some parts
premarked. No special tools or equipment needed; no
special skills or previous experience necessary to
construct shell. Some carpentry and trade skills
helpful but not essential.

**MANUFACTURER ASSISTANCE:** Manufacturer or
dealer will consult on all aspects of design. Financing
available.

**SALES AREA:** National.

# Serendipity
Pier 9, The Embarcadero
San Francisco, CA 94111
(415) 986-8108

**MODELS:** 15 stock models; modifications possible;
approximately 20% of the houses are custom
designed.

**SQUARE FOOTAGE:** 752 to 2,800 square feet.

**PRICE:** $12,637 to $38,284.

**COMPLETENESS OF PACKAGE:** About 33%
complete.

**CONSTRUCTION: Floors.** *First floor:* Beam and joist
framing • Plywood combined subfloor/
underlayment • Flooring not provided
*Second floor/loft:* Same as first floor
**Walls.** *Exterior walls:* Stud framing • Exterior
plywood siding • No sheathing needed • Interior wall
surface not provided
*Partition walls:* Not provided
**Roof.** Rough-sawn beam framing • Resawn-grooved
plywood or tongue-and-groove pine decking • Roof
protection and roofing not provided
**Windows/Doors.** Double-glazed, aluminum-framed
sliding windows with screens • Stopped-in glass
frames • Stopped-in glass not provided • Prehung
solid-core birch exterior doors • Double-glazed,
aluminum-framed sliding patio doors with screens •
Interior doors not provided

**MANUFACTURER PROVIDES:**
Structural plans (including foundation)  Blueprints
Specifications

*Photos Courtesy Serendipity*

First floor framing and combined subflooring/underlayment
Second floor/loft framing and combined subflooring/underlayment
Exterior wall framing and siding
Roof framing and decking   Operable windows
Exterior doors   Stairways   Exterior trim
Caulking   Some fasteners and builders' hardware

**BUYER PROVIDES:**
Formal mechanical plans   Foundation
First and second floor/loft flooring   Ceiling materials
Interior wall surface   Partition walls
Roof protection and roofing   Flashing
Guttering system   Stopped-in glass
Interior doors   Interior trim
Interior and exterior applied finishes   Vapor barriers
Insulation   Weatherstripping
Some fasteners and builders' hardware
Electrical system   Plumbing system and fixtures
Heating/cooling system   Ventilating system
Appliances   Cabinetry

**OPTIONS AVAILABLE:** Post and girder floor system for pier foundation; decks; garages; increased strength of structural members for additional snow load; shingles; rigid insulation; interior paneling; interior doors; trimwork; cabinetry; countertops; appliances; plumbing and electrical fixtures; carpeting.

**SPECIAL FEATURES:** Innovative award-winning designs; unique foundation system for minimum site disturbance and sloping-site construction; beam and combined subfloor/underlayment floor system; passive solar designs and options.

**EASE OF CONSTRUCTION:** Aimed at the do-it-yourselfer. All principal components are precut, marked, and coded to assembly plans. Some on-site cutting, trimming, and fitting required. Although construction manual is not provided, plans are explicit and fully detailed. Carpentry skills or experience not needed to assemble shell; basic woodworking skills advised for interior finish and completion of house.

**MANUFACTURER ASSISTANCE:** Manufacturer and/or dealers will help as needed through the planning and design selection process, cost calculations, financing, and contracting arrangements. Guidelines are furnished for each step in the buying/building process.

**SALES AREA:** National.

# Shelter-Kit, Inc.
Dept. CG
P.O. Box 1
Tilton, NH 03276
(603) 934-4327

**MODELS:** 3 basic units; modifications possible; only

*Photos Courtesy Shelter-Kit, Inc.*

10% of the houses are sold as is. Most buyers add extensions or units.

**SQUARE FOOTAGE:** 1) 144 square feet; 2) 512 square feet; 3) 960 square feet.

**PRICE:** 1) $3,300; 2) $5,932; 3) $8,913.

**COMPLETENESS OF PACKAGE:** About 75% complete.

**CONSTRUCTION: Floors.** *First floor:* Joist or truss framing • Pine tongue-and-groove board subflooring with joist framing • Plywood tongue-and-groove subflooring with truss framing • Underlayment and flooring not provided
*Second floor/loft:* Truss framing • Plywood tongue-and-groove subflooring • Underlayment and flooring not provided
**Walls.** *Exterior walls:* 4×4 post framing • Stud fill-in framing • Exterior pine tongue-and-groove clapboard or rough-sawn plywood siding • Interior wall surface not provided
*Partition walls:* Not provided
**Roof.** Rafter framing • Plywood sheathing • Roll roofing or asphalt shingles • Roof protection not provided
**Windows/Doors.** Double-glazed, aluminum-framed sliding windows with screens • Single-glazed, aluminum-framed sliding exterior doors with screens • Interior doors not provided

**MANUFACTURER PROVIDES:**
Foundation plans   Specifications
Construction manual
First floor framing and subflooring
Second floor/loft framing and subflooring
Exterior wall framing and siding
Roof framing, sheathing, and roofing   Windows
Exterior doors   Exterior trim   Caulking
Some fasteners and builders' hardware
Wood preservative
All necessary tools and equipment

**BUYER PROVIDES:**
Formal mechanical plans   Foundation
First floor underlayment and flooring
Second floor/loft underlayment and flooring
Ceiling materials   Interior wall surface
Partition walls   Roof protection   Flashing
Guttering system   Interior doors   Stairways
Interior trim   Interior and exterior applied finishes
Vapor barriers   Insulation   Weatherstripping
Some fasteners and builders' hardware
Electrical system   Plumbing system and fixtures
Heating/cooling system   Ventilating system
Appliances   Cabinetry

**OPTIONS AVAILABLE:** Double-glazed patio doors; prehung solid-core exterior doors; double-glazed windows; skylights; passive or active solar design service.

**SPECIAL FEATURES:** Flexible module system incorporating decks and open or closed porches. Basic units can be mixed and matched in a variety of ways. Very seldom is one unit purchased alone. Shell is designed for pier foundation, which can be installed by an inexperienced owner-builder. Modified post-and -beam construction allows great design flexibility. Extreme ease and simplicity of construction. Ideally suited to solar heating. All necessary tools and equipment included in kits.

**EASE OF CONSTRUCTION:** Especially designed for owner-builders with no skills or experience. Shell erection is quite simple and not demanding physically. All necessary components and supplies are precut and predrilled. All necessary hand tools and equipment (including two stepladders) are included.

**MANUFACTURER ASSISTANCE:** Will advise or counsel at the factory, by mail, or by phone concerning designs and planning, siting and orientation, solar heating, construction, or any similar associated matters.

**SALES AREA:** National.

# Aladdin Company
901 Saginaw Street
Bay City, MI 48706
(517) 895-8545

**MODELS:** 64 stock models; modifications possible.

**SQUARE FOOTAGE:** 736 to 2,600 square feet.

**PRICE:** $8,792 to $32,000.

**COMPLETENESS OF PACKAGE:** About 33% to 40% complete, based on do-it-yourself building.

**SPECIAL FEATURES:** Many options available; 6 month financing available; brick-veneer designs offered; designed for owner-building.

**SALES AREA:** National.

# Carroll Homes, Inc.
2434 Forsyth Road
Orlando, FL 32807
(305) 678-7700

**MODELS:** 8 stock models; modifications possible; custom design available.

**SQUARE FOOTAGE:** 938 to 1,772 square feet.

**PRICE:** $12,973 to $22,965.

**COMPLETENESS OF PACKAGE:** About 45% to 50% complete.

**SPECIAL FEATURES:** Porch decking material available; modified post- and -beam frame; insulated structural first-floor panels optional; insulated structural wall panels standard.

**SALES AREA:** Alabama, Florida, Georgia, North Carolina, South Carolina, Tennessee.

# Heritage International
4625 S. 2300 E, Suite 206
Salt Lake City, UT 84117
(801) 272-4481 or (800) 453-0402

**MODELS:** 115 stock models; modifications possible; custom design available.

**SQUARE FOOTAGE:** 800 to 3,500 square feet.

**PRICE:** $25,000 to $250,000.

**COMPLETENESS OF PACKAGE:** About 40% complete.

**SPECIAL FEATURES:** All Weather Wood Foundation; floor trusses available; floors, walls, and roof can be panelized; earth shelter housing available; wide range of options.

**SALES AREA:** National.

# Nor-Wes Cedar Homes
11120 Bridge Road
Surrey, BC, Canada V3V3T9
(604) 580-2023

**MODELS:** 27 stock models; modifications possible; custom design available.

**SQUARE FOOTAGE:** 645 to 2,766 square feet.

**PRICE:** $18,000 to $96,000.

**COMPLETENESS OF PACKAGE:** About 50% complete.

**SPECIAL FEATURES:** Red cedar interior and exterior; specially engineered truss system; many custom interior features including spiral stairs; unusual contemporary designs.

**SALES AREA:** National and Canada.

## President Homes

Division of Harvey Builders, Inc.
4808 N. Lilac Drive
Minneapolis, MN 55429
(612) 537-3622

**MODELS:** 54 stock models; modifications possible; custom design available.

**SQUARE FOOTAGE:** 768 to 1,728 square feet.

**PRICE:** $21,200 to $43,000.

**COMPLETENESS OF PACKAGE:** About 100% complete, based on do-it-yourself building.

**SPECIAL FEATURES:** Financing available; shell erected by manufacturer's crew; cabinets, plumbing, and electrical packages standard; many options.

**SALES AREA:** Illinois, Indiana, Iowa, Kansas, Michigan, Minnesota, Missouri, Montana, North Dakota, South Dakota, Wisconsin, Wyoming.

## Wickes Lumber

515 N. Washington Avenue
Saginaw, MI 48607
(517) 754-9121

**MODELS:** 23 stock models; modifications possible.

**SQUARE FOOTAGE:** 720 to 1,800 square feet.

**PRICE:** $7,200 to $32,000.

**COMPLETENESS OF PACKAGE:** Withheld.

**SPECIAL FEATURES:** Wood Bavarian shutters available; fireplace packages; various interior finishing packages; electrical, plumbing and heating packages; many options.

**SALES AREA:** East of the Mississippi, plus California.

# Panelized Houses

Of all manufactured houses, the panelized types are undoubtedly the most popular. Of the many thousands that are erected throughout the country each year, about half are constructed by small con-tractors and do-it-yourself buyers on individual building sites. The other half are built by developers and large production builders in developments and subdivisions for sale to the general public. Many other types of manufactured houses are also panelized to some degree; some domes, log houses, and post-and-beam houses have some panelized sections.

Panelized construction means that sections of the house, primarily walls but sometimes floors and roofs, are preassembled. The degree of completeness of the sections varies from one manufacturer to another. Three methods of assembling panelized components are common. The first is the nailed-up section, where the parts are assembled with nails or other fasteners just as they would be in a contractor-built house. The second is a section where plywood or other coverings are glued and fastened to one side of a framework; sometimes the glue is bonded in a hot press. The third is the sandwich panel, with the frame and insulation covered on both sides with panels that are glued and secured with nails or screws. The last two methods are stronger and generally to be pre-ferred where there is a clear-cut choice.

Panelized sections are made in a factory, where equipment, processes, and procedures are used that would be impossible in the field. This can result in walls, floors, and roofs that are built to more exacting standards. Full wall sections, for example, can be made without seams, and with windows installed and sealed. Such construction nearly eliminates any possibility of air infiltration. Sections can be glued and then cured in a hot press, producing panels that are stronger than ones put together with nails. Also, materials not often found in house construction, steel framing for example, are sometimes used.

## Two Types of Construction

Panelized construction can be classed in two different categories: open-wall, and closed-wall. Both terms refer particularly to exterior walls, but interior parti-tion walls, roofs, and floors are sometimes panelized as well.

Open-wall construction is just what the name im-plies—when the wall sections are built, the interior covering is left off. The assembly consists of the wall frame and sheathing, or both sheathing and siding. Often the insulation is installed, windows may or may not be preinstalled, and doors are generally put in at the job site. Wiring and plumbing are installed after the shell has been erected, to allow for inspection by local building officials. This procedure offers added flexibility in selecting interior wall surface coverings.

Open-wall house packages usually come with pre-assembled roof trusses or precut rafter frame assemblies; roofs are not panelized. Interior partition walls come as preassembled frames only, or as uncut or precut framing materials. Floors are usually sup-plied as unassembled precut joist frame systems with plywood subflooring. In some cases a completely panelized floor arrangement is used. Where the houses are designed for conventional foundations the panels are open—there is no added covering on the bottom. A few houses are designed for an open pier or pedestal-and-post foundation, and these floor panels are closed with a plywood bottom for added protection.

The closed-wall construction method is more complex, and considerably less common. With this method a wood or steel frame from 4 to 14 inches thick is assembled and covered on one side with exterior sheathing. Insulation is installed, along with electrical wiring and plumbing as required. A vapor barrier is put on, the interior is covered with drywall or some other surface covering, and exterior siding is applied. Depending upon the specific manufacturer's building system, the exact materials will vary. Sometimes a layer of building paper is put on the outside, or added rigid thermal insulation is used, and the exterior siding may be left off for on-site application. Windows are sometimes preinstalled and sometimes not; prehung doors are installed at the job site.

Closed-wall house packages often come with similar closed-panel roof sections. These can be complete with a drywall or similar surface covering as a ready-to-finish ceiling that is secured to a beam or open truss roof frame. Or, the roof might be a conventional truss or rafter system that is assembled in the usual fashion. Interior partition walls are usually closed panels, although they may be assembled frames or even precut components. Floors are either panelized—open for the first floor, and open or closed for the second floor—or supplied as precut components.

In addition, closed-wall panelized house packages are sometimes furnished with a completely preassembled and prefinished mechanical or utility core. This module, typically 10 by 15 feet, includes the main electrical service entrance, a "wet" wall that contains most of the plumbing system, a water heater, complete bathroom(s), kitchen with cabinetry and basic appliances, and the heating/cooling system. Exactly what is included depends upon the specific manufacturer, and the specifications of the particular house.

Panelized houses can also be classified by the size of the panels used in construction. The larger panels range up to 40 feet long and 8 feet high. These panels can be extremely heavy, and must be set in place by a crane. Assembly of these shells, usually a bolt-together process, must be done by a trained professional crew. Closed-wall houses and a few open-wall types use these large panels. In houses made up of a number of smaller panels, the sections are typically 8 by 8 feet or less. Those that include windows are fairly heavy, but they can still be handled and maneuvered by three or four workers. The majority of the open-wall panelized houses are in this class. In some instances, where the sections are large and heavy, they can be placed by hand, but a boom truck or crane makes assembly faster and safer.

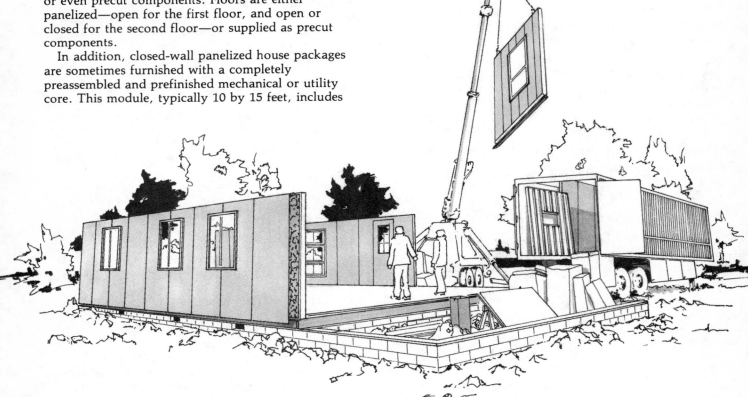

*Panelized houses often can be made weathertight in a day or less.*

# Construction Advantages

The main advantage to panelized construction is that the shell is put up quickly. Because many components are preassembled, shell assembly takes less time than for a comparable contractor-built or precut house. The larger the panelized sections are, the fewer parts there are to handle, and the shell erection goes even faster. Nearly all of the closed-wall houses made up of large panels are assembled and made weathertight in less than a day.

Swift shell erection offers other advantages too. The total time necessary for construction can be shortened. Completion times vary considerably, but it is not at all unusual for a buyer to move into a finished house a month after the foundation is constructed. Once the shell is up, it can be locked with all tools, equipment, and materials stored inside. This eliminates theft problems, vandalism, and weather damage.

Panelizing can be advantageous in other ways, too. Because the builder can rapidly assemble the house with a minimum of on-site labor, costs may be lowered. For the buyer who wants to do the major portion of the construction himself, the small-panel models are ideal because a lot of the hard work has already been done. And, the do-it-yourselfer who wants to do part, but not all of the building, can choose a house in varying stages of completion.

Panelized construction can be found in the entire range of house styles; literally anything is possible from traditional to contemporary to futuristic. The range of sizes runs from about 300 square feet to 4,000 square feet. House packages can be obtained as little more than shells, ready for interior and exterior finishing, or as nearly completed houses. Many manufacturers offer a wide range of options and possible modifications, as well as custom design services. Although they are built differently, panelized houses look the same as other houses—appearance can be anything desired, including the log-look. Prices are competitive and run from a low of $4,000 to more than $150,000. Finished costs are comparable to any other kind of house construction.

# Affordable Luxury Homes, Inc.

U.S. 224 W.
P.O. Box 368
Markle, IN 46770
(219) 758-2141

**MODELS:** 40 stock models; modifications possible; approximately 75% of the houses are custom designed.

**SQUARE FOOTAGE:** 720 to 2,977 square feet.

**PRICE:** $8,995 to $42,393.

**COMPLETENESS OF PACKAGE:** About 33% to 50% complete.

*Photos Courtesy Affordable Luxury Homes, Inc.*

**CONSTRUCTION: Floors.** *First floor:* Joist framing • Tongue-and-groove subflooring • Particle board underlayment • Flooring not provided
*Second floor/loft:* Same as first floor
**Walls.** *Exterior walls:* Closed sections, windows not installed • Stud framing • Polystyrene insulation • Exterior plywood sheathing • Interior drywall • Exterior siding not provided
*Partition walls:* Preassembled stud framing • Wall surface not provided
**Roof.** Closed sections for A-frame and cathedral designs; other types not panelized • Truss or rafter framing • Plywood sheathing • Felt roof protection • Asphalt shingles or cedar shakes
**Windows/Doors.** Double-glazed, wood-framed double-hung windows with screens • Prehung steel insulated exterior doors • Double-glazed, wood-framed patio doors with screens • Interior doors not provided

**MANUFACTURER PROVIDES:**
Structural plans (including foundation)   Blueprints
Specifications
First floor framing, subflooring, and underlayment
Second floor/loft framing, subflooring, and underlayment

Exterior wall framing and sheathing   Interior drywall
Partition wall framing   Complete roof system
Windows   Exterior doors   Vapor barriers
Insulation on some models   Caulking
Some fasteners and builders' hardware
Some electrical wiring

**BUYER PROVIDES:**
Formal mechanical plans   Foundation   Flooring
Ceiling materials   Exterior wall siding
Partition wall surface   Flashing   Guttering system
Interior doors   Stairways   Interior and exterior trim
Interior and exterior applied finishes
Insulation on some models   Weatherstripping
Some fasteners and builders' hardware
Most of the electrical system
Plumbing system and fixtures
Heating/cooling system   Ventilating system
Appliances   Cabinetry

**OPTIONS AVAILABLE:** Panelized first floor system; panel sections (floor, walls, or roof) in thicknesses up to 14 inches; shingles or shakes; exterior siding.

**SPECIAL FEATURES:** Several panel thicknesses; great thermal efficiency; use throughout of stable and noncombustible expanded polystyrene insulation; very low outside-air infiltration factor; great structural strength and integrity; panelized first floor available; will adapt the building system to nearly any custom design; chalets and A-frames of somewhat different construction available; special panelized system available for do-it-yourselfers.

**EASE OF CONSTRUCTION:** Most homes built by owner-builder. 30% of those owner-builders are complete novices. Shell usually assembled by a professional crew with the help of a crane or boom truck.

**MANUFACTURER ASSISTANCE:** Manufacturer, factory representative, or dealers will offer advice, counsel, and help in whatever areas questions or problems arise, within reason, and will guide the buyer through the entire process of design selection, construction, and finishing. Construction superintendent available from factory if required.

**SALES AREA:** National.

# American Timber Homes, Inc.

P.O. Box 496
Escanaba, MI 49829
(906) 786-4550

**MODELS:** 25 stock models; modifications possible; approximately 95% of the houses are custom designed.

**SQUARE FOOTAGE:** 600 to 3,212 square feet.

**PRICE:** $18,728 to $79,273.

*Photos Courtesy American Timber Homes, Inc.*

**COMPLETENESS OF PACKAGE:** About 40% complete.

**CONSTRUCTION: Floors.** *First floor:* Not provided *Second floor/loft:* Joist framing • Plywood subflooring • Underlayment and flooring not provided
**Walls.** *Exterior walls:* Open sections, windows not installed • 2×6 stud framing • Exterior plywood sheathing • Exterior building paper underlayment • Exterior rough-sawn white cedar siding • Interior rough- or smooth-sawn paneling for some models *Partition walls:* Stud framing • Wall surface not provided
**Roof.** Exposed log truss, conventional truss, or conventional rafter framing • Tongue-and-groove decking for truss framing • Sheathing for conventional rafter framing, underlayment, and roofing not provided
**Windows/Doors.** Double-glazed, wood-framed casement, double-hung, sliding, picture, bow, and bay windows with screens as necessary • Prehung metal insulated doors • Sidelight and/or double doors on

some models • Double-glazed, wood-framed sliding patio doors with screens • Prehung birch or pine interior doors

## MANUFACTURER PROVIDES:
Structural plans (including foundation)   Blueprints
Specifications   Construction manual
Second floor/loft framing and subflooring
Second story ceiling
Exterior wall framing, sheathing, and siding
Interior wall paneling on some models
Partition wall framing   Roof framing
Roof decking for some models   Windows
Interior and exterior doors   Stairways and railings
Porch decking, steps, and railings on some models
Some interior trim   Exterior trim
Some fasteners and builders' hardware

## BUYER PROVIDES:
Formal mechanical plans   Foundation
Complete first floor
Second floor/loft underlayment and flooring
First story ceiling   Interior wall surface if applicable
Partition wall covering
Roof sheathing, roof protection, and roofing   Flashing
Guttering system   Porch floor framing if applicable
Some interior trim
Interior and exterior applied finishes   Vapor barriers
Insulation   Weatherstripping   Caulking
Some fasteners and builders' hardware
Electrical system   Plumbing system and fixtures
Heating/cooling system   Ventilating system
Appliances   Cabinetry

**OPTIONS AVAILABLE:** Smooth or rough-sawn pine, white cedar, or aged barnwood interior paneling package; open sun decks; attached garage; masonry-level interior finishing package; triple-glazed windows; variety of exterior doors; triple-glazed patio doors; rigid insulation; wood circular stairs; screening for covered porches; wide range of solar comfort and water heating equipment.

**SPECIAL FEATURES:** Full line of specially designed solar models; use of open log or timber trusses; white cedar exterior siding; panelized sections small enough to be emplaced by hand; optional cedar back walls in clothes closets.

**EASE OF CONSTRUCTION:** House package is not designed for erection by amateur builders, but there is ample opportunity for owner involvement, especially in completion of interior. Principal components are precut; wall sections are panelized for ease of assembly. Panelized sections and small trusses can be emplaced by hand, but large trusses should be set by crane or boom truck. At least one experienced supervisor should be on hand throughout construction.

**MANUFACTURER ASSISTANCE:** Works closely with buyer and contractor throughout entire process of selecting and constructing a house package; helps supervise purchase of materials bought locally; helps contractor with construction details and cost estimating. Provides a construction supervisor to oversee shell erection. Inspects the house after completion. Manufacturer works with buyer to develop a personalized, or completely customized, design and plan.

**SALES AREA:** National.

# Boise Cascade Corp.
Housing Division
Kingsberry Homes
P.O. Box 8358
Boise, ID 83707
(208) 384-6161

**MODELS:** 375 stock models; modifications possible; approximately 25% of the houses are custom designed.

**SQUARE FOOTAGE:** 800 to 3,000 square feet.

**PRICE:** Sold to approved builders/contractors only: Finished price from $26,000 to $250,000.

*Photos Courtesy Boise Cascade Corp.*

**COMPLETENESS OF PACKAGE:** Homes usually delivered to buyer 100% complete. Sold to builders/contractors at 50% complete.

**CONSTRUCTION: Floors.** *First floor:* Joist framing • Plywood subflooring • Underlayment and flooring not provided
*Second floor/loft:* Same as first floor
**Walls.** *Exterior walls:* Open sections, windows installed • Stud framing • Exterior plywood sheathing • Exterior siding and interior wall surface not provided
*Partition walls:* Stud framing • Wall surface not provided
**Roof.** Rafter or truss framing • Plywood sheathing • Roof protection and roofing not provided
**Windows/Doors.** Single-glazed, wood-framed double-hung windows • Metal insulated exterior doors • Interior doors not provided

**MANUFACTURER PROVIDES:**
Structural plans (including foundation)
Mechanical plans   Blueprints   Specifications
Construction manual
First floor framing and subflooring
Second floor/loft framing and subflooring
Exterior wall framing and sheathing
Partition wall framing   Roof framing and sheathing
Windows   Exterior doors
Some fasteners and builders' hardware

**BUYER PROVIDES:**
Foundation   First floor underlayment and flooring
Second floor/loft underlayment and flooring
Ceiling materials   Exterior wall siding
Interior drywall   Partition wall surface
Roof protection and roofing   Flashing
Guttering system   Interior doors   Stairways
Interior and exterior trim
Interior and exterior applied finishes
Vapor barriers   Insulation   Weatherstripping
Caulking   Some fasteners and builders' hardware
Electrical system   Plumbing system and fixtures
Heating/cooling system   Ventilating system
Appliances   Cabinetry

**OPTIONS AVAILABLE:** Two- and four-foot house extensions; ½ bath; garages, ¾-inch tongue-and-groove plywood roof sheathing or subflooring; carports; patios; various exterior sidings; insulation; various exterior doors; double-glazed windows; full or partial brick veneering; appliances; several kitchen cabinet designs; plumbing fixtures; roofings; floorings.

**SPECIAL FEATURES:** Sold to and built by contractors only; power roof ventilation system; wide range of other options.

**EASE OF CONSTRUCTION:** Homes are built only by qualified contractors, usually as a turnkey job; owners can do some finishing work, according to contract terms established.

**MANUFACTURER ASSISTANCE:** All reasonable assistance is given by regional representatives working together with contractors, in all phases of planning, purchasing, and building.

**SALES AREA:** East of the Rockies, excluding North Central states (Michigan, Minnesota, Nebraska, North Dakota, South Dakota) and Southwest states (Arizona, Montana, Utah, Wyoming).

# Rondesics Homes Corp.
527 McDowell Street
Asheville, NC 28803
(704) 254-9581

**MODELS:** 6 stock models; modifications possible.

**SQUARE FOOTAGE:** 350 to 2,119 square feet.

**PRICE:** $5,155 to $36,403.

**COMPLETENESS OF PACKAGE:** About 40% complete.

**CONSTRUCTION: Floors.** *First floor:* Beams under closed sections • 2×4 framing • Fiberglass insulation • Plywood subflooring • Particle board underlayment • Flooring not provided
*Second floor/loft:* Not provided
**Walls.** *Exterior walls:* Open sections, windows installed • Stud framing • Fiberglass insulation • Exterior redwood siding • No sheathing needed • Interior wall surface not provided
*Partition walls:* Not provided
**Roof.** Precut beam and purlin framing (truss framing on one model) • Plywood sheathing • Fiberglass insulation • Felt roof protection • Asphalt shingles • Steel compression cabling system
**Windows/Doors.** Double-glazed, aluminum-framed sliding windows with screens • Prehung fir exterior doors • Double-glazed, aluminum-framed sliding patio doors with screens • Interior doors not provided

**MANUFACTURER PROVIDES:**
Structural plans (including foundation)   Blueprints
Specifications   Construction manual
First floor framing, subflooring, and underlayment
Exterior wall framing and siding
Complete roof system   Windows   Exterior doors
Decks on some models   Exterior trim
Some fasteners and builders' hardware

**BUYER PROVIDES:**
Formal mechanical plans   Foundation
First floor flooring   Complete second floor
Ceiling materials   Interior wall surface   Partition walls
Flashing   Guttering system   Interior doors
Stairways   Interior trim
Interior and exterior applied finishes   Vapor barriers
Insulation   Weatherstripping   Caulking
Some fasteners and builders' hardware
Electrical system   Plumbing system and fixtures
Heating/cooling system   Ventilating system
Appliances   Cabinetry

**OPTIONS AVAILABLE:** Packages for slab, pier, or

*Photos Courtesy Rondesics Homes Corp.*

perimeter foundations; chalet-type roof assembly; 2×6 wall or floor framing with thick insulation; added deck sections; outside stairways; spiral stairways; Andersen windows; steel foundation/support columns; additional exterior doors.

**SPECIAL FEATURES:** Round units that can be stacked or connected cluster-fashion; redwood siding and decking; flexibility of floor plan; special roof

design with compression cabling system; wide variety of options available.

**EASE OF CONSTRUCTION:** Very simple. Excellent possibilities for maximum owner involvement in construction and finishing. No previous experience or skills required for shell assembly. Principal components precut; floor and wall sections panelized for rapid, easy assembly. Minimum on-site cutting, fitting, and trimming needed for shell assembly.

**MANUFACTURER ASSISTANCE:** Offers help in design selection, modifications, and custom planning, interior planning, selection of options and procurement of materials; will help with construction questions or problems; construction superintendent available for on-site assistance if required.

**SALES AREA:** National.

# Wausau Homes, Inc.

P.O. Box 1204
Wausau, WI 54401
(715) 359-7272

**MODELS:** 25 sample models; 99% of the houses are custom designed.

**SQUARE FOOTAGE:** 960 to 2000+ square feet.

**PRICE:** $29,000 to $175,000 finished.

**COMPLETENESS OF PACKAGE:** Choice of four packages: 1) 64% complete 2) 83% complete 3) 91% complete 4) 100% complete.

**CONSTRUCTION: Floors.** *First floor:* Open sections • Joist framing • Insulation • Tongue-and-groove plywood subflooring • Underlayment and flooring not provided
*Second floor/loft:* Same as first floor
**Walls.** *Exterior walls:* Closed sections, windows installed • Stud framing • Fiberglass insulation • Vapor barrier • Exterior polystyrene sheathing • Exterior hardboard siding • Interior drywall
*Partition walls:* Closed sections • Stud framing • Unfinished lauan paneling wall surface
**Roof.** Closed sections • 2×6 or 2×8 rafter framing • Fiberglass insulation • Plywood sheathing • Building paper roof protection • Asphalt shingles • Interior drywall
**Windows/Doors.** Single-glazed, wood-framed double-hung and sliding windows with storm sash • Prehung metal insulated exterior doors • Prehung hollow-core interior doors

**MANUFACTURER PROVIDES:**
Structural plans (including foundation)
Typical mechanical plans   Specifications
First floor framing and subflooring
Second floor/loft framing and subflooring
Exterior walls   Partition walls   Complete roof system
Flashing   Windows   Interior and exterior doors

*Photos Courtesy Wausau Homes, Inc.*

Stairways and railings   Some interior trim
Exterior trim   Vapor barriers   Insulation
Weatherstripping   Caulking
Some fasteners and builders' hardware
Electrical system   Plumbing system and fixtures
Heating/cooling system   Ventilating system
Appliances   Cabinetry

**BUYER PROVIDES:**
Formal mechanical plans if needed   Foundation
First floor underlayment and flooring
First floor insulation if needed
Second floor/loft underlayment and flooring
Guttering system   Some interior trim
Interior and exterior applied finishes
Some fasteners and builders' hardware

**OPTIONS AVAILABLE:** Triple-glazed windows;
patio doors; various interior doors; casement
windows; deluxe lighting package; garages; ceramic
tile bathroom; cabinets and appliances; several
heating systems.

**SPECIAL FEATURES:** An unusual, and effective,
means of custom designing. The buyer first chooses a
style and size of house, then chooses from many
different "zones" or floor plans to fit that style. Four
different stages of completeness are also offered.
Buyers can leave all construction responsibilities to
the manufacturer or take as much as 35% of the
responsibilities upon themselves. Specific features
include: Complete, self-contained, entirely

preassembled and prefinished bath/kitchen/utility
core; all plumbing and wiring installed; cabinetry and
appliances preinstalled. All panel joints made with
thermal breaks; very high thermal efficiency and low
infiltration factor; practically seamless construction;
fully vented roof assembly.

**EASE OF CONSTRUCTION:** The package is always
assembled by dealer/builder's crew; whatever is not
included in the chosen package is often done by
contractor, but can be done by a do-it-yourselfer.

**MANUFACTURER ASSISTANCE:** Manufacturer
and/or dealer provides any help or counsel needed,
within reason, in selection of zones and design, floor
plan, and options; dealer/builder's crew assembles
package; dealers can arrange for turnkey job.

**SALES AREA:** 500 mile radius of Wausau,
Wisconsin.

# Acorn Structures, Inc.
Box 250
Concord, MA 01742
(617) 369-4111

**MODELS:** 50 stock models; modifications possible;
custom design available.

**SQUARE FOOTAGE:** 800 to 3,200 square feet.

**PRICE:** $40,000 to $160,000+.

**COMPLETENESS OF PACKAGE:** Withheld.

**SPECIAL FEATURES:** Active and passive solar
designs available; solar hot water systems available;
multi-family units and specialized structures available.
Choice of three different packages.

**SALES AREA:** National.

# Deltec Homes
537 Hazel Mill Road
Box 6931
Asheville, NC 28806
(704) 253-0483

**MODELS:** 13 stock models; modifications possible;
custom design available.

**SQUARE FOOTAGE:** Log (8 models): 320 to 1,570
square feet; round (5 models): 300 to 1,200 square
feet.

**PRICE:** Log: $7,916 to $29,143; round: $5,907 to
$29,787.

**COMPLETENESS OF PACKAGE:** About 40%
complete.

**SPECIAL FEATURES:** Hand-peeled log siding; round
house easily stacked up to three stories; cedar or

Douglas fir exterior siding for round models; high energy efficiency; decks and porches included.

**SALES AREA:** Rocky Mountain states and east.

# First Colony Homes
Division of J&J Construction, Inc.
P.O. Box 224
Calverton, VA 22016
(703) 788-4222

**MODELS:** 25 stock models; modifications possible; custom design available.

**SQUARE FOOTAGE:** 864 to 2,700 square feet.

**PRICE:** $9,715 to $30,295.

**COMPLETENESS OF PACKAGE:** About 33% complete.

**SPECIAL FEATURES:** Many energy-saving features; both traditional and contemporary house lines.

**SALES AREA:** Delaware, Maryland, New York, North Carolina, Pennsylvania, South Carolina, Virginia, Washington D.C., West Virginia.

# Helikon Design Corp
Box 48
Cavetown, MD 21720
(301) 824-2254

**MODELS:** 2 basic modules in 64 standard plans; modifications possible; custom design available.

**SQUARE FOOTAGE:** 1,000 or 2,000+ square feet.

**PRICE:** $17,850 to $22,800.

**COMPLETENESS OF PACKAGE:** About 33% complete.

**SPECIAL FEATURES:** Requires less energy than conventional house; solar greenhouses and garages available; Andersen or Certainteed windows standard; turnkey construction available.

**SALES AREA:** National.

# Heritage International
4625 South 2300 East, Suite 206
Salt Lake City, UT 84117
(800) 453-0402 or (801) 272-4481

**MODELS:** 115 stock models; modifications possible; custom design available.

**SQUARE FOOTAGE:** 800 to 3,500 square feet.

**PRICE:** $25,000 to $250,000.

**COMPLETENESS OF PACKAGE:** About 60% to 95% complete.

**SPECIAL FEATURES:** All Weather Wood Foundations available; special do-it-yourself program; earth shelter housing options; wide range of additional options.

**SALES AREA:** National.

# Hexagon Homes
905 N. Flood
Norman, OK 73069
(405) 321-2880

**MODELS:** 1 basic module; modifications possible; custom design available.

**SQUARE FOOTAGE:** 718+ square feet.

**PRICE:** $14,500+.

**COMPLETENESS OF PACKAGE:** About 50% complete.

**SPECIAL FEATURES:** Easily expandable; great flexibility; all finishing materials included; low maintenance.

**SALES AREA:** National.

# Hilton Lifetime Homes Corporation
36 Glenola Drive
P.O. Box 69
Leola, PA 17540
(717) 656-4181

**MODELS:** 89 stock models; modifications possible; custom design available.

**SQUARE FOOTAGE:** 768 to 2,576 square feet.

**PRICE:** $17,595 to $67,695.

**COMPLETENESS OF PACKAGE:** About 50% complete.

**SPECIAL FEATURES:** 3 different lines of homes; wide range of options; packages complete with kitchens and utilities.

**SALES AREA:** New England, mid-Atlantic states, Kentucky, North Carolina, eastern Ohio, Virginia, West Virginia.

# Homecraft Corp.
Interstate 85 & US Route 58
South Hill, VA 23970
(804) 447-3186

**MODELS:** 330 stock models; modifications possible.

SQUARE FOOTAGE: 670 to 3,500 square feet.

PRICE: $10,000 to $40,000 (to builders/contractors only).

COMPLETENESS OF PACKAGE: About 33% complete.

SPECIAL FEATURES: Wide choice of designs and architectural styling.

SALES AREA: Canada to Florida, west to Indiana.

# Mayhill Homes Corp.

Box 1778
Gainesville, GA 30503
(404) 536-9871

MODELS: Over 100 stock models; modifications possible; custom design available.

SQUARE FOOTAGE: 800 to 2,400 square feet.

PRICE: Withheld.

COMPLETENESS OF PACKAGE: About 65% complete.

SPECIAL FEATURES: Sell to builder/contractors only; pass-through windows from kitchen to outside; one extremely high thermal efficiency model built around wood-burning stove heating system; walk-in master bedroom closets; innovative cathedral-ceiling insulation method; six passive solar models.

SALES AREA: Southeastern and Midwestern United States.

# Midwestern Homes, Inc.

Box 640
Rapid City, SD 57701
(605) 394-5000

MODELS: 60 stock models; modifications possible; custom design available.

SQUARE FOOTAGE: 900 to 2,716 square feet.

PRICE: Withheld.

COMPLETENESS OF PACKAGE: About 90% complete.

SPECIAL FEATURES: Sell to builder/contractors only; clear-span floor trusses; packages very complete; many options.

SALES AREA: Colorado, Idaho, Illinois, Iowa, Kansas, Minnesota, Mississippi, Montana, Nebraska, North Dakota, Oklahoma, South Dakota, Utah, Wisconsin, Wyoming.

# Modular Homes, Inc.

North Main St.
Newcastle, CA 95658
(916) 663-3333

MODELS: Custom design only.

SQUARE FOOTAGE: 500 to 5,000 square feet.

PRICE: $10,000 to $63,750.

COMPLETENESS OF PACKAGE: About 33% complete.

SPECIAL FEATURES: Cedar or redwood plank exterior siding; passive solar designs; modular methods compatible with virtually any active solar system.

SALES AREA: Mostly Western United States and Hawaii.

# National Homes

Box 7680
Lafayette, IN 47903
(317) 448-2000

MODELS: Over 350 designs; modifications possible; custom design available.

SQUARE FOOTAGE: 800 to 5,000 square feet.

PRICE: $18,000 to $200,000.

COMPLETENESS OF PACKAGE: Withheld.

SPECIAL FEATURES: Professional consultants available at no extra cost; total building program; exceptional range of designs and options.

SALES AREA: Eastern and Rocky Mountain states.

# Nationwide Homes

P.O. Box 5511
1100 Rives Road
Martinsville, VA 24112

MODELS: 20 stock models; modifications possible; custom design available.

SQUARE FOOTAGE: 800 to 2,350 square feet.

PRICE: $7,000 to $20,000.

COMPLETENESS OF PACKAGE: About 30% complete.

SPECIAL FEATURES: Sold only through dealers; wide range of designs; complete custom design available; Energy Miser package available.

SALES AREA: Delaware, Kentucky, Maryland, North Carolina, New Jersey, Pennsylvania, South Carolina, Tennessee, Virginia, West Virginia.

# Northern Homes

Box 515
Chambersburg, PA 17201
(717) 264-5132

**MODELS:** 20 stock models; modifications possible; custom design available.

**SQUARE FOOTAGE:** 960 to 3,200 square feet.

**PRICE:** $15,000 to $65,000.

**COMPLETENESS OF PACKAGE:** About 40% complete.

**SPECIAL FEATURES:** High energy efficiency; very complete basic package.

**SALES AREA:** New England and the North Central States.

# Passive Solar Variant Homes by Savell

575 Birch Court, Suite A
Colton, CA 92324
(714) 825-4615

**MODELS:** Custom design only.

**SQUARE FOOTAGE:** 800 to 5,000 square feet.

**PRICE:** $10,400 to $85,000.

**COMPLETENESS OF PACKAGE:** About 40% complete.

**SPECIAL FEATURES:** Passive solar design with concrete wall construction; walls preconstructed off site; high energy efficiency.

**SALES AREA:** National.

# Pioneer Log Homes

Box 267
Newport, NH 03773
(603) 863-1050

**MODELS:** 11 stock models; modifications possible; custom design available.

**SQUARE FOOTAGE:** 676 to 1,632 square feet.

**PRICE:** $12,526 to $19,438.

**COMPLETENESS OF PACKAGE:** About 40% complete.

**SPECIAL FEATURES:** Garages available; log siding on heavy frame construction; very high thermal efficiency; log-look exterior; conventional or log-look interior; low maintenance.

**SALES AREA:** East of Mississippi River.

# Scholz Homes

3103 Executive Parkway
Toledo, OH 43606
(419) 531-1601

**MODELS:** 200+ stock models; modifications possible; custom design available.

**SQUARE FOOTAGE:** 900 to 5,000 square feet.

**PRICE:** $8,000 to $90,000.

**COMPLETENESS OF PACKAGE:** About 15% to 35% complete.

**SPECIAL FEATURES:** Sold only to independent building contractors; tremendous range of designs and sizes, modest through luxurious.

**SALES AREA:** East of the Rockies, excluding New England States, North Dakota, South Dakota.

# Shelter, Inc.

P.O. Box 108
Oakland, MD 21550
(301) 334-4445

**MODELS:** 33 stock models; modifications possible; custom design available.

**SQUARE FOOTAGE:** 1,048 to 3,000 square feet.

**PRICE:** $10,000 to $35,000.

**COMPLETENESS OF PACKAGE:** About 20% complete.

**SPECIAL FEATURES:** Prebuilt pocket-wall panels for storage of rigid movable window insulation panels; octagon and hexagon shapes; air-lock entries; aluminum exterior siding; heat-zoned interiors.

**SALES AREA:** Maryland, Ohio, Pennsylvania, Virginia, West Virginia.

# Southern Structures, Inc.

Box 52005
Lafayette, LA 70505
(318) 856-5981

**MODELS:** 5 stock models; modifications possible.

**SQUARE FOOTAGE:** 1,395 to 3,000 square feet.

**PRICE:** $18,000 to $28,000.

**COMPLETENESS OF PACKAGE:** About 60% complete.

**SPECIAL FEATURES:** Dormer windows for the roof/walls; financing available; designed to withstand hurricane force winds; steel structures; complete prebuilt kitchen-bath module; high energy efficiency.

**SALES AREA:** National; will export.

## Topsider Homes

Highway 601
P.O. Box 849
Yadkinville, NC 27055
(919) 679-8846

**MODELS:** 6 stock models; modifications possible; custom design available.

**SQUARE FOOTAGE:** 465 to 1,000 square feet.

**PRICE:** $18,900 to $26,000.

**COMPLETENESS OF PACKAGE:** About 60% complete.

**SPECIAL FEATURES:** High wind load modifications; energy packages; roof insulation options to R 40; garages and deck packages; jacuzzi tub option.

**SALES AREA:** National, will export.

## West Coast Mills, Inc.

887 N.W. State Avenue
Box 480
Chehalis, WA 98532
(206) 748-3351

**MODELS:** 45 stock models; modifications possible; custom design available.

**SQUARE FOOTAGE:** 1,100 to 1,905 square feet.

**PRICE:** $15,000 to $20,000.

**COMPLETENESS OF PACKAGE:** About 33% complete.

**SPECIAL FEATURES:** Flexibility in modification or plans.

**SALES AREA:** Western United States, Alaska and Hawaii.

## Wick Homes

Wick Building Systems, Inc.
P.O. Box 188
Mazomanie, WI 53560
(608) 795-2261

**MODELS:** 81 stock models; many modifications possible.

**SQUARE FOOTAGE:** 800 to 3,000 square feet.

**PRICE:** $22,000 to $90,000.

**COMPLETENESS OF PACKAGE:** About 75% complete.

**SPECIAL FEATURES:** High energy efficiency; solid oak prefinished trim; oak parquet or plank hardwood floors available; power attic ventilator; wide range of structural and decorative options.

**SALES AREA:** Arkansas, Illinois, Indiana, Iowa, Kansas, Michigan, Minnesota, Missouri, Nebraska, North Dakota, Ohio, South Dakota, West Virginia, Wisconsin.

## Woodmark Chalet Homes, Inc.

P.O. Box 404
Forest Lake, MN 55025
(612) 462-2114

**MODELS:** 6 stock models; modifications possible; custom design available.

**SQUARE FOOTAGE:** 800 to 2,184 square feet.

**PRICE:** $15,000 to $25,900.

**COMPLETENESS OF PACKAGE:** About 40% complete.

**SPECIAL FEATURES:** Trapezoid windows; low maintenance; easily adaptable to solar heating units; electrical and plumbing packages available.

**SALES AREA:** National.

# Modular/Sectional Houses

Modular/sectional houses are unlike any other type of manufactured house—they are almost entirely factory-built. When the house arrives at the building site—usually in two or more big sections—it's about 95 percent finished. Very little remains to be done, in most cases, to make the house ready for occupancy. Buyers can, however, elect to do some additional painting, papering, and similar interior decorating chores after the builder has completed construction.

Most modular/sectional houses are made up of two modules; typically the house is split down the middle lengthwise, with each half complete and self-supporting. At the site, each module is either slid onto a waiting foundation or lifted into place with a crane. The two halves are connected and the finishing details are completed. Larger houses are built in the same basic fashion. Three or more modules are arranged on the same or slightly differing levels and secured together. Two-story houses are also feasible, and are made by placing second-level modules atop the first-level ones with a crane.

Modular/sectional houses are sometimes confused with mobile homes, but there is a big difference. Although the sections are often transported to the building site on wheels much as mobile homes are, and some of the houses might resemble mobile homes, there are key differences.

First, the modular/sectional house is designed to be permanently secured to a foundation. Usually this is either a full-perimeter crawl space or a full basement,

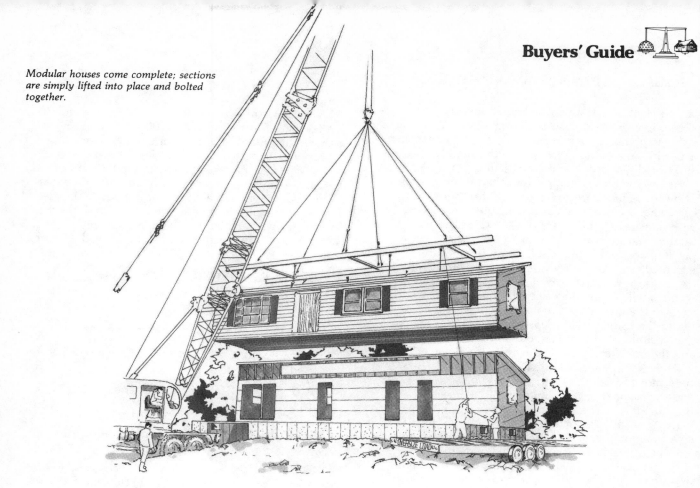

*Modular houses come complete; sections are simply lifted into place and bolted together.*

but a slab, pier, or All Weather Wood type might be used. Second, modular/sectional houses are built to standards set by various national, state, and local building codes, and must meet certain requirements applicable to factory-built houses. To ensure that the requirements are met, independent inspections take place within the manufacturer's plant. Mobile homes, on the other hand, are built to conform to entirely different codes, and in most areas their placement and use is covered by different laws and regulations.

Finally, modular/sectional houses are built with materials and methods that are common to the housing industry in general, but not to the mobile home field. Their construction is almost identical with any contractor-built house.

# Assembly Line Construction

Modular/sectional houses are constructed under controlled, indoor conditions. Weather problems are never a factor, waste is reduced, working conditions are ideal by comparison with those found at a building site, and as a result cost levels can be kept low. Construction quality is monitored closely so that standards are maintained. The end result is a well-built house at a reasonable cost.

Another advantage is that many of the equipment and construction procedures that are utilized can't usually be duplicated in the field. Floor and wall sec-

tions, for example, are usually glue-bonded—sometimes using a hot press. When nails or screws are added, the strength of the construction is increased.

Most modular/sectional homes are built with conventional materials and systems, but there are some differences. Floors are generally made with a conventional joist frame, and the subflooring and underlayment are glue-bonded to one another and to the frame. Exterior walls are made in much the same way, with a stud frame—either 2×4's or 2×6's are used—to which exterior sheathing and interior drywall or wall surface covering are glue-bonded. The walls are fiberglass-insulated, and may include insulating sheathing as well.

A variety of exterior sidings is used, with prefinished or primed hardboard being the most common. Load-bearing interior walls use 2×4 stud frame construction; non-load-bearing walls are sometimes of lighter 2×3 construction. Roof construction is either a conventional truss or rafter frame, with plywood sheathing and asphalt shingles or other roofing material. Structural components and coverings are joined with fasteners as well as adhesives. Nails are commonly used, but many manufacturers use screws for greater holding power. The modules typically have good structural rigidity, because they must be moved about and perhaps hoisted with cranes. Energy efficiency, maintenance factors, and general upkeep are about the same as for any conventional frame house.

# Houses Are Nearly Complete

As the shell of a modular/sectional unit begins to take shape, interior work also is started. Professionals install the plumbing and wiring, and the heating system is put in. All of these systems are thoroughly checked and tested before the house leaves the factory.

As the shell nears completion, the finishing work is also done. Floors are covered with sheet vinyl and carpeting, walls are taped, and painted or finished with paneling. Ceilings are typically finished with a sand or texture paint. All molding and trimwork is put in place, plumbing and lighting fixtures are mounted, and cabinets are installed. In short, the entire house is finished, except at the points where the sections will eventually join. There are some variations in the degree of completeness when the house leaves the factory. This depends not only on the particular house, but the manufacturer's building system and the specifications laid down by the buyer.

After the modules that make up the house have been moved into place and secured to one another and the foundation, the builder will take care of finishing tasks. The extent of the work to be done varies, but at least some trimwork must be done to cover the joints where the modules come together, and the utilities must be connected and checked.

In most cases there is little opportunity for the do-it-yourselfer. Some owners, however, elect to repaint walls, apply wallpaper, or take care of other interior decorating chores. Outside work, such as building decks or porches, constructing a garage, or making a patio can be done by the buyer, or can be left to the builder. In cases where the house is set on a full basement, the owner can also do the finishing and decorating there. The foundation itself often must be built by the manufacturer's builder, or an approved contractor. Thus, most modular/sectional houses are essentially ready-to-live-in homes for the great majority of buyers. Occupancy is sometimes possible only a few days after the house has been set on the foundation.

## An Economical Selection

Because of the difficulties—and the expense—of transporting large house sections over long distances, most manufacturers of modular/sectional houses sell and erect their products only in limited areas. Most also do not sell direct to the consumer, but only to their own builders or dealers. However, there are numerous manufacturers, so there is an excellent range of models and designs available almost anywhere in the country.

At one time most houses of this type were rather small and unstylish, but that has changed over the past few years. Now you can choose from many standard models, most can be modified to some degree, and some custom designing is possible. The range of options, choices, and extras that many manufacturers

offer—some even include drapes and furniture—gives the buyer plenty of latitude in both interior and exterior decor.

Living space in stock models ranges from less than 1,000 square feet to well over 2,000. Some of the manufacturers that offer custom design and engineering service can factory-build sectional houses of almost any size. Prices are comparable to—and often less than—those for other types of completed houses. A finished house can be purchased for $35,000 or less. Because a modular/sectional house requires little or no extra work or materials, the manufacturer's package price is frequently the total cost of the house.

# Dynamic Homes, Inc.

525 Roosevelt
Detroit Lakes, MN 56501
(218) 847-2611

**MODELS:** 60 stock models; modifications possible; no custom design.

**SQUARE FOOTAGE:** 816 to 2,200 square feet.

**PRICE:** $35,000 to $115,000.

**COMPLETENESS OF PACKAGE:** About 90% complete.

**CONSTRUCTION: Floors.** *First floor:* Joist framing • Insulation if required • Plywood subflooring • Particle board underlayment • Sheet vinyl and carpet flooring *Second floor/loft:* Same as first floor

*Photos Courtesy Dynamic Homes, Inc.*

**Walls.** *Exterior walls:* Stud framing • Fiberglass insulation • Vapor barrier • Exterior sheathing • Exterior hardboard siding • Interior drywall wall surface
*Partition walls:* Stud framing • Drywall wall surface
**Roof.** Truss framing • Vapor barrier • Cellulose insulation • Plywood sheathing • Felt roof protection • Asphalt shingles
**Windows/Doors.** Double-glazed, wood-framed casement and sliding windows with screens • Steel insulated exterior doors • Double-glazed, wood-framed sliding patio doors with screens • Hardboard hollow-core interior doors

**MANUFACTURER PROVIDES:**
Complete house, finished

**BUYER PROVIDES:**
Foundation    Guttering system    Appliances

**OPTIONS AVAILABLE:** All Weather Wood Foundation; added wall insulation; triple-glazed windows; fireplaces; foyer plans; kitchen layouts; appliances; complete interior decorating service; garages; guttering system; heating systems; flooring; exterior sidings; interior paneling; cabinetry; countertops; fixtures.

**SPECIAL FEATURES:** High energy efficiency; flexibility of design; glued subfloor and underlayment for extra-strong and squeakfree floors; All Weather Wood Foundations available and built by certified installers; complete professional interior decorating service available; wide range of options; unique four-module two-story design available; wide variety of floor plans.

**EASE OF CONSTRUCTION:** Foundation is built by Dynamic dealer/builder; house moved onto foundation and set up by Dynamic factory crew; all finish work is completed by Dynamic dealer/builder; turnkey job for buyer. Owner involvement only in finishing basement level if desired.

**MANUFACTURER ASSISTANCE:** Factory and/or dealer/builder offers full-service help, from finding suitable building site, through design and option selection. Will help arrange financing. Manufacturer constructs additional desired elements such as driveway, decks, and even does final clean-up.

**SALES AREA:** Iowa, Minnesota, Montana, North Dakota, South Dakota, Wisconsin, Wyoming.

# Golden West Homes

1308 East Wakeham
Santa Ana, CA 92705
(714) 835-4200

**MODELS:** 35 stock models; modifications possible.

**SQUARE FOOTAGE:** 800 to 1,920 square feet.

**PRICE:** $24,000 to $60,000.

*Photos Courtesy Golden West Homes*

**COMPLETENESS OF PACKAGE:** About 80% complete.

**CONSTRUCTION: Floors.** *First floor:* Joist framing • Plywood subflooring • Particle board underlayment • Sheet vinyl and carpet flooring
*Second floor/loft:* No 2-story models
**Walls.** *Exterior walls:* Stud framing • Fiberglass insulation • Exterior hardboard siding • Interior drywall wall surface
*Partition walls:* 2×3 and 2×4 stud framing • Drywall wall surface
**Roof.** Truss or rafter framing • Plywood sheathing • Fiberglass insulation • Vapor barrier • Felt roof protection • Asphalt shingles
**Windows/Doors.** Single-glazed, aluminum-framed double-hung windows • Steel insulated exterior doors • Hollow-core interior plywood doors

**MANUFACTURER PROVIDES:**
Complete house, finished

**BUYER PROVIDES:**
Foundation    Guttering system

**OPTIONS AVAILABLE:** Double-glazed windows and patio doors; various ceiling materials; various exterior sidings; various interior wall coverings; floor coverings; plumbing fixtures.

**SPECIAL FEATURES:** Special flame-spread rated materials used in some areas for greater safety; higher than normal heating system and fire-safety standards used in construction.

**EASE OF CONSTRUCTION:** Modules or sections completely built and almost entirely prefinished at factory; set on buyer's foundation and assembled/completed by contractor. Only potential areas of owner involvement might be in foundation construction, minor interior finishing and/or decorating, and construction of outside items such as decks or garage.

**MANUFACTURER ASSISTANCE:** Dealer will assist throughout entire process, from planning and design selection through completion of house; shipping by Golden West trucks.

**SALES AREA:** Arizona, California, Idaho, Montana, Nebraska, and Washington.

# RODA Corp.

57475 CR 3 Rte 3
Elkhard, IN 46517
(219) 293-7551

**MODELS:** 66 stock models; modifications possible; approximately 50% of the houses are custom designed.

**SQUARE FOOTAGE:** 900 to 2,800 square feet.

**PRICE:** $29,000 to $55,000.

**COMPLETENESS OF PACKAGE:** About 80% complete.

*Photos Courtesy RODA Corp.*

**CONSTRUCTION: Floors.** *First floor:* Joist framing • Laminated wood or plywood tongue-and-groove subflooring • Sheet vinyl and carpet flooring *Second floor/loft:* Same as first floor.
**Walls.** *Exterior walls:* Stud framing • Fiberglass insulation • Exterior hardboard siding • Interior drywall wall surface
*Partition walls:* 2×4 or 2×3 stud framing • Drywall wall surface
**Roof.** Rafter or truss framing • Plywood sheathing • Fiberglass insulation • Felt roof protection • Fiberglass or asphalt shingles
**Windows/Doors.** Double-glazed, wood-framed casement and double-hung windows with screens • Steel insulated exterior doors • Double-glazed, wood-framed sliding patio doors with screens • Hardboard hollow-core interior doors

**MANUFACTURER PROVIDES:**
Complete house, finished

**BUYER PROVIDES:**
Foundation    Guttering system    Appliances

**OPTIONS AVAILABLE:** Appliances; decks; whirlpools; fireplaces; flower boxes; drapery packages with hardware; alternate choices in flooring, wall coverings, countertops, windows, entry doors, patio doors, exterior siding, kitchen cabinets, and heating systems.

**SPECIAL FEATURES:** Good range of options; houses very energy-efficient; heavily-insulated models.

**EASE OF CONSTRUCTION:** Modules or sections completely built and almost entirely finished at factory; set on buyer's foundation by dealer/builder's professional crew, and assembled. Only areas of possible owner involvement are in foundation construction, decks, and some interior finishing.

**MANUFACTURER ASSISTANCE:** Dealer/builder will provide all reasonable help in planning, selecting options, securing financing, and similar matters. Takes care of set-up and completion of house, and will handle interior finishing, foundation construction, and contracted extras. Shipping by RODA Corp. trucks.

**SALES AREA:** Illinois, Indiana, Kentucky, Minnesota, Ohio, Pennsylvania, and Wisconsin.

# Trademark Homes, Inc.

2109 4th Avenue South
Clear Lake, Iowa 50428
(515) 357-8131

**MODELS:** 40 floor plans with 101 stock variations; modifications possible.

**SQUARE FOOTAGE:** 768 to 1,800 square feet.

**PRICE:** $22,500 to $47,500.

*Photos Courtesy Trademark Homes, Inc.*

**COMPLETENESS OF PACKAGE:** About 95% complete.

**CONSTRUCTION: Floors.** *First floor:* Joist framing • Plywood subflooring • Particle board underlayment • Sheet vinyl and carpet flooring
*Second floor/loft:* Same as first floor
**Walls.** *Exterior walls:* Stud framing • Fiberglass insulation • Vapor barrier • Exterior plywood sheathing • Exterior hardboard siding • Interior drywall wall surface
*Partition walls:* Stud framing • Drywall wall surface
**Roof.** Truss framing • Fiberglass insulation • Vapor barrier • Plywood sheathing • Felt roof protection • Asphalt shingles
**Windows/Doors.** Single-glazed, wood-framed sliding windows with storms and screens • Steel insulated exterior doors with combination storm/screen doors • Hardboard hollow-core interior doors

**MANUFACTURER PROVIDES:**
Complete house, finished

**BUYER PROVIDES:**
Foundation   Guttering system   Appliances

**OPTIONS AVAILABLE:** Fireplaces; appliances; additional insulation; triple-glazed windows; dormers; exterior styling changes; kitchen and bath wallpapers; oak interior trimwork and doors; choices in cabinetry; exterior sidings.

**SPECIAL FEATURES:** Uses all stress-graded lumber;

epoxy/nailing system of framing for strength and rigidity; two-story models available.

**EASE OF CONSTRUCTION:** Modules completely built and almost entirely finished at factory, set on buyer's foundation and assembled/completed by dealer/builder's professional crew. Only potential areas of owner involvement in construction might be foundation, some interior decorating, and outside items such as a deck.

**MANUFACTURER ASSISTANCE:** Dealer/builder will assist throughout entire process, from planning and design selection through completion of house, including contracted extras if desired. Shipping by Trademark trucks.

**SALES AREA:** Illinois, Iowa, Minnesota, Missouri, Montana, Nebraska, North Dakota, South Dakota, Wisconsin.

# Westville Homes Corp.
Railroad Avenue
Plaistow, NH 03865
(603) 382-6505

**MODELS:** 15 stock models; modifications possible; approximately 5% of the houses are custom designed.

**SQUARE FOOTAGE:** 864 to 1,392 square feet.

**PRICE:** $23,000 to $36,000.

**COMPLETENESS OF PACKAGE:** About 90% complete.

**CONSTRUCTION: Floors.** *First floor:* Joist framing • Fiberglass insulation • Vapor barrier • Plywood tongue-and-groove subflooring • Plywood tongue-and-groove underlayment • Sheet vinyl and carpet flooring
*Second floor/loft:* Same as first floor.
**Walls.** *Exterior walls:* Stud framing • Fiberglass insulation • Vapor barriers • Exterior plywood sheathing • Exterior vinyl, hardboard, or plywood siding • Interior drywall wall surface
*Partition walls:* Stud framing • Drywall wall surface
**Roof.** Truss framing • Fiberglass insulation • Vapor barrier • Plywood sheathing • Felt roof protection • Asphalt shingles
**Windows/Doors.** Double-glazed, wood-framed double-hung and sliding windows with screens • Steel insulated exterior doors • Hardboard hollow-core interior doors

**MANUFACTURER PROVIDES:**
Complete house, finished

**BUYER PROVIDES:**
Foundation   Guttering system   Appliances

**OPTIONS AVAILABLE:** Foundation; guttering system; appliances; higher R-value insulation; red cedar shingle exterior siding; wood-framed storm windows; aluminum storm doors; 2-foot structure

add-ons; double-glazed patio doors; alternative choices in cabinetry, carpeting, and vinyl floor covering; heating systems.

**SPECIAL FEATURES:** Many energy-saving features standard; glued and fastened construction throughout; recessed entrance foyers; all hardwood interior trim; many material and color options available.

**EASE OF CONSTRUCTION:** Modules or sections completely built and almost entirely prefinished at factory; set on buyer's foundation by dealer/builder's professional crew, and assembled/completed. Finishing consists of some interior painting/papering, exterior painting in some cases; can be done by dealer/builder or by owner. Other potential areas of owner involvement include foundation construction, deck, patio, and garage.

**MANUFACTURER ASSISTANCE:** Dealer/builder will assist through entire process, from planning and design selection through completion of house, including contracted extras if desired. Shipping by Westville trucks.

**SALES AREA:** New England, New York, Pennsylvania.

Photos Courtesy Westville Homes Corp.

# Arabi Homes, Inc.
Box 117
Arabi, GA 31712
(912) 273-6050

**MODELS:** 20 stock models; modifications possible; custom design available.

**SQUARE FOOTAGE:** 912 to 1,632 square feet.

**PRICE:** $25,000 to $50,000.

**COMPLETENESS OF PACKAGE:** About 100% complete.

**SPECIAL FEATURES:** Choice of exteriors; garages available; energy-efficient homes available.

**SALES AREA:** Southeastern United States.

# The Builders
Box 235
Winter, WI 54896
(715) 266-2311

**MODELS:** 60 stock models; modifications possible; custom design available.

**SQUARE FOOTAGE:** 864 to 2,128 square feet.

**PRICE:** $30,000 to $70,000.

**COMPLETENESS OF PACKAGE:** About 85% to 90% complete.

**SPECIAL FEATURES:** 1 year warranty to original owners; duplexes, 4-plexes, and townhouses available.

**SALES AREA:** Minnesota, Wisconsin.

# Cardinal Industries, Inc.
2040 S. Hamilton Road
Columbus, OH 43227
(614) 861-3211

**MODELS:** 10 stock models; modifications possible.

**SQUARE FOOTAGE:** 864 to 2,000+ square feet.

**PRICE:** $25,000 to $60,000.

**COMPLETENESS OF PACKAGE:** About 100% complete.

**SPECIAL FEATURES:** Additions easy to build onto basic home (expandable home with options and features); energy efficient envelope system; heat pumps; air conditioning; appliances; garages available.

**SALES AREA:** Ohio and adjacent states, Florida and adjacent states.

# Grizzly Manufacturing

Box 1070
Hamilton, MT 59840
(406) 363-2387

**MODELS:** 23 stock models; modifications possible; custom design available.

**SQUARE FOOTAGE:** 864 to 1,456 square feet.

**PRICE:** $28,000 to $42,000.

**COMPLETENESS OF PACKAGE:** About 100% complete.

**SPECIAL FEATURES:** 3 series of homes; mobile/modular construction allows either 15 or 30 year financing; cedar shakes, dormers, fireplaces available; exterior trim of redwood or pine; numerous options.

**SALES AREA:** Idaho, Montana, Nevada, Utah, Wyoming.

# Harrington Homes

Box 269
Lewiston, NC 27849
(919) 348-2531

**MODELS:** 15 stock models; some modifications possible.

**SQUARE FOOTAGE:** 960 to 2,162 square feet.

**PRICE:** $26,000 to $45,000.

**COMPLETENESS OF PACKAGE:** About 90% to 100% complete.

**SPECIAL FEATURES:** Some models designed for brick veneer; packages very complete.

**SALES AREA:** East Coast states.

# Intermountain Precision-Bilt Homes, Inc.

2525 N. Hwy. 89-91
Ogden, UT 84404
(800) 453-4692
(801) 782-8090

**MODELS:** 11 nonchangeable floor plans and additions; mainly custom design.

**SQUARE FOOTAGE:** 800 to 3,000 square feet.

**PRICE:** $31,000 to $45,000.

**COMPLETENESS OF PACKAGE:** About 100% complete.

**SPECIAL FEATURES:** Custom-made kitchen cabinets; expandable foam blown into all joints and openings in exterior walls.

**SALES AREA:** Arizona, Colorado, Idaho, Montana, Nevada, South Dakota, Utah.

# Kober Homes

Box 20875
Billings, MT 59104
(406) 656-3650

**MODELS:** 30 stock models; modifications possible; custom design available.

**SQUARE FOOTAGE:** 816 to 2,108 square feet.

**PRICE:** $35,000 to $125,000.

**COMPLETENESS OF PACKAGE:** About 95% complete.

**SPECIAL FEATURES:** Duplex and triplex models; triple-glazed windows; 10 year warranty under Home Owners Warranty program in states having building associations; garages, decks available; many options.

**SALES AREA:** Montana, North Dakota, South Dakota, Wyoming.

# Lancer Homes Inc.

Box 1200
Corona, CA 91720
(714) 371-0860

**MODELS:** 50 stock models; modifications possible; custom design available.

**SQUARE FOOTAGE:** 900 to 2,200 square feet.

**PRICE:** $25,000 to $66,600.

**COMPLETENESS OF PACKAGE:** About 95% complete.

**SPECIAL FEATURES:** Wide variety of options; energy-efficient design; conventional house packages.

**SALES AREA:** Western United States.

# Mill-Craft Homes

Box 327
Tower Road
Waupaca, WI 54981
(715) 258-8531

**MODELS:** 80 stock models; modifications possible; custom design available.

**SQUARE FOOTAGE:** 864 to 1,700 square feet.

**PRICE:** $20,000 to $35,000.

**COMPLETENESS OF PACKAGE:** About 95% complete.

**SPECIAL FEATURES:** Sold exclusively through dealers; garages available; redwood, cedar, and aluminum siding; brick veneer available.

**SALES AREA:** Illinois, Iowa, Michigan, Minnesota, Missouri.

# Mod-U-Kraf Homes, Inc.
Rocky Mount, VA 24151
(703) 483-0291

**MODELS:** 60 stock models; modifications possible.

**SQUARE FOOTAGE:** 988 to 2,328 square feet.

**PRICE:** $30,000 to $100,000.

**COMPLETENESS OF PACKAGE:** About 95% complete.

**SPECIAL FEATURES:** Energy efficient; various energy packages.

**SALES AREA:** Delaware, Kentucky, Maryland, North Carolina, Ohio, Pennsylvania, Tennessee, Virginia, West Virginia.

# Nationwide Homes
P.O. Box 5511
1100 Rives Road
Martinsville, VA 24112
(703) 632-7101

**MODELS:** 60 stock models; modifications possible; custom design available.

**SQUARE FOOTAGE:** 768 to 3,300 square feet.

**PRICE:** $16,500 to $40,000.

**COMPLETENESS OF PACKAGE:** About 60% complete.

**SPECIAL FEATURES:** Sold only through dealers; wide range of designs; complete custom design.

**SALES AREA:** Delaware, Kentucky, Maryland, New Jersey, North Carolina, Pennsylvania, South Carolina, Tennessee, Virginia, West Virginia.

# New Era Homes, Inc.
Industrial Park—Box 656
Belington, WV 26250
(304) 823-2600

**MODELS:** 25 stock models; modifications possible; custom design available.

**SQUARE FOOTAGE:** 816 to 1,800 square feet.

**PRICE:** $16,000 to $150,000.

**COMPLETENESS OF PACKAGE:** About 95% complete.

**SPECIAL FEATURES:** Triple-glazed windows; passive solar design available.

**SALES AREA:** West Virginia.

# Poloron Homes of Pennsylvania, Inc.
74 Ridge Road—Box 306
Middleburg, PA 17842
(717) 837-0051

**MODELS:** 175+ stock models; modifications possible; custom design available.

**SQUARE FOOTAGE:** 864 to 3,000 square feet.

**PRICE:** $20,000 to $60,000.

**COMPLETENESS OF PACKAGE:** About 100% complete.

**SPECIAL FEATURES:** Double- or triple-glazed double-hung windows; oak or pine kitchen cabinets; energy efficient.

**SALES AREA:** Northeast states.

# R-Anell Homes
P.O. Box 236
Denver, NC 28037
(704) 483-5511

**MODELS:** 28 stock models.

**SQUARE FOOTAGE:** 933 to 1,905 square feet.

**PRICE:** $22,000 to $50,000.

**COMPLETENESS OF PACKAGE:** About 100% complete.

**SPECIAL FEATURES:** Polybutylene water lines; aluminum siding.

**SALES AREA:** Georgia, Kentucky, North Carolina, South Carolina, Tennessee, Virginia, West Virginia.

# Timberland Homes
7418 S. 212th
Kent, WA 98031
(206) 872-8810

**MODELS:** 11 stock models (includes 2 duplexes); modifications possible; custom design available.

**SQUARE FOOTAGE:** 864 to 1,600 square feet.

**PRICE:** $23,000 to $50,000.

**COMPLETENESS OF PACKAGE:** About 100% complete.

**SPECIAL FEATURES:** Choice of siding; cedar shakes; garages available; many options; lauan trim; acoustic ceilings.

**SALES AREA:** Alaska, Hawaii, Idaho, Montana, Oregon, Washington.